Skinhead

REGGAE HIT THE TOWN

AKA THE HISTORY OF SKINHEAD REGGAE
1968-1972

JOHN BAILEY

THE HISTORY OF SKINHEAD REGGAE
1968 – 1972
JOHN BAILEY

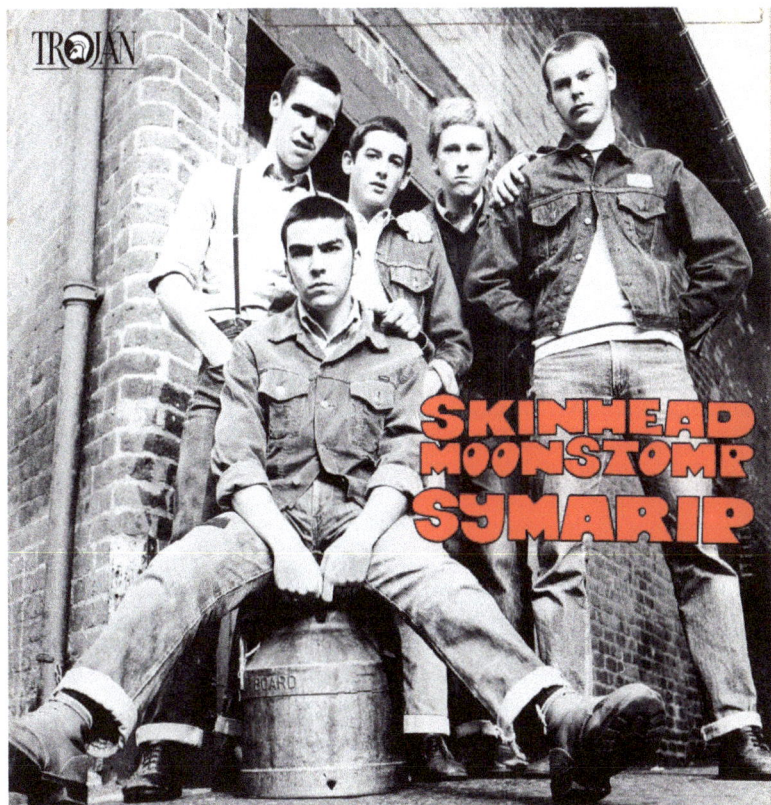

This book is dedicated to all the traditional skinheads of 69

Well before we explore the golden age of reggae I would just like to say compiling the book has been a true labour of love. When I first made contact with Universal Music to enquire about the use of their images I was told that this was a work long overdue, a statement that came up time and time again in conversations, some by e-mail to Jamaica and some by the good old fashioned telephone. I would first of all like to acknowledge Emperor Rosko for his generous contribution of the foreword. When I asked him about his top ten he said *"did I forget anyone, you bet, there was only room for ten so I keep my closing mention for the guy who eclipses everyone with more songs for my top ten than there is space for"*. The Emperor placed Let Your Yeah Be Yeah by The Pioneers at number one and that leads very aptly to my thanks to Sydney, Jackie and George, who were a significant part of the golden age of reggae. Special thanks go out to Jackie for the interview and permission to use the photographs of the group within the book.

The chapter covering Toots and of course The Maytals has been enhanced with the quotes from Toots surrounding the first reggae sound and the inspiration for him writing 54-46, a true skinhead classic, and I thank Mike Cacia, Toots manager, for granting permission.

My appreciation goes out to Simon Lindsay and Samantha Hales for their time spent sorting permission to be granted for the images of all of the Trojan album covers and vinyl labels used in the book, the Trojan catalogue is now solely owned by Universal Music. Island Records were originally founded by Chris Blackwell and Graeme Goodall in Jamaica as far back as 1959 and are now part of Universal Music. I would like to acknowledge the help from Nicola Kennedy for arranging the granting of permission for the use of all Island images in the book. Nicola also kindly arranged with Juliet Henzell, daughter of the late Perry Henzell, for her kind permission for the use of The Harder They Come album cover and text. The Pama label images and album art work are now included with kind permission arranged by Jessica Munro at Phoenix Music International (PMI) who are making the all important Pama back catalogue available digitaly remastered for the very first time. My thanks go to Claire Tilley head of marketing at John Blake publishing for the use of the image from Want Some Aggro by Cass Pennant and Micky Smith and for the permission to use an extract from the book, both remain © *John Blake Publishing Ltd.* It has been a long but enjoyable haul contacting various people who were involved in the reggae scene back in the late 60s to get permission for images to be used and my thanks also go to Junior Lincoln in Jamaica for the inclusion of his Bamboo label.

I was delighted to include the words from Ian R Smith, member of The Inner Mind, described as the greatest white reggae band on earth by Pama, telling of his experiences with Pama and other labels and how he formed his own Hot Lead label. Ian provided a fascinating collection of posters from the golden age of reggae

Chris Brown, author of Booted and Suited, has also kindly recalled his memories of how we used to get hold of the music during those early years.

Bunny 'Striker' Lee, the great producer of Jamaican music, and the originator of reggae, and a true gentleman, has also generously given an interview for the book and I thank Young 'Striker' Lee for organising the event.

For the quote on the front cover, *"No true Skinheads are racist. Without the Jamaican culture Skinheads would not exist. It was their culture mixed with British working class culture that made Skinhead what it is"*, I thank Roddy Moreno of The Oppressed.

Best not to forget to give a mention for the 'Traditional Skinhead of 69'.

They say that you should always leave the best 'till last, so therefore my final acknowledgements are to the artists and producers that brought us the golden age of reggae, the list is long and sadly as you may well know some have passed on. My gratitude goes out to The Pioneers, Max Romeo, Jimmy Cliff, Dave & Ansel Collins, Toots And The Maytals, Greyhound, Derrick Morgan, Dandy, Eric Donaldson, Lee 'Scratch' Perry, Bunny 'Striker' Lee. The list just goes on and on and I mention with a hint of sadness my posthumous appreciation to Desmond Dekker, Nicky Thomas, Judge Dread, Leslie Kong and Clancy Eccles to name but a few for their immeasurable contribution to the golden age of reggae.

Since the first edition was published I am saddened to hear of the passing of Bunny 'Striker' Lee, who I was privileged to interview, Fredrick 'Toots' Hibbert, U Roy and Johnny Nash.

All Trojan and subsidiary labels and album artwork licensed from and © Universal Music
All Island labels and album artwork licensed from and © Universal Music
Al Pama labels and album artwork licensed from and © Phoenix Music international (PMI)
CBS labels and album art work licensed from and © Sony Music Entertainment
Bamboo and subsidiary labels © Junior Lincoln.
Unity label originally included with kind permission from Bunny 'Striker' Lee
Rhino images by kind permission of www.covers 33.co.uk

Whilst every possible effort has been made to ensure the copyright owners of any work have been traced, there may be some omission of credit to which I apologise. I would however like to acknowledge the help in my relentless quest from David Rodigan, Adrian Sherwood, The Apollo Club London, Michael De Koningh, author of Young Gifted & Black and Tighten Up. Also help from Ian R Smith who worked with Pama during the golden years and the Pama Forum.

22nd November 1969

Upsetters, Pioneers fly in, hoping for a white Christmas

The Pioneers and Upsetters have arrived in London from Jamaica. The Pioneers are here for a six week promotional tour following the success of their record Long Shot Kick The Bucket in the UK charts.

LONG SHOT
THE PIONEERS
TROJAN RECORDS TBL103
Released 1969

TROJAN RECORDS

Island Music
℗ 1969

Barron/Cook/Robinson

TR-672 A
TMR. 269

LONG SHOT KICK THE BUCKET
THE PIONEERS
Produced by: L. Kong

Contents

Foreword	8
Introduction	10
Skinheads and Reggae	11
Symarip	16
Trojan Records	18
Pama Records	20
The Inner Mind	22
The Labels	24
A Musicians Tale	60
Tell It Like It Was	63
Desmond Dekker	66
Max Romeo	73
The Pioneers	79
Jimmy Cliff	92
Bob & Marcia	98
Nicky Thomas	103
Dave & Ansel Collins	108
Greyhound	113
Toots & The Maytals	120
Judge Dread	126
Chartbusters	128
Leslie Kong	158
Bunny 'Striker' Lee	162
Lee ' Scratch' Perry	168
Harry J	175
Dandy	179
Clancy Eccles	186
Eric Donaldson	189
Derrick Morgan	192
Dennis Alcapone	197
U-Roy	202
Bob Marley & The Wailers	205
Johnny Nash	210
The Various Artists	214
The Albums	227
Tighten Up	228
Reggae Chartbusters	246
Club Reggae	258
Straighten Up	270
Pama Albums	276
Reggae Hit The Town Again	289
The Harder They Come	290
Conclusion	293
Index	296

FOREWORD

Thanks for asking me to participate in this long overdue book, there is reggae and then reggae as it was, and before reggae blue-beat / ska! I could just list the chart guys but there is so much more fun stuff out there so I will give you my top 10 list, these are songs I still play weekly! But to the student of music and the fan of reggae this book will be a treasure.

Thank you John for writing about music I call infectious! It grabs you and moves you without one being aware, one finds one tapping one's feet to the rhythm without thinking about it, I loved reggae the first listen.

I started off with blue-beat / ska in the 50s! I even put my first purchase on the 10 list!

Enjoy this and treasure it, a music bible for the worthy! The guys and gal's who partied at the Apollo Club in London, just to mention one of the many will relive the good times with this book and many thanks for helping me enjoy the party scene so much.

And yes, to set the book straight I did play Wet Dream a few times before the Beeb banned it, (with a big grin on my face !)

Emperor Rosko

ALCAPONE by ROSKO (Rosco) released on Trojan TR-7758 1970

RADIO ONE
Friday 22nd January 1971

07.00: **Tony Blackburn**

10.00: **Jimmy Young**

12.00: **Richard Park**

14.00: **Barry Mason**

15.02: **Terry Wogan**

17.00: **Rosko Round Table**

18.00: **Alan Black**

AT 4003

JAMAICA SKA
(Lee)
THE SKA KINGS

Emperor Rosko started his broadcasting career as a Pirate radio DJ although his first opportunity to broadcast came whilst in the US Navy where he presented a show on an aircraft carrier. He joined the pirate radio station, Radio Caroline, from a ship off the coast of England in 1966. There his pacey American style soon made Rosko one of the stations best loved DJs. Rosko was then heard on Radio Luxembourg. Following his tenure on the pirate ships he became one of Radio One's first signings in 1967, initially recording shows in France for the Midday Spin programme. On his first Midday Spin show Rosko introduced himself like, 'I am the Emperor, the geeter with the heater, your leader, your groovy host from the West Coast, here to clear up your skin and mess up your mind. It'll make you feel good all over'. He highlighted the new Motown, reggae, and rock music.

From 1970 he presented the Friday Roundtable where new records were reviewed by a panel, and had a Saturday lunchtime slot where you could always be assured to hear some reggae, at that time still an occasional event at the beeb. He stayed with Radio One until September 1976.

The Emperor has since been heard on the Classic Gold network and REM.FM, his programme being pre-recorded in California. He's currently running Rosko Radio on *www.emperorrosko.net*

Rosko's top tunes:

RADIO ONE
Saturday 24th April 1971

1. Let Your Yeah Be Yeah –The Pioneers
2. Red Red Wine –Tony Tribe
3. Double Barrel –Dave And Ansil Collins
4. Al Capone –Prince Buster / Emperor Rosko
5. Wet Dream–Max Romeo
6. Liquidator –Harry J All Stars
7. Wonderful World Beautiful People –Jimmy Cliff
8. Jamaica Ska–Ska Kings
9. Israelites–Desmond Dekker
10. Help Me Make It Through The Night –John Holt

8.32   **Ed Stewart**

9.55:   **Noel Edmonds**

12.00: **The Rosko Show**

14.00 : **Johnny Moran**

15.00: **John Peel**

17.00: **Johnnie Walker**

18.00

9

INTRODUCTION

The relationship between the original skinheads of the late
1960s and reggae music are often a source of debate, as to the
uninitiated they seem curious partners. The raw unpretentious
sounds of reggae, with the enduring overtones of rocksteady were in
great contrast to the mainstream progressive rock and pop that was the
mainstay of the BBC playlists at that time. The music was often first heard
at the school disco as very little reggae received air play on the BBC. What
is in no doubt by the summer of 69 skinheads and reggae were inseparable,
a phase that was to last until 1972.

Reggae evolved in 1968, superseding rocksteady as Jamaica's dominant
musical style, characterised by a guitar rhythm that accentuated the second
and fourth beat in each bar, with the rhythm guitar either emphasising the
third beat or holding the chord on the second beat until the fourth is
played. The shift from rocksteady to reggae was pioneered by Bunny Lee
with the organ shuffle sound featuring initially on Clancy Eccles Say What
Your Saying, Lee 'Scratch' Perry's People Funny Boy and the Pioneers 1967
track Long Shot Bus' Me Bet. Early 1968 saw the release of the true reggae
sound with Nanny Goat by Larry Marshall and No More Heartaches by
The Beltones.

In 1969 a record produced by Bunny Lee took the charts by storm and
become an anthem for the skinhead. Despite the ban by the BBC Max
Romeo's Wet Dream reached number ten on the UK chart and was
reputed to have sold over 250,000 copies. The two main players vying for
success were Pama, a label formed in 1967 by brothers Harry, Jeff and Carl
Palmer with a base in North London, and Trojan, with a base in Neasden
North West London. Trojan formed as a result of a tie in with Lee
Gopthal's (B&C) and Island record owner Chris Blackwell, and went on to
release over 20 hit singles, receiving plenty of air play. Their success with
the British charts was thanks in the main to the skinheads embracing the
music and adopting it as their own.

The book tells the story of the rise of reggae, and its followers, the
skinheads, from1968 to its height and subsequent demise as by the end of
1972 reggae had again evolved to what some say was, watered down and
string laden, a very far cry from the original raw sounds of the late 1960s
which the remaining skinheads could
no longer empathise.

By the summer of 1972 the youth had moved on, growing their hair a bit, not too long, and wore a baseball shirt, probably with a number seventeen on. All of the major artist of the time, some who have sadly passed on are reviewed with their singles and chart positions, their albums and of course the compilation budget LP's that were to become a mainstay, and a very important part of the skinheads collection. The leading producers of the day without whom none of this could have happened are also reviewed.

The story ends with one of the most influential pieces of work ever to emanate from Jamaica, a masterpiece that would catapult reggae to the world stage. The feature film The Harder They Come, complete with its soundtrack, became one of the most acclaimed compilation albums of reggae ever released.

SKINHEADS AND REGGAE

Where did it all begin? Well we need to go back to the early 1960s, a time before the hippie movement when the British youths were divided into primarily two groups based on their musical tastes.

The mods had formed an allegiance to R&B and British rock bands like The Who and Small Faces; perhaps most significantly they had taken to Jamaican ska. The mods rode scooters and had a tendency toward dressing well. Their rival group with far more progressive musical taste, the rockers, rode motorcycles and wore leather jackets.

When the psychedelic 1960s hit Britain the mods split into a wide variety of fashions and styles including hippies and the skinhead. This period is where the style of the skinhead was first defined. Skinhead fashion was intended to show a pride in the traditional English working-class look. The hard mod's who couldn't empathise with the hippie attitude and style got harder, and with a little influence from the Jamaican rude boys the traditional skinhead was born. The Jamaican ska the mods had endeared earlier in the decade, many now the elder brothers of the emerging skinheads, had slowed to the more romantic rocksteady rhythm, but by 1968 with poverty, violence, and political unrest in Jamaica the music upped its tempo again and began to evolve into reggae.

Reggae can be distinguished from rocksteady by the slightly faster beat marked out by the drummer using the hi-hat, heavy organ lines, lower mixing of the bass, and electronically doubled rhythm guitar strokes. What was in no doubt by the summer of 69 skinheads and reggae were inseparable, a phase that continued until 1972.

Reggae during this period can be classified as skinhead reggae with the skinheads playing a major part in the promotion of the emerging sounds from Jamaica. For the first time Jamaican music was beginning to be noticed outside of the island. 1969 saw the new Jamaican music being bought in increasing quantities and enjoying an unrivalled success from international audiences, with reggae now charting in the UK.

As to who produced that first reggae sound is a matter of conjecture but certainly to the fore were The Maytals with Do The Reggay, and Lester Stirling's Bangarang, produced by Bunny Lee, who has always claimed it as the first reggae record. In 1969 a record produced by Bunny Lee took the charts by storm despite the ban by the BBC. The record always referred to as "a record by Max Romeo" during a rundown of the charts was of course Wet Dream reaching number ten and selling over 250,000 copies. The record was a huge hit for Pama who released it on their Unity label on UN-503.

1969 saw reggae emerge as a true force with one theory suggesting that the skinheads took to the raw unpretentious sound as a reaction to the main stream music of the day, a statement that would reflect their fashion that had to some extent been copied from their black friends, including half mast trousers and almost shaven heads.

The most influential record was Skinhead Moonstomp, a single, inevitably followed by the album of the same name. One of the first reggae records to bring together the skins and Jamaican music, released in 1968, was the Dandy produced Skinheads A Message To You. The record was released on Trojan's Downtown label, DT-450, by Desmond Riley. But the embryo of the union between the music and the youth without doubt was Desmond Dekker's 007 and Israelites, both released on the Pyramid label.

The original skinheads, who later became known as traditional skins, had their own distinctive look of the era, they wore their hair cropped but not shaven, feathered was the order of the day for the skinhead girl. The look that set the skinhead apart was unique and consisted of a quality Ben Sherman shirt with button down collars, or a Fred Perry polo shirt, Levis 501 red tab jeans or Levi Sta-Prest trousers.

I recall sitting in the bath with a brand new pair of Levi jeans on in order for them to shrink, to provide the classic tight skinhead look. The jeans were worn with the compulsory turn up of about an inch at the bottom so they sat at what was described as half mast, revealing the shine of your boots. Unlike the rude boys of Jamaica no matter how hard you were it was essential to have a coat for the winter in the UK. A Harrington jacket or Crombie overcoat if funds would stretch were the order of the day.

Levi Sta-Prest trousers were a relatively new brand that did exactly what it said on the label, they could be taken from the dryer, that is if you were fortunate to have had one back then, with no need to iron, and the creases did stay in. Levi Strauss & Co began production of these trousers as early as 1964. Mainly a khaki shade of green with two-tone becoming more popular as the era progressed.

A Levi denim jacket was also an essential part of the skinheads wardrobe, with sleeves tucked up and the Levi badge taken from the inside and sewn above the left front chest pocket.

We must not forget the most essential part of the look, the half mast jeans were held up with braces about a half inch wide and crossed at the back.

The appearance was complete with a pair of boots, originally hobnail, it didn't matter if they were DM's or not, but soon Dr. Martens became the preference with the eight-eyelet Cherry Red, known as the 1460 so named as they began production on 1 April 1960, becoming the mainstay. The same look was often achieved courtesy of some vigorous polishing of a pair of brown DM's with ox blood or red polish. The Dr. Martens air filled soles were invented by a German doctor, Klaus Martens, in 1947. In 1960 the Griggs company acquired a license to manufacture the air cushioned footwear in the UK, introducing for the first time the distinctive yellow welt stitch, a two-tone grooved sole edge and the unique sole pattern. The original Dr. Martens boots became popular during those early skinhead days. Brogues or loafers were also worn by the skinhead when the occasion suited.

Like most things today the manufacturers were quick to take advantage of the skinhead uniform and what had been top quality clothing, including the Ben Sherman shirt and the Levi Sta-Prest trousers, began to be mass produced, flooding the market with far inferior garments at odds to the original quality that had endured them to the skinhead. I'm still the proud owner of my first Ben Sherman shirt and to this day the quality is unbelievable, looks and feels like new despite being over 40 years old, although it's not worn for a couple of reasons!

The skinheads had identified themselves to the rude boy culture of their new Jamaican friends and with their Dr. Marten boots, half mast Levis held up with bracers and cropped hair they looked formidable and intimidating to the masses.

Although they embraced the music and brought about its chart success they were also seen by some as influential in its downfall. In several interviews it has been well documented that Pama owner Harry Palmer has cited the influence of the skinhead on the record shop owners as damaging to the business. Many had refused to continue stocking the music Pama was producing for fear that their record shop would be overrun with the working class youth on a Saturday, a daunting proposition to other customers, causing a general loss of business.

The original skinheads were influenced by Jamaican music and the Jamaican rude boys following on from the mod movement. Unlike later generations that took the name the skinheads of 69 were fashioned on those elements alone and did not regard attitudes toward racism and politics as central to their subculture, how could they be racist, many danced the night away with their new West Indian friends.

I recollect a story surrounding Max Romeo who had just finished a performance at a school in Guilford, including of course Wet Dream to an audience of mainly white skinheads. On the way out a white man said something like, "how you doing Mr Black", Max replied, "alright Mr White", the man then spat at Max, the skinheads who were following Max turned and beat the white man up.

The sight of cropped heads and the sound of hefty boots entering the disco was enough to send many fleeing but the real aggro was reserved for the football terraces, a place where rival skinhead gangs, sometimes from the same clubs, ultimately aspired to be the hardest of them all. The aggro was well organised and each club had their own identity.

WANT SOME AGGRO?

The book, Want Some Aggro, tells of the time when skinhead gangs were staring out all over. Written by Cass Pennant and the late Micky Smith it tells the true story of West Ham's first Guv'nors from the late 60s to the early 70s. The following extract from season 69-70 is included with kind permission of John Blake Publishing Ltd.

The Man U game came around and as planned about a hundred of us met up at Mile End at 10 *o'clock*. We got to the tube at Euston and waited around. About 12 we knew the train was close because Old Bill started to appear and some sussed us out. We told them that we were Cockney Reds and were waiting for the main fans to come down as Upton Park was a bad place to go. They seemed to swallow this and, as there had been no aggro on the station, left us alone. We teamed up and decided to get them on the tube as it was too open at Euston and there were too many Old Bill around.

Two trains came in and a massive mob of Man U got off, all chanting and letting people know that they were there - scarves, the lot. We let the first lot go and joined the second lot. Coming off the platform we all walked down to the tube and once on the train the Old Bill left. They had done their bit and it wasn't their problem anymore.

We waited for a couple of stations and then started. One of our lads nicked a Man U scarf and was trying to burn it with his lighter. The Man U fans didn't like that and about six of them fronted him. That was the signal. One bloke swung up on the overhead handles and kicked this Man U bloke in the face. He went down and the rest soon got a good slapping. As the train pulled into the station a load got off; the ones we had done got thrown off.

The train moved off and we went down to the next carriage. It was half packed with Man U fans and once we were all in, we steamed in. They were shouting and screaming. We just hit and kicked at them and trampled over them. At Tottenham Court Road station most of them pilled out and ran.

The aggro continued later on that day on the terraces inside Upton Park with several small scuffles breaking out, but nothing as violent and organised as was witnessed in the mid seventies, scenes that were replicated at many football grounds.

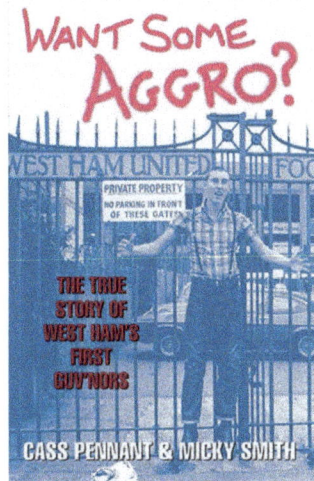

By the dawn of 1971 many skinheads had grown their hair a bit and became known as suedeheads whilst some still maintained the style and others became boot-boys. Much of the disruption at football matches in the early 1970s was blamed on the skinhead culture, but in reality it was the clubs well organised and disciplined fans.

SYMARIP

Enter Symarip AKA The Pyramids. The Pyramids had launched themselves onto the UK music scene as Prince Buster's backing group during his earlier tours of the UK. The Pyramids recorded many singles including Feel Alright /Telstar TR-7755, and To Sir With Love TR-7770, both released on Trojan in 1970. They made a name for themselves as Symarip, one of the first reggae bands to target the skinhead. First to come was the single on Treasure Isle in 1969, Skinhead Moonstomp / Must Catch A Train TI-7050, the former based on Derrick Morgan's Moon Hop. An album was inevitable with a compilation released on Trojan in 1970.The LP featured twelve boot-stomping tracks. Skinhead Moonstomp, Skinhead Girl and Skinhead Jamboree were all great stomping records with Chicken Merry having a semblance to Long Shot. A couple of instrumental's completed what was described at the time as the perfect party album. The original single sold well and an extensive tour of the UK followed with many venues thronged with stomping skinheads. 1970 saw the release on the Joe label JRS-9 by Joe The Boss titled Skinhead Revolt with Skinhead Train released on Explosion EX-2045, by The Charmers.

Essentially Derrick Morgan had Moon Hop released by Pama on Crab CRAB-32. When Roy Ellis and the band were in the studio Graeme Goodhall suggested they should take the rhythm from Derrick Morgan's Moon Hop and sing something about the skinheads. Roy just rapped some words that came into his head. With the cut complete in one take Graeme Goodhall said it's perfect for the white skinhead kids to dance to. However there was a problem as the Pyramids were contracted to President Records so couldn't release the track on a Trojan label. Problem solved, they just spelt the name Pyramids backwards without the D and Symarip were launched.

Skinhead Moonstomp was issued on Treasure Isle TI-7050, the B side featured Must Catch A Train.

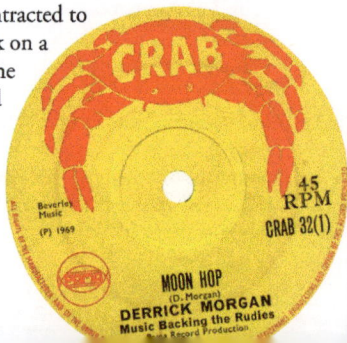

SKINHEAD MOONSTOMP
SYMARIP
TROJAN RECORDS   TBL102
Released 1970

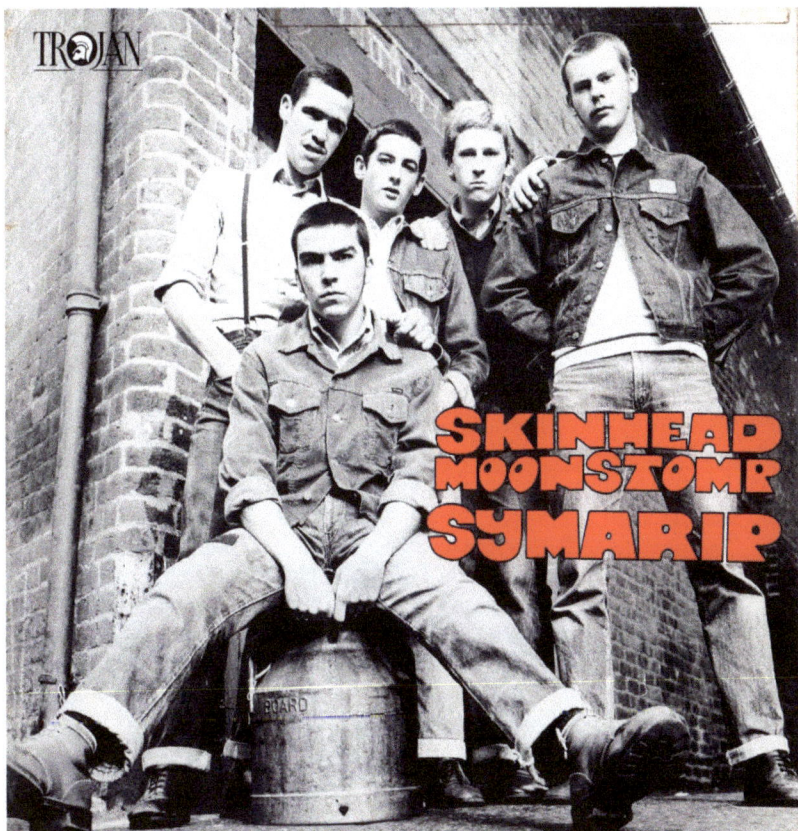

Side 1
1. SKINHEAD MOONSTOMP   2. PHOENIX REGGAE
3. SKINHEAD GIRL   4. TRY ME BEST
5. SKINHEAD JAMBOREE   6. CHICKEN MERRY

Side 2
1. THESE BOOTS ARE MADE FOR WALKING
2. MUST CATCH A TRAIN
3. SKINFLINT
4. STAY WITH HIM
5. FUNG SHU
6. YOU'RE MINE

TROJAN

The story of Trojan began during 1967 when the label was set up as a platform for productions from Duke Reid. The name Trojan is believed to have its origin in Jamaica as the huge truck Duke Reid used to transport his sound system around was a seven ton Leyland Trojan truck. The label soon folded but in 1968 was resurrected to become the biggest distributor of reggae in the UK by Lee Gopthall. Gopthall had been running a record store with previous business connections to Chris Blackwell who had already established Island records a decade earlier.

Reggae had hit the charts in the form of Desmond Dekker's Israelites issued on the Pyramid label and Max Romeo's risqué Wet Dream issued by Trojan's rival to be, Pama. Trojan's initial plan was to act as a feeder from Island Records releasing productions from Jamaica onto the UK market. The company enjoyed unparalleled success on the UK chart with hits from Lee 'Scratch' Perry's Upsetters, Desmond Dekker and Dave And Ansel Collins with their number one Double Barrel in 1970.

The tracks were supplied from the likes of Duke Reid and Leslie Kong back in Jamaica with the singles transferred to budget priced LP's once potential sales had peaked. Trojan released the Tighten Up, Reggae Chartbusters and Club Reggae series that became extremely popular with the growing fan base of skinheads, who had embraced the music along with their new West Indian friends. Trojan had established over thirty subsidiary labels between 1968 and 1972 catering for the output from different producers. The highlights include Clandisc associated with Clancy Eccles, Duke Reid for Duke Reid productions, Downtown exclusively for Dandy, Harry J for Harry Johnson productions and Dynamic for releases from Byron Lee's Dynamic Jamaican studio to name but a few.

Why did it all go wrong? Earlier in the decade Trojan was turning out an enormous amount of reggae and enjoyed several chart hits, but perhaps there lay the problem. Trojan began adding strings and horn arrangements to sweeten the sound, aiming to appeal to the mainstream, a sound different to the one that had brought about the love affair with the skinhead. Just listen to Long Shot Kick The Bucket, Return Of Django or It Mek, all no nonsense raw sounds that the youth of the day could identify with. Island pulled out of the partnership in 1971, a move that coincided with a declining interest in reggae.

TROJAN

Dominating the UK reggae market since their launch in 1968 to cater for the growing West Indian community Trojan had released over 180 singles on various labels by the dawn of 1969. Traditionally Jamaican music, ska and rocksteady had found success in the singles market with LP's seen as a luxury item. Trojan revolutionised the album market launching a budget price series TTL in early 1969. Its inaugural release Tighten Up was a compilation of the most popular recent singles, a format that would give wider access to the music, priced at just 14/6d.

It was a must have for the skinheads that had embraced the incessant dance music, originating from Jamaica, now being released in the UK. Those budget priced albums had a modest expectation from Trojan but would soon become a winning formula and the Tighten Up series had arrived. With the success of Tighten Up and the hits continuing on the chart an inevitable album was issued titled Reggae Chartbusters on the slightly pricier TBL series, a release that became the catalyst for another series, although running to just three volumes. Trojan's next series saw the release of Club Reggae showcasing the hits that were popular in the clubs again with the same formula as Tighten Up with a compilation of recent singles where sales had peaked. The budget priced compilations proved a very popular choice with the record buying public. However the reggae sales eventually began to suffer as the skinheads faded away and both Trojan and their rival Pama by the end of 1972 were releasing an extensive amounts of weak, watered down and string laden reggae, which found no favour with the remaining skinheads or indeed the general record buying public, the love affair was well and truly over.

Trojan skinheads were influenced by the traditional late 1960s culture and were named after Trojan Records embracing Jamaican music and the rude-boy style.

Many stories have been told of the struggle of the artists in Jamaica and it was perhaps highlighted for the first time in The Harder They Come when Ivan is offered 20 Dollars for his song. The producer called the shots with both Trojan and Pama approached by the likes of Bunny Lee, Leslie Kong and Lee 'Scratch' Perry for their own label identifying their work. At the height of the golden age of reggae Trojan and Pama alone accounted for over 40 labels, producing a staggering amount of music. This continued until production started to decline around 1971. It has been said that Trojan ensured the records most likely to succeed would be released on the main Trojan imprint with this theory backed up with the success of Desmond Dekker, Jimmy Cliff, Bob & Marcia, The Pioneers and Greyhound, the main exception being Dave And Ansel Collins success on Trojan's Winston Riley's Techniques label.

PAMA

Pama was set up by the Palmer brothers, Harry, Jeff and Carl, initiated when Harry, born in Clarendon, Jamaica, set up a record shop in north London. Harry produced and released a single through Island by Joyce Bond, Do The Teasy on WIP-6010, a take on Hopeton Lewis' Take It Easy. In spite of this little interest was shown for the Clancy Eccles track What Will Your Mama Say so they distributed the single independently on Pama PM-701 in 1967. The label soon became a major out pouring for reggae with the business run from the back room of their estate agency office in Harrow, later relocating to 78 Craven Park Road, Harlesden.

The breakthrough came for Pama when Harry Palmer established a link with the Jamaica producer Bunny 'Striker' Lee. Lee was able to supply almost unlimited material that had already achieved success on his native Jamaican Unity label. The second release on the Unity label in the UK was Last Flight To Reggae City by Stranger Cole then came Bangarang which had proved to be a massive hit in Jamaica and often cited as the first reggae record.

The label, unlike its competitor Trojan, only enjoyed one top ten hit, but what a hit it was. Max Romeo's Wet Dream produced by Bunny Lee and released on the Unity label took the charts by storm in 1969 with its risqué lyrics never receiving any airplay (apart from the outings courtesy of Emperor Rosko) but still sold over 250,000 copies, and remained on the UK charts for a respectful twenty five weeks. Another hit for Pama was Derrick Morgan's Moon Hop, released on the Crab label with the record soon establishing itself as a favourite with the emerging skinheads, reaching number 49 in the UK chart.

It was no secret that a great rivalry existed between Pama and Trojan, a contention that had been fuelled by Bunny Lee who had licensed Derek Morgan's Seven Letters to both companies. Pama, like Trojan, had several subsidiary labels, including Unity and Crab associated with Bunny Lee and the Punch label for the output from Lee 'Scratch' Perry. When Trojan introduced the very successful Tighten Up series Pama responded with their own version aptly titled Straighten Up.

Additional labels were soon launched with the emergence of Crab and Gas. Beverley Music appeared on many Pama labels, not a connection with Leslie Kong but a reference to a member of the Palmer family.

Further labels soon followed including Escort, perhaps best known for the original issue of Bob & Marcia's Young Gifted And Black, a version with no strings attached. Bob Andy was said to be surprised when it was issued by Pama along with some concern from Trojan, as a result it was hastily replaced on the same label and number with a somewhat uninspiring version from Denzil And Jennifer. What followed has been well documented with the release being put out by Trojan complete with the string arrangement by Johnny Arthey, the record became an all time classic hit. The record did however emphasize the difference in the reggae to come out over the next couple of years as it had highlighted that Trojan were prepared to sweeten tracks with strings added to ensure success in the pop market.

The Punch label was without doubt the most distinctive to emerge from the Pama stable. The design portrayed a fist smashing into the top 20 chart with the label initially concentrating on the sounds that were gripping the skinheads. One was the follow up to the Upsetters Return Of Django, Clint Eastwood, a record that it was claimed if distribution had not hampered its progress would have been another chart success for Pama. Another record that was issued on both Pama's Punch label and Trojan was Dave Barker's Shocks of Mighty although Barker was said to have been unaware of the Pama issue. Increasingly with the same artist appearing on both Pama and Trojan several singles were released simultaneously although it would be covered up by a change of title and artist on the credits. Other labels in competition with the big two at the time were Junior Lincoln's Bamboo and Melodisc.

By the end of 1971 the companies production from Jamaica was beginning to dry up with Trojan now fully established as the main producer with several chart successes to their name. The sound originating from Pama and its subsidiaries still held true to the unpretentious sounds that had earlier catapulted reggae to the fore back in 1968, unlike its rival Trojan. However by 1972 only Bullet, Camel, Pama Supreme, Punch and the main Pama label remained from the heyday of a dozen or so subsidiaries, all turning out vast amounts of reggae singles, and several albums.

The company would survive beyond 1972 but by 1974 had gone out of business. The Straighten Up series that Pama launched to rival Trojan's innovative compilation series of budget albums ran to just three volumes issued through to the end of 1972 with other compilations titled This Is Reggae and Hot Numbers. To the skinhead and the collector of reggae the label had come to personify a certain sound, ask any reggae connoisseur from 68-72 about a label and they would identify the sound and the producer, for it was the producer who was king at that time.

ARAWACK VERSION
I. Smith
THE INNER MINDS
Produced by Ian Smith

THE INNER MIND

During the late 60s there were a handful Jamaican musicians living in London who would support stop-over recording stars from Jamaica on tour, including the likes of Prince Buster. By 1969 with reggae now charting other artists arrived in Britain with Desmond Dekker leading the way, although The Aces refused to travel with him. Within a few months the bustling capital became home to Derrick Morgan, Jimmy Cliff, Owen Gray, sometimes known as Grey, and of course Laurel Aitken.

Most of the artists were unknown in Britain, apart that was from their recording talents and many a promoters tale has been told of the same artist topping the bill at different far apart venues on the same night.

The backing for many of the artists new UK releases were from British based musicians and one group from Yorkshire, The Inner Mind, were destined to become one of Pama's backing bands, earning the title as The Greatest White Reggae Band on Earth. The group had formed in 69 and comprised Ian R Smith, Organ and Piano, Jimmy Walsh on drums, Dave Tattersall bass and Finley Topham guitar. Ian generously reveals his personal recollections during the golden age of reggae later in the book titled A Musician's Tale. The Inner Mind backed many of Pama's established reggae acts such as Laurel Aitken, Owen Gray, Winston Groovy and Alton Ellis.

BAMBOO CLUB
EASTER
HOLIDAY ATTRACTIONS

THURSDAY April 8th
The fantastic DUKE with his latest soul sounds
Guests 20p
Members 15p

FRIDAY April 9th
The fabulous INNER MIND—Great Raggae Show
Guests 30p
Members 20p

SATURDAY April 10th
The Really Dynamic OWEN GRAY
Backed by the INNER MIND BAND
A Fantastic Raggae and Soul Show
Guests 75p
Members 50p

SUNDAY April 11th
Special Easter Sunday Show—Dancing to the gre
INNER MIND
SPECIAL DANCING COMPETITION
Free Tickets for Easter Monday Show for the twel
best dressed Girls and Boys
Members 30p

EASTER MONDAY April 12th—The one and only
BIG, BIG DANCE—STON GRO
don't make me cry
INER MI

LONDON APOLLO CLUB
375, HIGH ROAD, WILLESDEN, N.W.10
01-459 7842

PRESENTS

AUGUST
Thursday, 19th
DISCO SPECIAL
NEW 1100 WAT SOUND
JOHN CROW SKANK
AND FUNKY RECORDS NIGHT

Friday, 20th
THE MOHAWKS

Saturday, 21st
THE INNER MIND

Sunday, 22nd
THE FASCINATIONS
From America

Coming Attraction
Saturday 28th
THE DRIFTERS

SUNDAY 29th
JOYCE BOND

PLEASE DRESS SMARTLY or YOU WILL BE REFUSED ADMISE

Their first release was an instrumental on the Shades label SHA11 Dreams Of Yesterday, a track that did receive extensive air play including outings on Radio One. But in those days distribution and promotion was atrocious, preventing records being available to larger audiences, holding the record back, unlike Trojan who had enjoyed their extensive network of connections.

Fledgling record companies began to emerge and one was Ian R. Smith's Hot Lead Records based in Yorkshire. The Inner Mind had releases on Pama's New Beat label with one of their biggest in 1970 Pum Pum Girl NB-069, although erroneously credited as a Laurel Aitken production on the label. Singles on Bullet BU-465 Arawack Version, and Devil Woman BU-490 were released in 1971. Pama also released an unauthorised record on the Pama Supreme label PS-352 in 1972 titled Breakdown Rock which just happened to be Dreams Of Yesterday crediting the artist as The Harlesden Monks. Without doubt Ian Smith's biggest success came in 1973 after the skinhead era had run its course with the release on Hot Lead of Doggie Bite Postman, under the guise of Smithy, a record it was said to have sold faster than it could be pressed. The record was a brilliant risqué version of Maga Dog HL-12 with the B side featuring an instrumental version Teeth Marks, very reminiscent of skinhead reggae at its best. The Inner Mind were described as 'The Greatest White Reggae Band on Earth'.

The history of the labels that launched the sounds of Jamaica to the UK is up next. The influence of these charismatic labels during the golden age should never be understated.

REGGAE TOP 50

PAMA RECORDS
78 CRAVEN PARK ROAD
HARLESDEN · LONDON · NW10
Telephone: 01-965 2267-8-9

BOSS SOUNDS ON PAMA

RR 6th. AUGUST 1971

THIS WEEK	LAST WEEK			THIS WEEK	LAST WEEK	
1	1	GUILTY - TIGER	CA 70	26	21	RICE & PEAS Dandy
2	2	JUST MY IMAGINATION The Charmers	SUP 220	27	44	GIRL TELL ME WHAT
3	3	FAREWELL MY DARLING Eugene Paul	PS 317	28	22	PEACE TREATY The
4	4	MONKEY SPANNER Larry & Lloyd	NB 080	29	29	I FOUND A MAN Eu
5	6	PUT YOUR SWEET LIPS Raphel Stewart	PS 71	30	26	GROOVE ME Owen
6	5	EVERY NIGHT Ruddy & Skitto	SUP 218	31	13	SEX EDUCATION Th
7	11	CO CO The Marvels	NB 018	32	42	SILHOU ETTES Winst
8	8	MY LOVE Rupie Edwards All-Stars	BU 462	33	27	RUN BABYLON The Ma
9	7	LET THE POWER FALL Max Romeo	PS 306	34	34	LET IT FALL Eugene & Bu
10	10	CHIE-CHIE BUD Max Romeo	PH 73	35	28	CANDIDA Owen Gray
11	9	CRYING Stranger Cole	CA 72	36	32	YOU INSPIRE ME Busty Brown
12	14	BLACK EQUALITY Max Romeo	CA 65	37	30	DON'T LET THE TEARS FALL Eugene
13	20	JOHN CROW SKANK Derrick Morgan	PS 321	38	33	MY WAY D. Dennis
14	24	BLACK MAN'S PRIDE Alton Ellis	BU 466	39	37	MY LOVE COME TRUE Slim Smith
		DON'T YOU WEEP Mx Romeo	PS 381	40	41	DON'T GET WEARY Tony Brevett
		CHANGED D.D. Dennis	PS 304	41	38	MY SWEET LORD Fitzroy Sterling
			NB 086	42	50	ARAWACK VERSION Inner Minds
				43		HAILES SELAISE Laurel Aitken
						RVATION The Ethiopians
						Lloyd Jackson

ARAWACK VERSION
I. Smith
THE INNER MINDS
Produced by Ian Smith

	PS
ERT	851
SUP	224
PM	820
BU	465
23 NB	032
SUP	226
PS	308
CA	67

AMALGAMATED RECORDS

AMG 8

B&C Musi
℗ 1968

THEM A LAUGH AND A KI KI
(Soulmates)
THE SOULMATES
Producer: J. A. Gibson

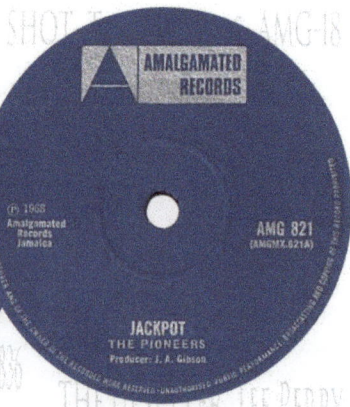

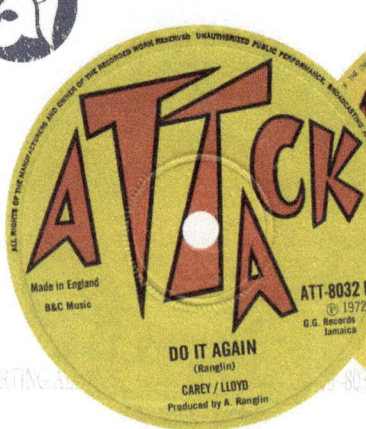

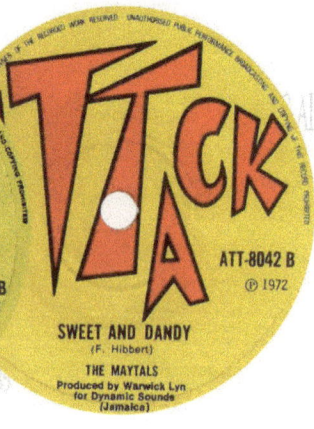

AMALGAMATED RECORDS

℗ 1968
Amalgamated
Records
Jamaica

AMG 821
(AMGMX.621A)

JACKPOT
THE PIONEERS
Producer: J. A. Gibson

ATTACK

Made in England
B&C Music

ATT-8032 B
℗ 1972
G.G. Records
Jamaica

DO IT AGAIN
(Ranglin)
CAREY / LLOYD
Produced by A. Ranglin

ATTACK

ATT-8042 B
℗ 1972

SWEET AND DANDY
(F. Hibbert)
THE MAYTALS
Produced by Warwick Lyn
for Dynamic Sounds
(Jamaica)

BIG

Made in England
B&C Music
℗ 1971

BG 319-A
Produced by:
Gaylads

CAN'T HIDE THE FEELING
(The Gaylads)
THE GAYLADS
Produced by: Gaylads

BIG

BG 319-B
Produced by:
Gaylads

CAN'T HIDE THE FEELING
VERSION TWO
(The Gaylads)
THE GAYLADS

THE LABELS

TROJAN

AMALGAMATED
(PREFIX) AMG

The label was set up in 1968 by B&C to issue production from Joe Gibbs.

The most notable recordings were from The Pioneers including such classic offerings as Long Shot, Jackpot and Mama Look Deh. The label also issued Wreck A Buddy by The Soul Sisters and Them A Laugh And A Ki Ki by The Soulmates, both featuring on Tighten Up Volume 2 TBL 132 in 1970, a re-issue of TTL 7, originally released by Trojan during 1969. The first single on the Amalgamated label was Please Stop Your Lying by Errol Dunkley AMG-800. Amalgamated produced over seventy good quality recordings right up until early 1971 with Joe Gibbs productions switched to the Pressure Beat label created in 1970.

ATTACK
(PREFIX) ATT

Graeme Goodall launched the Attack label in 1969.

The label initially concentrated on British reggae with The Pyramids in their various guises having the lion's share of the production. The label ceased production in 1970 with just a mere twenty three records ever released before the label folded. It was however revived by Trojan in 1972 seeing some good quality singles including Scorpion and Do It Again by Lloyd & Carey, Starting All Over Again by Hopeton Lewis and another release of The Maytals Sweet And Dandy as the B side to It Was Written Down on ATT-8042. The label continued record production for Trojan well into the decade.

BIG
(PREFIX) BG

Rupie Edwards was the main producer for the Big label with perhaps its most notable offering from The Gaylads with Can't Hide The Feeling, a track featured on Club Reggae Volume 2. The label ceased production at the end of 1972 perhaps not one of Trojan most significant contributors.

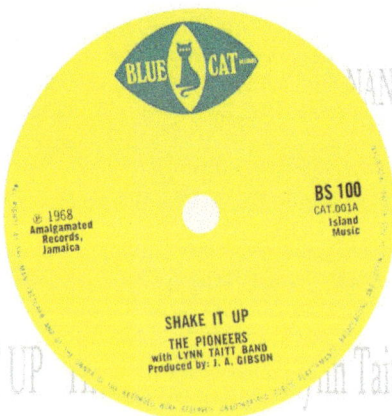

BIG SHOT
(PREFIX) BI

The first release on Big Shot was Reggae Girl BI-501 in late 1968 at the dawning of the golden age of reggae. The label released over one hundred and twenty singles. Two of the early offerings featured on the highly acclaimed Tighten Up Series, Sufferer by The Kingstonians and John Jones by Rudy Mills on Volume 2. Queen Of The World by Lloyd And Claudette continued the success, the track issued on BI-546 in 1970 had an outing on Volume 3 and Niney's Blood & Fire featured on Volume 4. 1972 saw the release of the labels British chart success in the shape of Big Six and Big Seven by Judge Dread.

BLUE CAT
(PREFIX) BS

Blue Cat was a label launched in 1968 only lasting until 1969 but issuing over fifty singles in the first year.

Nana by the Slickers and a couple of tracks by The Maytones with Billy Goat and Loving Reggae are the singles that stand above the others issued on the label. During the final few releases the label design changed to a more traditional white and orange Trojan style design.

BREAD
(PREFIX) BR

Trojan established Bread in 1970 as a label for Jackie Edwards productions. The labels output was leant toward the commercial sound with the most notable singles being Johnny Gunman, a track featuring on Club Reggae Volume 3, Your Eyes Are Dreaming by Danny Ray and Jackie Edwards and BR-1108 I Do Love You C/W Who Told You So? by Jackie Edwards. The label issued just twenty singles ceasing production in 1973.

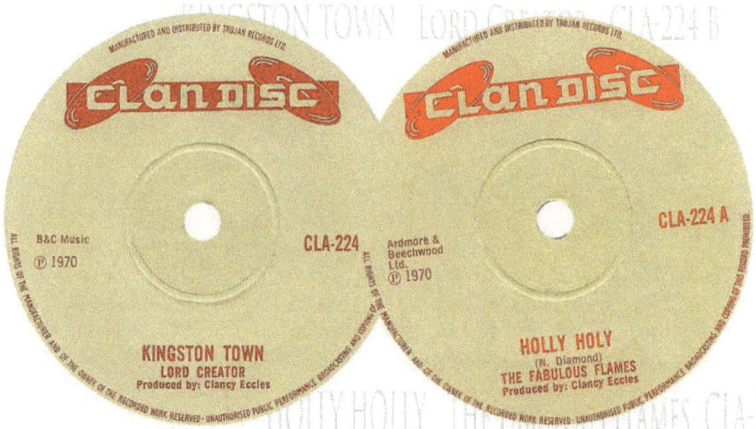

CLANDISC
(PREFIX) CLA

The name should be easily identified with the legendary Clancy Eccles. The label was launched by Trojan in 1969 and has to be one of the most notable for quality recordings. The label offered a mix of productions and releases by Clancy Eccles including Herbsman Shuffle by King Stitt and Unite Tonight by Clancy, superb offerings that featured on the Tighten Up series. Holly Holy by The Fabulous Flames and Sweet Jamaica, sung admirably by Clancy were both excellent tracks that featured on Club Reggae Volume 1 and Volume 2 respectively.

Other notable offerings were Open Up and Rod Of Correction again from Clancy, the later another track to feature on the Tighten Up series, this time Volume 5 in 1972.

DOWNTOWN
(PREFIX) DT

Downtown was set up exclusively for Robert Livingstone Thompson in 1968, better known as Dandy, RLT or Boy Friday to name but a few. The label not only issued productions by Dandy but also his excellent vocal talents including, Move Your Mule and Reggae In Your Jeggae. Prior to the latter Dandy had released Come Back Girl in 1968 on DT-402, using the forthcoming rhythm track for Reggae In Your Jeggae. One of the most notable singles released in 1969 on DT-419 was the skinhead favourite Red, Red Wine by Tony Tribe, although some copies incorrectly crediting the recording to Tony Tripe. Skinheads A Message To You calling for calm from Desmond Riley on DT-450, Dandy And Audrey forming a duet for Morning Side Of The Mountain and Version Girl, performed admirably by Boy Friday issued on DT-470 were all notable recordings.

Dandy moved on to record on the Horse label in the guise of Dandy Livingstone, a move that saw him enjoy success in the British charts albeit at the end of the golden era in the autumn of 1972.

DT-410 A
BOS 36

B&C/Island
Music
(P) 1969

REGGAE IN YOUR JEGGAE
DANDY
Produced by: Brother Dan

29

DUKE
(PREFIX) DU

The Duke label was formed in 1968 to issue productions from Duke Reid.

The Duke label ranks amongst the best for a variety of releases with undoubtedly the biggest success in terms of sales going to Boris Gardner's Elizabethan Reggae DU-39 reaching number 14 in the British charts in March 1970. Quality recording are not the monopoly of the charts and the label boasted many fine offerings ranging in styles from Clancy Eccles Auntie Lulu C/W Bag A Boo, Home Without You by The Beltones and The Law by Andy Capp, a track that featured on Club Reggae. Geronimo by The Pyramids and To The Fields by Herman were other excellent tracks, the latter also featured on the early Club Reggae albums. Bald Headed Teacher from Max Romeo and Save The Last Dance For Me by The Heptones shows just how varied the offering was. The label eventually ceased production in 1973.

DUKE REID
(PREFIX) DR

The label became an outlet for Ewart Beckford, better known by his stage name U.Roy or sometimes Hugh Roy, the pioneer of toasting. The originator as he was known had an excellent stream of offerings on Duke Reid despite the label only releasing twenty four singles. The limited number of releases contributed to the labels production of first class reggae issued from 70 to 72. U.Roy was responsible for a third of the output with such classic tracks as Wake The Town, Wear You To The Ball, with John Holt, and Version Galore. Another notable offering came from Hopeton Lewis with Boom-Shacka- Lacka a track that also featured on Club Reggae.

TR⊙JAN TOP 50 & New Releases.

LAST WEEK	THIS WEEK				W/E 24th March 1972
4	1	TR	7854	BUT I DO	BOB AND MARCIA
1	2	TR	7852	MOTHER AND CHILD REUNION	THE UNIQUES
2	3	TRM	9001	CHOPSTICKS/I'VE GOT IT/PUT IT ON	DELTONES
5	4	RAN	521	IT'S NOW OR NEVER	JIMMY LONDON
2	5	TR	7853	I AM WHAT I AM	GREYHOUND
3	6	HJ	6640	COME BACK AND STAY	FABULOUS FIVE
8	7	DYN	427	ALCAPONE GUNS DON'T BARK	DENNIS ALCAPONE
10	8	TR	7850	YESTERDAY MAN	NICKY THOMAS
13	9	GD	4021	RIOT	SOUL SYNDICATE
15	10	DYN	428	JUST A DREAM	SLIM SMITH
50	11	GD	4023	HIGH SCHOOL SERANADE	LENNOX BROWN
20	12	BR	1107	JOHNNY GUNMAN	JACKIE EDWARDS
	13	BI	598	SOMETIMES GIRL	THE CABLES
		US	377	ALPHA AND OMEGA	DENNIS ALCAP...
		...P	786	I NEED YOUR LOVING	SLIM SMITH
		...	7856	FOR YOUR PRECIOUS LOVE	VIC TAYLO...
			6510	SHANKY DOG	BUNNY...

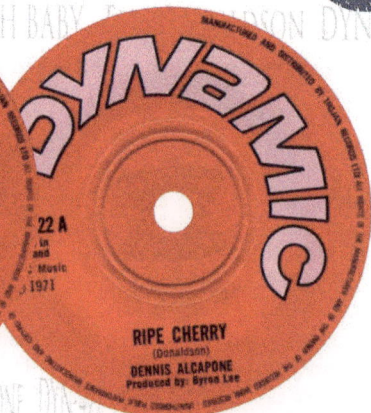

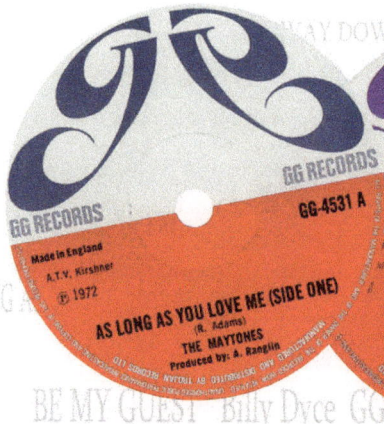

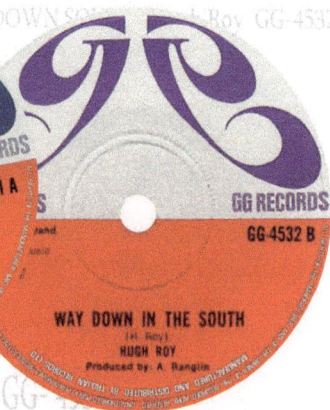

DYNAMINC
(PREFIX) DYN

Dynamic was launched as the UK outlet for producer Byron Lee who owned the Dynamic Studios back in Jamaica. Other producers used the label including Lee Perry and Bunny Lee who were also using Lee's studio back in Jamaica. The most notable and by far the best selling single was Cherry, Oh Baby, the 1971 festival winner from Eric Donaldson released on DYN-420, a record produced by Bunny Lee. The outstanding offerings included several other tracks from Eric including, Blue Boot, Miserable Woman and Love Of The Common People, the latter featured as the backing track for another inspired talk over from Dennis Alcapone, Alcapone's Guns Don't Bark. Johnny Too Bad by the Slickers was another gem, a track that featured on the forthcoming soundtrack of the Jamaican film The Harder They Come.

EXPLOSION
(PREFIX) EX

The name Explosion conjures up a real foot stomping vision, but the leaning was toward the commercial sounds, with very few tracks standing head and shoulders above the seventy or so singles released from 69 to 72. Man From Carolina by The GG All Stars who were in fact The Slickers, Skinhead Train by The Charmers and an inspiration from Neville with I Love Jamaica, a reggae backing with a calypso slant on the vocals also produced by Neville, and Slim Smith's The Time Has Come are though worthy of a spin. The label had three different designs during its time, the white, the red and an uninspiring yellow version.

GG
(PREFIX) GG

GG was producer Alvin Ranglin's main outlet on Trojan Records. The label featured Verne & Son's Little Boy Blue who's rhythm track resurfaced on the ribald offering from Judge Dread, Big Six. A large contribution came from The Maytones with some of their best in the form of As Long As You Love Me and Black & White. Good reggae sounds came from Lonely Nights from Eric Donaldson and Charlie Ace with Ontarius Version. The same rhythm track was used for It's Been A Long Time, an instrumental on GG-4504A from Winston Wright. Curiously this time the B side featured a vocal rendition Feel It More And More by Paulette & Gee. The same track was released on Pama's Crab label, albeit with a slight change of title to Feel It and credited to Sisters.

COME DOWN PART 1
(Hibbert)
CAREY AND LLOYD
A Dynamic Sounds Production

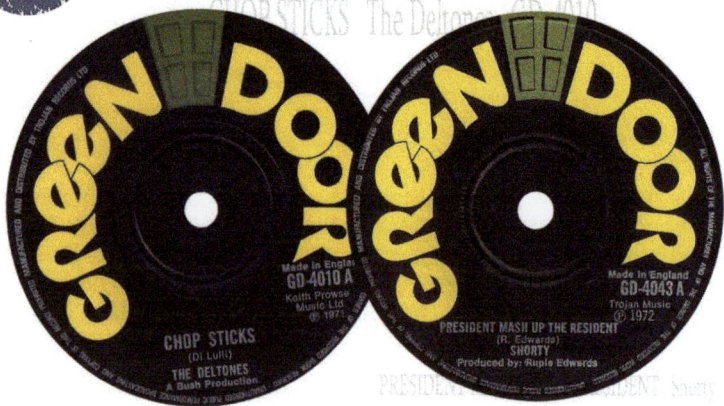

Made in England
Trojan Music
℗ 1972

COME DOWN PART 1
(Hibbert)
CAREY AND LLOYD
A Dynamic Sounds Production
MANUFACTURED AND DISTRIBUTED BY TROJAN RECORD

GR-3025 B

Made in England
Trojan Music
℗ 1972

COME DOWN PART 2
(Hibbert)
THE DYNAMITES
Dynamic Sounds Production
MANUFACTURED AND DISTRIBUTED BY TROJAN RECORDS LTD.

Made in England
GD-4010 A
Keith Prowse
Music Ltd
℗ 1971

CHOP STICKS
(Di Lulli)
THE DELTONES
A Bush Production

Made in England
GD-4043 A
Trojan Music
℗ 1972

PRESIDENT MASH UP THE RESIDENT
(R. Edwards)
SHORTY
Produced by: Ruple Edwards

Made in England
Trojan Music
℗ 1972

HJ-6640 A

COME BACK AND STAY
(F. Campbell)
FABULOUS FIVE INC.
A Harry J. Production

HJ-6640 B

COME BACK AND STAY—VERSION
(F. Campbell)
THE PETER ASHBOURNE AFFAIR
A Harry J. Production

34

GRAPE
(PREFIX) GR

The label was set up in 1969 to release producer Joe Sinclair's work. Just a few notable tracks stand out with some of the earlier contributions appealing to the skinheads. One being Skinhead A Bash Them by Claudette & The Corporation and Guns Of Navarone from Freddie Notes & The Rudies, although no match for the original classic ska track from the Skatalites issued on Island Records WI-168 in 1965. Another fine fast moving excellent dance crasher was Come Down from Lloyd & Carey.

GREENDOOR
(PREFIX) GD

The label kicked off in 1971, a relatively late starter, but delivered some classic tracks released during the years 71 to 72. The backbone of the output erred toward pure Jamaican with the first release reflecting the emerging sound of roots from The Charmers with Rasta Never Fails. The labels list of artists reads like a who's who of reggae and included Ken Boothe and The Heptones with Lively Up Yourself and Guava Jelly coming from Bob Marley & The Wailers. The quality didn't stop there with Hypocrite from The Heptones, A Sugar from Roy Shirley - Altyman Reid - and President Mash Up The Resident from Shorty.

HARRY J
(PREFIX) HJ

The iconic Harry J label was established to release the UK production from Harry Johnson, with the labels two most famous chart hits being HJ-6605 Young Gifted And Black by Bob & Marcia and HJ-675 Liquidator from Harry J All Stars, the latter appeared on Trojan 600 series TR-675 but with a Harry J label. Late 1972 saw the release of the upbeat Come Back And Stay by The Fabulous Five on HJ-6640 and Down Side Up by Harry J All Stars, featuring on Tighten Up Volume 6.

Come Back And Stay was the Fabulous Five's first recording and became a massive number one hit in Jamaica. The B side, Version, sounding very much like Scotty inadvertently had an outing on Club Reggae Volume 3. They also backed Johnny Nash on his successful album I Can See Clearly Now.

HIGH NOTE RECORDS

B&C Music
℗ 1970

HS-04

STAY A LITTLE BIT LONGER
(D. Stewart)
DELANO STEWART
Produced by: S. Pottinger

HIGH NOTE RECORDS

Made In
England
Copyright
Control
℗ 1971

HS-054 A

JOY TO THE WORLD
(H. Axton)
JULIAN AND THE CHOSEN FEW
WITH THE GAYTONES
Produced by: S. Pottinger

SUZANNE,
BEWARE
OF THE
DEVIL
(Thompson/Molby)
DANDY
LIVINGSTONE
Trojan
Music
℗ 19

HORSE

HOSS-16 A

HOSS 16A

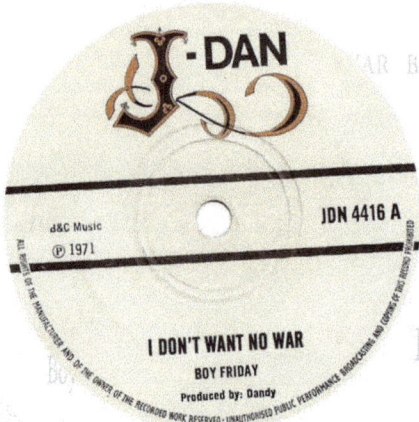

J-DAN

d&C Music
℗ 1971

JDN 4416 A

I DON'T WANT NO WAR
BOY FRIDAY
Produced by: Dandy

HIGHNOTE
(PREFIX) HS

High Note was mainly launched for the release of material from producer Sonia Pottinger. Notable singles are ABC Rocksteady by The Gaylads HS-001, Stay A Little Bit Longer from Delano Stewart, a track incidentally that featured on Tighten Up Volume 3 and Joy To The World by Julie Ann (actually Judy Mowatt) & The Chosen Few. That track went on to gain an outing on Tighten Up Volume 5 (where it is credited to Julien & The Chosen Few). Dance With Me from Delano Stewart and The Hippy Boys and Reggae Pressure are also worthy of a mention.

HORSE
(PREFIX) HOSS

The label was seen by Trojan as a pop label very much aimed at the mainstream rather than the skinhead. Its most notable release has to be Suzanne Beware Of The Devil on HOSS-16 from Dandy Livingstone towards the end of 1972. Very little of the labels offering would make it onto an album of purist reggae; however that was the labels intention from the outset.

A couple of tracks worth a mention would be John Holt with The Further You Look, on HOSS-22, and a sublime reggae version of Tchaikovsky Piano Concerto No 1 by The Neasden Connection, on HOSS-17, produced by Robert Thompson AKA Dandy.

J-DAN
(PREFIX) JDN

The label lasted only a year set up by Trojan as a sister label to Dandy's Downtown. Only seventeen singles were released but none stand out as classic tracks. Most of the production came from the Music Doctors and Boy Friday, not surprising given they are pseudonyms for Dandy.

JACKPOT
(PREFIX) JP

Jackpot ran similar to Pama's Unity label being the UK version of Bunny Lee's Jamaican Jackpot label. That said the label had few outstanding releases, however one exception was Delroy Wilson's Better Must Come JP-763, a song used by the Jamaican PNP in 1972 during their successful election campaign. The track proved worthy of an outing on Trojan's Tighten Up Volume 5. Other tracks worthy of a mention include the 1972 release Guilty by Ken Parker, not to be confused with the single by Tiger produced by Laurel Aitken and released on Pama's Camel label CA-70 a year earlier. Girl Of My Dreams from Dave Barker was another exception.

JOE
(PREFIX) JRS

The Joe label was aimed squarely at the rapidly emerging skinheads although the output only ran to seventeen singles with the release of tracks such as Trial Of Pama Dice, Skinhead Revolt and The Informer. All the releases in the series were produced by Joe Mansano who ran a record shack in Brixton.

MOODISC
(PREFIX) MU

Harry Mudie productions were released on Moodisc from 1970 to 1971 having previously issued work through Trojan's rival Pama. Cornel Campbell & The Eternals Let's Stay Together and an early release from I Roy with Musical Pleasure are two that are noticeable.

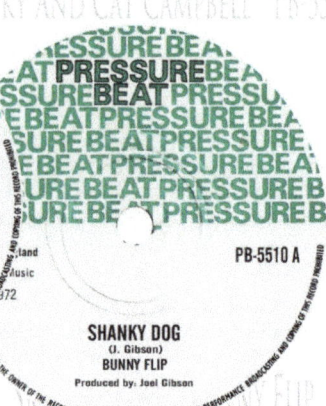

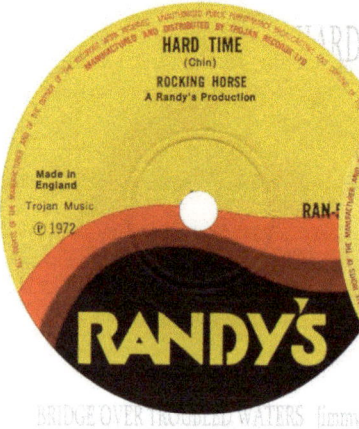

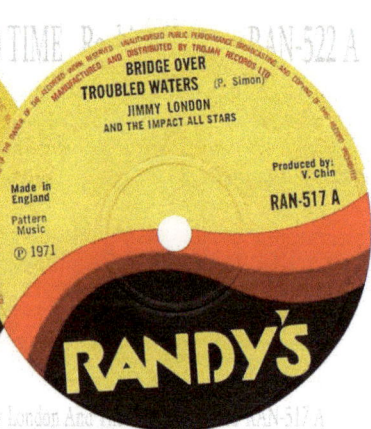

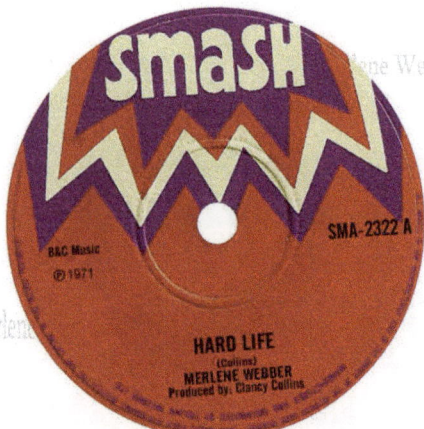

PRESSURE BEAT
(PREFIX) PR

Pressure Beat had a limited amount of releases continuing from where Joe Gibbs Amalgamated label left off. Perhaps the most notable being Them A Fe Get A Beatin from Peter Tosh on PB-5509 in 1972 and Shanky Dog from Bunny Flip toasting over Peter Tosh's Maga Dog on PB-5510.

RANDY'S
(PREFIX) RAN

The label was launched in 1970 to issue production from the late Vincent Chin's Jamaican Randy's and Impact labels. Randy's feature high on the list of Trojan's subsidiary labels with a reputation for some excellent offerings. Jimmy London & The Impact All Stars featured with Bridge Over Troubled Water, released in 1971 on RAN-517 making it onto Trojan's Tighten Up Volume 5. An instrumental version had been released the previous year credited to Randy's All Stars on RAN-507. The equally impressive follow up to Bridge was A Little Love RAN-520, a track that really showcased the vocal talents of Jimmy. The Impact All Stars featured once again with Rocking Horse on Hard Time RAN-522, a track included on the eagerly awaited 1972 Trojan release Club Reggae Volume 3.

SMASH
(PREFIX) SMA

Another label launched to act as an outlet for a Jamaican label in the UK, this occasion it was supposed to be Bunny Lee's Smash label. Things never went to plan although the label did have a couple of exceptionally good releases including Hard Life with a heavily accentuated rhythm from Merlene Webber on SMA-2322, with the track featured on Tighten Up Volume 4 and Wake The Nation from Hugh Roy on SMA-2313.

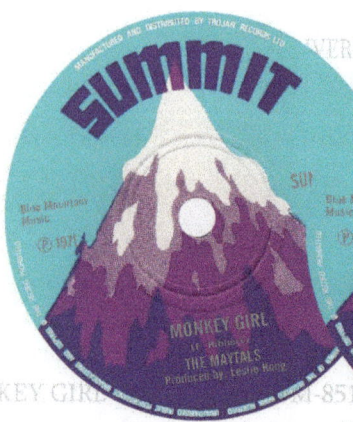

SONG BIRD
(PREFIX) SB

The label launched in 1969 was initially given over in the main to Lloyd Charmers productions and Trojan's own Joe Sinclair. The early releases included Riding For A Fall from Derrick Harriott on SB-1013 and Singer Man SB-1019 by the Kingstonians, a track included on Tighten Up Volume 3. Derrick Harriott came again with Groovy Situation, SB-1042 which was later released on Trojan TR-7887, the single making it onto the first Volume of Club Reggae. Good Ambition by The Ethiopians, Riddle I This from Scotty & Derrick, Know For I, Bongo Herman & Bunny and Lot Wife SB-1062 by The Ethiopians are all excellent tracks that would find their way onto any best of album.

SPINNING WHEEL
(PREFIX) SW

Launched in 1970 the label released less than a dozen singles and folded after just a year.

SUMMIT
(PREFIX) SUM

Summit was launched to provide Trojan with an outlet for work from the up and coming Leslic Kong's Beverley's Records in Jamaica. Following Leslie Kong's sudden death in August 1971 Trojan continued releasing his work posthumously, but when these ran out so did the labels direction.

The excellent work from Leslie Kong is clear to see on the labels output with the classic tracks including The Melodians Rivers Of Babylon on SUM-8508 and The Pioneers Starvation SUM-8511. The Maytals Monkey Girl on SUM-8513 and their One Eye Enos SUM-8520 were also classic reggae of the highest standard, as was a cover of Dawn's Knock Three Times by Brent Dowe. Other gems included It's You and Walk With Love from The Maytals.

Song bird

SINGER MAN
(C. Bernard/D. Harriott)
THE KINGSTONIANS
Produced by:
Derrick Harriott

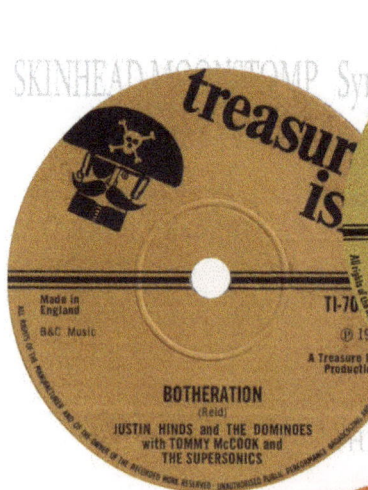

TECHNIQUES
(PREFIX) TE

Winston Riley productions were showcased on the Techniques label launched in 1970. The highlight of not only the label but for Trojan was the release of TE-901 Double Barrel by Dave & Ansel Collins, with the follow up TE-914 Monkey Spanner both providing massive hits in the UK. The remainder of the output from the label was eclipsed by those two gems from Dave Barker and Ansel Collins.

TREASURE ISLE
(PREFIX) TI

Treasure Isle was an Island label from 1967 to 1968. Re launched by Graeme Goodall's Doctor Bird group in 1969. Treasure Isle began with the early releases featuring the skinhead anthem Skinhead Moonstomp on TI-7050 and Pop A Top by Andy Capp TI-7052. Phyllis Dillon's TI-7058 One Life To Live, One Love To Give and Everybody Bawlin TI-7064 by U.Roy & The Melodians are the most notable offerings of classic reggae released in 1971 when the label came under the direct control of Trojan, who were then dealing with Duke Reid productions. One of Duke Reid's productions from 1965 issued on Island WI-171 was Bother Ration from Justin Hinds And The Dominoes, the track was updated and re released on TI-7063 in 1971 as Botheration with a strong reggae beat.

TROJAN
(PREFIX) TR 600 SERIES & TR 7000 SERIES

The second in Trojan's series, the first output from 1967-1968 putting out Duke Reid Productions. The second (600) series on an orange label ran from 1968 through to the end of 1969 releasing a century of singles. The series began with some fine work by Dandy prior to the launch of his Downtown label. The first release was Donkey Returns by The Brother Dan All Stars TR-60, released in July 1968. For the remainder of 1968 the label released some memorable tracks including Spanish Harlem from Val Bennett TR-611, Tighten Up by The Untouchables on TR-613, Place In The Sun by David Isaacs TR-616 and Stir It Up from Bob Marley & The Wailers on TR-617. Several of the best singles featured on Trojan's first budget priced compilation Tighten Up. Between the end of 1968 and December 1969 Trojan released a tremendous amount of quality material.

MONKEY SPANNER
(S. Riley / A. Collins)
DAVE & ANSEL COLLINS
Producer - Winston Riley

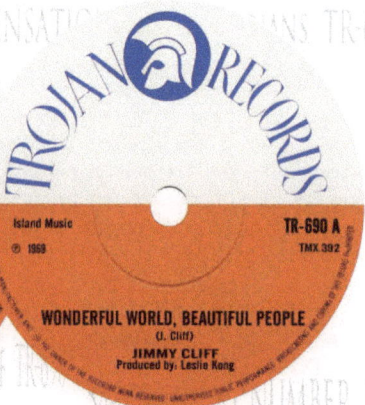

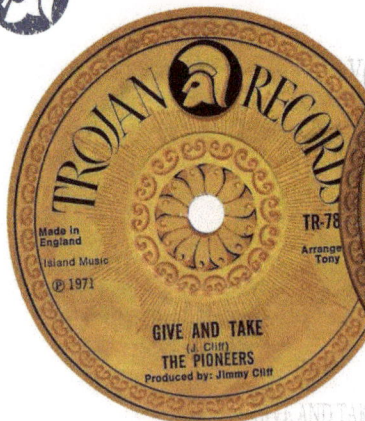

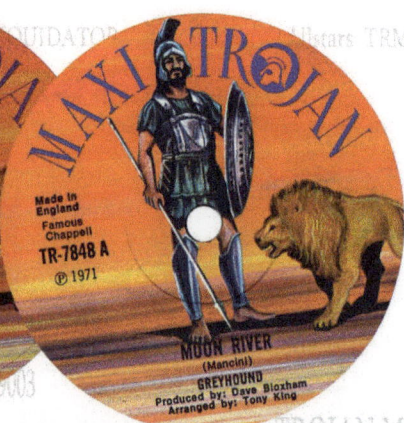

The highlights including amongst many was The Pioneers Long Shot Kick De Bucket TR-672 which appeared on both the orange and orange and white labels, and their Poor Rameses TR-698 on the orange and white label.

The (7000) series continued where the predecessor (600) had left off with more top quality recordings including several productions from Leslie Kong and Duke Reid, but the beginnings of the sweetening process had begun. Trojan who were now regularly gaining chart success with artists like Desmond Dekker, Jimmy Cliff and The Pioneers oversaw yet another change to the label, phasing out the iconic orange and white to the brown shield design. In order to sweeten the music Trojan acquired the services of Johnny Arthey to add strings and orchestras, the effect most recognisable on the UK versions of Harry J' Young Gifted And Black by Bob And Marcia and Love Of The Common People from Nicky Thomas issued on TR-7750, when compared with the original Jamaican recordings.

TROJAN
(PREFIX) TR 7000 SERIES (BROWN SHIELD)

By late 1971 most of the singles released were on the brown shield design with occasional orange and white label designs making an appearance, now with the popular single sleeve depicting the Trojan warrior. Most notable releases during this time, a time when reggae had evolved a long way from the early rocksteady influenced beat and with regular chart success becoming short lived were, Bob & Marcia with their version of Pied Piper issued on TR-7818, The Pioneers Let Your Yeah Be Yeah on TR-7825 and Greyhound with I Am What I Am on TR-7853.

TROJAN MAXI
(PREFIX) TR

Singles with two tracks on the B side were occasionally issued under the label of Trojan Maxi. The TR number followed on in the 7000 series until 1972 when Trojan Maxi Singles were launched carrying a TR 900 prefix, mainly releasing compilation of previous hit singles. Moon River by Greyhound TR-7848 made number 12 in the UK chart in February 1972 with the B side featuring I've Been Trying coupled with The Pressure Is Coming On.

RETURN OF DJANGO ... US-301 A

B&C/Island
Music

US-301 A
TMX.73

**RETURN OF
DJANGO**
(Lee Perry)

UPSETTERS

Produced by:
Lee Perry

℗ 1969

B&C/Island
Music

US-301 B
TMX.72

**DOLLAR IN
THE TEETH**
(Lee Perry)

UPSETTERS

Produced by:
Lee Perry

℗ 1969

DOLLAR IN THE TEETH UPSETTERS US-301 B

PICKNEY GAL Desmond Dekker PYR 6078

Beverleys
Copyright
Control
℗ 1969

PYR 60

IT MIEK

**DESMOND DEKKER
AND THE ACES**

Blue
Mountain
℗ 1969

PYR 6078 A

PICKNEY GAL
(Dacres)

DESMOND DEKKER
Producer: Leslie Kong/Philligree

IT MIEK Desmond Dekker And The Aces PYR 6078

WILD WORLD
(Stevens)
Produced by Cat Stevens

WIP-6087 A
(WIPX.1P)

Time:

Fre

JIMMY CLIFF

**THE BIGGER THEY COME
THE HARDER THEY FALL**
(Cliff)
Produced by: Jimmy Cliff and Guilly Bright
Recorded at: MUSCLE SHOALS, ALABAMA

JIMMY
CLIFF

WIP-6110

Island Music
Ltd.
℗ 1971
Time: 3.20

STRUGGLI

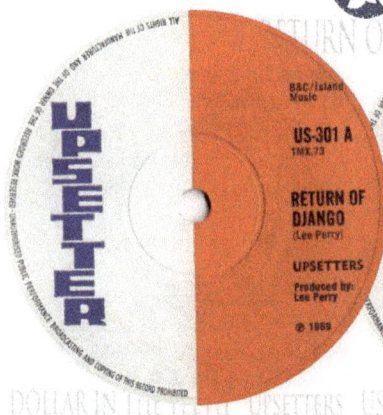

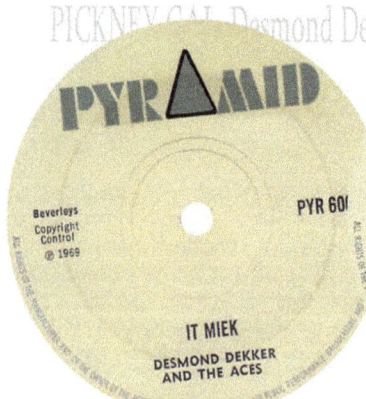

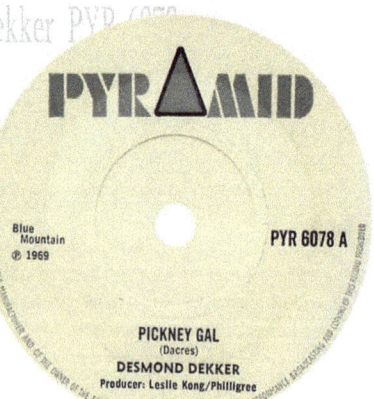

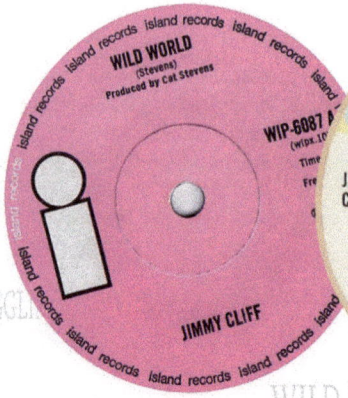

WILD WORLD Jimmy Cliff WIP-6087

UPSETTER
(PREFIX) US

One of the most identifiable of Trojan's subsidiary labels was set up for the output from Lee 'Scratch' Perry in 1969. The highlights included the Upsetters instrumental Return Of Django US-301 making it to number 5 on the UK chart in 1969 with the track featured on Trojan's first Reggae Chartbuster album. The label provided outlets for other artist including Bob Marley & The Wailers and Dave Barker. Additional notable releases amongst quality recordings were Duppy Conqueror on US-348 and Small Axe US-357 from Bob Marley & The Wailers and Well Dread US-373 featuring Dennis Alcapone toasting over the rhythm of Eric Donaldson's Cherry Oh Baby. The label continued to release material until early 1973.

PYRAMID
(PREFIX) PYR

The original label issued by the Doctor Bird group included Desmond Dekker's Israelites PYR-6058 and It Miek PYR-6068 amongst its output. Another notable release was Pickney Gal PYR-6078, the last of Desmond's recordings to be released on the Pyramid label and the last featuring The Aces. Trojan later revived the label after Doctor Bird had gone into liquidation.

ISLAND
(PREFIX) WIP

Chris Blackwell and Graeme Goodall had established Island as an outlet for Jamaican music in the UK as far back as 1959 with the company relocating to the UK in 1962. Without doubt the labels greatest asset was with Chris Blackwell's close friend Bob Marley who went onto become a worldwide superstar after the golden age of reggae had declined. Jimmy Cliff scored chart success with Island in 1970 with his version of a Cat Stevens penned song Wild World WIP-6087 peaking at a lofty number 8 in September that year.

Island were also responsible for bringing reggae to the world stage with the soundtrack from the Jamaican feature film The Harder They Come released on Island Records ILPS 9202 in 1972. At a time when the days were numbered for Trojan and Pama Chris Blackwell and Island were about to launch a reggae superstar, one that would inspire new life into reggae during the mid seventies, one that became a true legend.

BAMBOO RECORDS
(PREFIX) BAM

Junior Lincoln moved to North London in the early 60s at a time when very little Jamaican music was available, although artists such as Laurel Aitken and Jackie Edwards were performing live at venues in the capital. Ska had emerged as the dominant force in Jamaica during the early 60s and music was an essential element of life for the West Indians now living in England.

After a brief spell with Trojan Junior Lincoln set up his own Bamboo label from a shop at 88 Stroud Green in North London, Juniors Music Shop. The shop was always packed at weekends with his customers eager for the latest tunes that Junior always seemed to get hold of. Singles were released on the Bamboo label with the prefix BAM along with albums between 1969 and 1972.

The records were licensed in the main from Clement Coxone Dodd with some self produced. Subsidiary labels of Bamboo were launched releasing a range of material on Ackee and Banana with the most notable releases on Bamboo coming from Bob & Marcia, Ken Boothe, The Heptones, The Maytals and The Ethiopians.

CBS
(PREFIX) CBS

Reggae released on CBS came toward the end of the era when the pop influenced sound was clearly established. Paul Simon went to Jamaica to record Mother And Child Reunion released on CBSS-793 to ensure he had an authentic Jamaican beat, travelling to the Dynamic Studios in Kingston. At the time he commented that "the equipment was so antiquated and falling apart and a take would have to be interrupted when goats would walk through the studio", but he did achieve that authentic feel. In essence that was what reggae was all about, down to earth no nonsense raw sounds, who needed sophisticated equipment. CBS were also responsible for the release of material from Johnny Nash who achieved chart success with his version of the Bob Marley penned Stir It Up on CBSS-7800 peaking at number 13 during April 1972.

RHINO RECORDS
(PREFIX) RNO

Rhino Records was established at the end of the golden era in 1972 with the records manufactured and distributed by EMI. The label did enjoy chart success but it was with a much sweetened version of the real thing. The first release Mad About You by Bruce Ruffin on RNO-101 peaked at number 9 on the UK chart in July 1972. Desmond Dekker also released material on the label with Beware RNO-107 issued late in 1972.

PAMA

BULLET
(PREFIX) BU

Launched in 1969 Bullet was considered by many to be one of Pama's finest, releasing some excellent boss skinhead sounds amongst its quality output. Dandy Shandy Version 4 on BU-483 is up there with the best, a vibrant offering from Impact All-Stars, as is Motherless Children by Willie Francis on BU-415. The classic Maga Dog delivered with resounding vocals and a pulsating rhythm by Peter Tosh was issued on BU-486 in 1971. Aily And Ailaloo by Niney & Max, Rum Rhythm from Roy Shirley, The Samething For Breakfast by Winston Groovy & Pat Rhoden along with Here Come The Heartaches by Delroy Wilson and Rome by Lloyd Jones are more excellent examples. They were offerings of the purest sound of reggae that had hardened from rocksteady. An album Bullet - A World Of Reggae was issued on Pama SECO 19 during 1970.

CAMEL
(PREFIX) CA

Camel began with good quality productions and maintained the classic Pama reggae sound right through to the end of 72 with offerings from The Techniques with Who You Gonna Run To, the Upsetters A Few Dollars More, The Uniques Watch This Sound and Everybody Bawlin by Dennis Alcapone & Lizzy. Add to those Linger A While from John Holt, Nothing Can Separate Us from Owen Gray and the original Guilty by Tiger and you have some of the finest recordings from the era of skinhead reggae.

CRAB
(PREFIX) CRAB

The Crab label was in production from 1968 through to 1971 and seen as being Pama's most prolific with the skinhead in mind, releasing the sound that appealed to the youth of the day. The list is never-ending with almost a third of the output credited to Derrick Morgan. The original Moon Hop issued alongside such classic tracks as River To The Bank, Hard Time, Man Pon Moon and Make It Tand Dhay to name but a few. The Ethiopians came in with Reggae Hit The Town, The Kingstonians with Hold Down and The Versatiles with Children Get Ready, I Am King and Spread Your Bed.

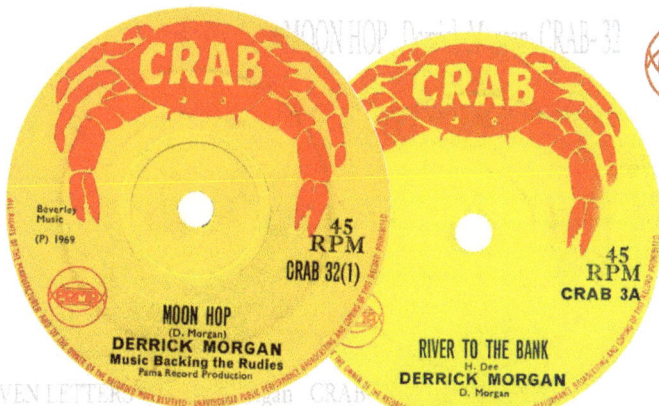

ESCORT
(PREFIX) ES

Perhaps one of Pama's lesser known labels albeit with a handful of gems and one oddity. ES-824 was a release of Young Gifted And Black by Bob Andy And Marcia Griffiths minus the strings that were such a prominent feature on the simultaneously released Trojan single, a record that was enjoying chart success. The oddity was more in the fact that Pama also released another version again on ES-824 Young Gifted And Black by Denzil And Jennifer replacing their Bob And Marcia version, but still under the same prefix ES-824. Some of the gems were Man From Carolina from the GG All Stars issued as the B side on ERT-835, Elizabethan Serenade by Sweet Confusion and What Am I To Do from Tony Scott.

GAS
(PREFIX) GAS

Gas was launched in 1968 following in the footsteps of Unity, Nu-Beat and Crab. The label seemed to lack direction, without doubt not the case with its forerunners. The label turned out several Bunny Lee productions, unusual as Lee already had his Unity label. The label released upward of seventy singles between 1968 and 1971. The inaugural release on GAS-100 was the excellent instrumental The Horse by Eric Barnet and another notable release was How Long Will It Take from Pat kelly.

NU-BEAT
(PREFIX) NB

Following Pama's success from late 1967 through to early 1968 their first subsidiary label Nu-Beat was launched to promote Jamaican releases. Dandy approached Pama with a view to issuing his work on Nu-Beat but the newly emerging Trojan offered Dandy his own Downtown label. One single did feature Dandy, Engine 59 on NB-005. By 1969 Nu-Beat had become an outlet for Laurel Aitken with a change of policy to releasing UK productions and a change of name to Newbeat. Pama's version of Monkey Spanner was released on NB-080. An Album of the labels best work was issued on Pama ECO 6 titled Nu-Beat's Greatest Hits during 1969 featuring artists Max Romeo, Derrick Morgan, Alton Ellis and Laurel Aitken.

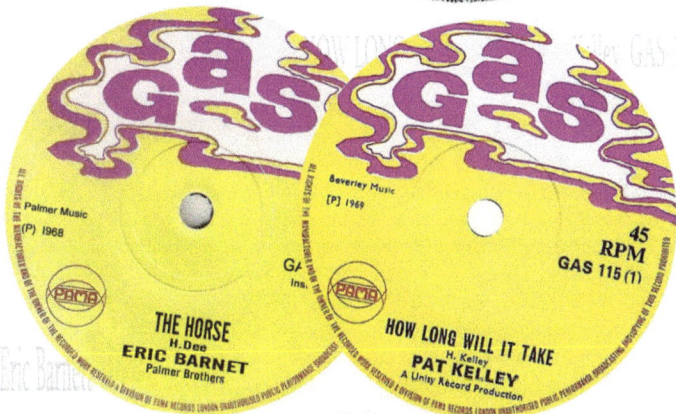

OCEAN
(PREFIX) OC

One of the last to be set up by Pama releasing just three singles by the end
of 1970.

PAMA
(PREFIX) PM

Pama's second release on the home label was What Will Your Mama Say
by Clancy Eccles PM-701, a record that enjoyed healthy sales and a few
airings on Radio One. The recordings came thick and fast including Lloyd
Tyrell's, AKA Lloyd Chalmers, Lloyd Terell or Lloyd Terrell, suggestive
Bang Bang Lulu on PM-710. Over one hundred and fifty singles were
released on the Pama label up to the end of 1972. Gems included PM-835
Way Down South from U. Roy and PM-856 Good Hearted Woman by
The Clarendonians.

Birth Control from Lloyd Terrell was issued on PM-792 in 1970, the
precursor for the album of the same title issued on SECO 32. Lloyd Terrell
AKA Lloyd Charmers et al also recorded a version released by Trojan on
the album Censored under the name of Lloydie & The Lowbites, but the
Pama one is by far and away the best. Byron Lee & The Dragonaires had a
cover version issued on Trojan TR-7736 the same year which was later
updated by The Specials as Too Much Too Young. Continuing the risqué
theme another single that was never going to receive airplay was Sex
Education by The Classics released on PM-830, the record produced by
Harry Palmer in 1971 was always a firm favourite at the school disco.

PAMA SUPREME
(PREFIX) PS

Amongst the last to be set up it was seen as Pama's commercial label
working with established artists in the UK. At the time it was described as
Pama's version of Trojan, lots of strings and things. The labels biggest
sellers by far were Max Romeo's Let The Power Fall PS-306, Denzil Dennis
with his version of South Of The Border PS-350 and Cynthia Richards
Jamaican offering Mr Postman on PS-366. At this time Trojan were issuing
reggae version of pop hits recorded in Jamaica and Pama would issue a
cover version of their own, usually far less commercial, although Trojan
inevitably had the upper hand.

PAMA
RECORDS

Palmer
Music

Beverley
Music

PAMA

Beverley
Music
(P) 1971

45
RPM

PM 830(I)
Made in
England

SEX EDUCATION
H. Dee
THE CLASSICS
Produced by H. Palmer

PAMA

45
RPM
PM 792(1)

BIRTH CONTROL
(L. Terrell)
LLOYD TERRELL
Distributed by
Pama Records London

Pama SUPREME

M.C.P.S.
(P) 1972

PAMA

45
RPM
PS 350(I)
Made in
England

SUPREME

45
RPM
PS 332(I)
Made in
England

SOUTH OF THE BORDER
Densil Dennis
Produced by Pama Records

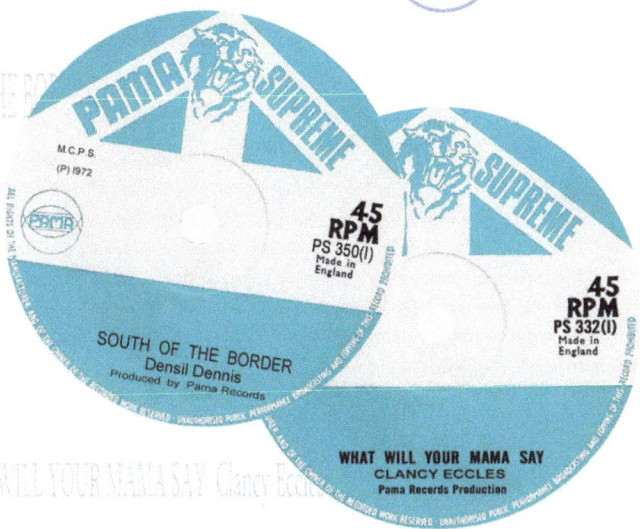

WHAT WILL YOUR MAMA SAY
CLANCY ECCLES
Pama Records Production

PUNCH
(PREFIX) PH

A label does not make a record great but in the case of Punch it gave a clearly defined image with a fist smashing into a 1969 top 20 chart. A favourite with the skinheads with the early releases concentrated on skinhead reggae from Lee 'Scratch' Perry. The label released the official follow up to his UK hit single Return Of Django, Clint Eastwood, released on PH-21. The record just failed to chart despite its popularity with the skinheads due it was said down to poor distribution, a decision that Perry admitted he had got wrong leasing the track to Pama. Perry released several strong selling singles notably Return Of The Ugly PH-18 and Dry Acid PH-19, both bought in great numbers by the West Indian community and the skinheads. Confusion was often in evidence when it came to Pama releases and one such incident fell around Dave Barker's Shocks Of Mighty released on Punch PH-25 and Trojan's Upsetter label at the same time, with Barker said to have been unaware of the Pama release. Other notable singles included Cherrio Baby by The Classics PH-79 and Johnny Too Bad by The Slicker, a group often wrongly attributed to be a pseudonym of The Pioneers, on PH-59 a track also released on Trojan's Dynamic label. Strange as it was an album of Punch's greatest hits was never forthcoming.

SUPREME
(PREFIX) SUP

The label issued just twenty-nine singles during its short rein from 1969 to 1971. One that stands out is a revived number from Ruddy & Sketto Ritch with Every Night issued on Supreme SU-218 in 1971.

UNITY
(PREFIX) UN

The label was set up to provide Pama with a solid link to Jamaican producer Bunny 'Striker' Lee, who could supply the label with a constant succession of quality Jamaican hits. This was seen as a long term venture with Pama paying for the records to be recorded in Jamaica. Bangarang UN-502 by Stranger Cole and Lester Sterling would prove very successful, trialling a new sound having a jerky organ line cited by many as to be the first authentic reggae record. Bunny Lee began issuing records in Jamaica using a similar Unity design with the label becoming synonymous with Bunny Lee productions. The fourth release on the label, Lee's production of Max Romeo's legendary Wet Dream UN-503 used Derrick Morgan's Hold You Jack rhythm track.

JOHNNY (TOO) BAD
The SLICKER
Distributed by
Pama Records London

CHERRIO BABY
THE CLASSICS

RPM
PH 59(1)
Made in
England

RPM
PH 79(1)
Made in
England

EVERY NIGHT
Ruddy & Sketto Rich
Produced by Laurel Aitken

Beverley
Music
(P.) 1971

45
RPM
SUP 218 (1)
Made in
England

MINI-SKIRT VISION
M. Romeo/H. Dee
MAX ROMEO
A Pama Records Production

Beverley Music
(P) 1969

45
RPM
UN 532 (1)

TWELFTH OF NEVER
J. Mathis
MAX ROMEO
D. T. Leigh

45
RPM
UN 511 (1)

A MUSICIANS TALE

Ian 'Smithy' Smith recalls his memories of reggae as a musician during the skinhead years.

'I joined an existing group as keyboard player, aged 18, in 1966. By 1968 the group's name (back then, they were called 'groups'; 'bands' were either Brass or Big Bands - and they played instruments and didn't just sing, look pretty and dance around!) had changed from The Inner Circle to The Inner Mind and our music had also changed from Atlantic Records-style soul, Small Faces, Spencer Davis Group stuff to include rocksteady, as it was known then, and reggae.

This was due to the boss of the Huddersfield West Indian Association, Errol Babb, bringing me seven records he wanted us to play at a forthcoming West Indian Dance. We were the only white people there on the night and when we featured these rocksteady tracks, the crowd went wild.

That was that, as far as we were concerned until six weeks later, we were appearing at Sheffield's Shades Club, I heard the D.J. playing one of the tracks we'd learned, Prince Buster's Shaking Up Orange Street, so we reintroduced the songs into the act and, yep, the crowd went wild again! From that moment onwards The Inner Mind became well known at most of the West Indian centres in the country – London's Apollo and Q(Cue) Club, Bristol's Bamboo, Club 67 at Wolverhampton and Santa Rosa, Birmingham, Bobby's in Mosside, Manchester, Leeds International Club, Huddersfield's Venn Street, Arawak, Shalimar and Fartown International Clubs etc.

It was somewhat of a strange coincidence that we ended up recording for Pama Records. Basically, besides our own show, over the months we'd backed Laurel Aitken (a lot), Owen Gray (several times), Winston Groovy (twice) & Alton Ellis, so Pama had heard of us and our reputation. We'd done a gig in High Wycombe with Owen and on the following night, we'd taken a gig at Pama's Apollo Club in Harlesden– just The Inner Mind.

When we got there, there seemed to be a sort of strange atmosphere and the boss (Jeff Palmer) started getting awkward with me. We set up our gear and then he said he wasn't going to pay us our full fee, no reason given. It was obvious he was just 'trying it on'; as we were down there from Yorkshire, reluctantly I said OK, we'll take the reduction; ten minutes later, he tried it on again saying he would pay us less. At that, the Yorkshire white reggae band said 'Stuff you', packed up and went north! That night, the Apollo ended up without an act or, at best, a last minute replacement. This was our first dealings with a Palmer brother and in hindsight - nothing really changed.

Don Auty was one of the employees at Pama's artiste's agency called 'Apollo Artists'. Don was, even then, an old-school theatrical agent, originally from Dewsbury/Batley in Yorkshire, who ended up firstly in the West End and then rather down-market in Harlesden. He persuaded us to give it one more try and we became a regular at the Apollo, on an agreed fee and billed as 'The Greatest White Reggae Band on Earth', somewhat of a change of heart on Jeff Palmer's part!

We began giving some of our recordings to Pama for release. Jeff even took us all out to a restaurant after a gig at the club to offer us a job as one of Pama's resident studio bands, alongside The Mohawks and, to a lesser extent The Rudies, but we declined. Surprise, surprise the money offered was absolutely dire and it would mean moving to London, which none of us wanted, and relying on Apollo Artists for most of our gigs, a bit iffy, to say the least, so we probably made the right decision. One act, we found out later, got gigs in Italy and had to sell their gear to get back home; whether that was due to the agency or the promoter was never made clear, but the result was the same.

Back then the gigs were a great experience - it was a completely underground scene; the music press looked down on the reggae market, university students hadn't started to pretend to like it yet and mainstream radio would have rather broadcast a political rant by Tony Benn, especially the BBC, than play a reggae record. It was a completely alien concept! We hardly ever played white venues during this period; universities stopped booking us (we weren't progressive rock etc.), dance clubs - er, discos – couldn't dance to us but we were on cloud nine at the gigs we did! Our records which were released under our own name or as backings for other artistes were just boosters for our reputation at the live gigs. We, as countless others, never got paid for the records we made.

During the skinhead years, we had records out on Pama's NewBeat & Bullet labels under our own name. They also released a track called Breakdown Rock on Pama Supreme Records as The Harlesden Monk; this was actually Dreams of Yesterday by The Inner Mind, released on Shades Records! which brings me to Pum Pum Girl on NewBeat Records. We'd done some backing tracks for Laurel Aitken at a studio down in London and at that session, we'd also done Witchcraft Man, destined to be our first single on Pama's NewBeat label. I'd given Laurel an acetate of eight tracks we'd recorded at 'Mat 'Mathias' King Street Studios in Huddersfield for the Shades label in Sheffield. Dreams' was released on Shades, followed up by Jesse James Hits Back.

In the meantime, Pama slipped out Pum Pum Girl, one of the above mentioned tracks on NewBeat, produced by me not Laurel Aitken as the label wrongly stated. They'd pressed it up from that copy of the acetate and had not used the original tape, cos of course they didn't have it.

Max Omare, at Shades, made them withdraw the single, and so potentially stopped the record being a massive seller although we probably wouldn't have got paid anyway! When Dreams was snuck out as Breakdown Rock it was no surprise. And that's why I set up Hot Lead Records and Castle Hill Music, to safeguard all my songs, productions & recordings.

Just a foot note, Pum Pum Girl was the Dreams Of Yesterday backing track with suggestive words added. I lived in Thornhill Lees, Dewsbury at the time; I caught the bus to Huddersfield one night to get to Mat's two track recording studio, nothing posh, just primitive, simple and great. I wrote the lyrics on the bus on the way there! So, had the mood taken me, it could've ended up a sentimental love song!"

Ian continued to say *"I did write some love songs but, for some reason, Pum Pum Girl and more so Doggie Bite Postman as 'Smithy All Stars', our biggest seller, were to be my legacy! Those days were, to me, golden days, an underground scene of music we loved, endless recording sessions & gigs, much merriment and booze, it couldn't last. The spoken intro to Dreams which was spliced off the Pama Supreme PS352 release says it all. 'I remember how it used to be, the pattern of time moves on regardless'. That's far too philosophical for reggae - no wonder they cut it off the record! Reggae is fun, sun and rum! I'm still at it, much older, no wiser but doing the odd gig with the old Inner Mind members, Jimmy Walsh (Drums) and Dave Tattersall (Bass)."*

Throughout Britain the story of how skinheads and reggae became intertwined has been told time and time again by many, all reiterating that the original skinhead was non racist and had no interest in politics, most coming from working class backgrounds. Reggae between 1968 -1972 can be classed as skinhead reggae, but what influence did the skinheads have in the development of the Jamaican music scene. The buying power of the youth had created an international audience away from Jamaica for the first time. The skinheads began to buy reggae at a rate never before seen outside of the island, and some records were now selling in sufficient quantities to begin charting in the UK, an event that forced the hand of the BBC to add the skinhead sounds to their restrictive playlists.

The top 100 selling singles of 1969 included Desmond Dekker's Israelites at number 21, Max Romeo at number 50 and Return Of Django / Dollar In The Teeth from the Upsetters at 51. Jimmy Cliff's Wonderful World, Beautiful People was placed at 67. Also featured were Johnny Nash with You Got Soul at 76 and Cupid at 88 with Desmond's It Mek at number 84. Harry J All Stars also made the top 100 with Liquidator positioned at 86. All in all not a bad result when you consider David Bowie was at 61 with Space Oddity and Bob Dylan was at 71 with Lay Lady Lay.

TELL IT LIKE IT WAS

I recall my first encounter with the incessant rhythm of Jamaican music, at the school disco, 007 Shanty Town would have been amongst the first, and on hearing the risqué but melodic Wet Dream I gathered together all the change I could and hurried to the local record store. My first purchase, a shiny vinyl single, released on what was to me at the time the obscure Unity label for about five bob. The sad thing was though I never had a record player to play it on, but my best mate Richard did, a posh radio-stereogram, and it was played over and over again. Richard I recall also built up a good collection of Trojan albums. In those early days with no radio exposure discovering the new sounds from Jamaica was always an exciting challenge.

Chris Brown, author of the skinhead book Booted & Suited, recalls the golden days in Bristol at a place I have fond memories of hanging about on a Saturday.

"If you wanted to buy your vinyl records there was a very well known shop on Picton Street called RCA records. That stood for Record Collectors Association. It was run by a guy called Ray and his dad. It was really the only place you could get West Indian music or soul music. Even then you wouldn't know the records because you couldn't hear this music at all, a lot of it was word of mouth. You would go down on the Saturday morning and they would just play music and you would try and buy it, I say try and buy it because a lot of people would say, "I'll have that one," and the RCA might only have one copy of it. It was a great little shop, full, absolutely jam packed with albums and singles. It just had a great vibe in there and was a really nice place to hang around on a Saturday and buy music".

The early development of West Indian music in Britain can be traced back to June 1948 with the merchant vessel Empire Windrush arriving at Tilbury carrying 492 passengers from Jamaica, all wishing to start a new life in the United Kingdom. Virgil Jack Williams recalls his arrival in Britain two decades later.

"I arrived in a cold damp London in 1962 having spent my early years growing up bathed by the warmth of the sun blessed West Indies, where blue beat, calypso and mento music always seemed to fill the balmy nights. In London at that time I was not allowed to soak up the nightlife in the pubs as all had banned entry with notices stating NO COLOUERED OR IRISH allowed.

Music was an inherent part of the West Indian culture and we would go to big dance hall events in West London, not far from where I was living at the time in Edgware Road. The dance halls were popular venues although no food was served, just drinks and a generous helping of great music, a combination of steel bands, calypso and ska.

I recall with fond memories one evening we had a visit from Cassius Clay, around the time of the great Cooper fight, his appearance caused a real stir and great interest. I was now living with a black family in London and although it was difficult to get hold of we did manage to come by some blue beat and ska records imported from Jamaica. The music was beginning to become more prevalent as the decade went on with ska now being played at the Hammersmith Palais and other clubs such as 'Burtons', a hot spot, and on one occasion Pan's People came to dance.

After the clubs we would go onto 'Blues Parties' often held in someone's house where a large sound system would be pumping out ska and rocksteady into the night, you didn't need to know the address you just had to follow the sound of incessant rhythms booming out. The MC would 'toast' over the music as the drink and food flowed freely including traditional rice peas, jerk chicken and red stripe, with the venues always packed. The opportunity to buy West Indian music was still very limited, and little if any was played on national radio, so the clubs and impromptu parties with their sound systems allowed us to soak up the music with all of our friends.

Towards the end of the decade record shops began to open specialising in the imported hits from Jamaica and would always be crowded on a Saturday, with everyone anxious to hear the latest tunes from back home. The youth both white and black with their cropped hair who rejected the hippie attitude and progressive music took an interest in reggae; much like their elder brothers did with ska earlier in the decade. Add to this mix the birth of record labels in the UK and soon reggae had found its rightful international acclaim. With the sound from the islands available to the mainstream record buying public for the first time, reggae was now charting".

Perhaps the following from 'Uncle Fee' will sum up how it all began for many of us back then.

"From a very early age I was influenced by music and I was brought up on a good diet of jazz. Dad had a drum kit in the front room and he and some of his pals would jam along to records. Whilst growing up during the early 60s, although not totally aware, the street and local area was slowly giving rise to a certain change. More and more West Indians (mainly Jamaicans) were coming here to live and bringing with them their rich and vibrant culture.

Houses were being painted in a way that the traditionally 'stuffy' English where totally unaware of, aromas and fragrances were equally baffling, filtering through the scent of good old fish and chips!

It was during this period that I became conscious of a different style of music that I was not very familiar with although I had heard stuff that I thought might have resembled it, from hearing tunes like Al Capone, Madness, and Bonanza Ska from early visits to a local 'dance hall' in Bush Hill Park. I would dance along to these as well as the latest pop hits. I was really unaware that I had been listening to early ska. It was not unusual for me to be found loitering up and down our street and hanging about outside the houses of our overseas friends just listening to what I could. The sound was always more powerful than our record player and it was not long after that I saw and heard my first 'Blue Spot Stereogram' The 'Spot' was the ultimate home accessory for any Jamaican household and would take pride of place in the front room normally adorned with lace and pictures.

It's now early 1968 and my 16th birthday is looming so I persuaded my Mum to let me have a party for a few friends. So I got a couple of crates of brown ale (for the men ha-ha) and some port and lemonade (for the girls). Oh we knew how to enjoy ourselves in the 'old days'!

While I am waiting for people to arrive my brother Eric turns up with a pile of tunes that Carlton Small had given him saying "let Brian use these for his party tonight". So there I am going through these tunes thinking bloomin' 'eck these are brilliant! All rocksteady stuff like Run Boy Run and a whole pile more of Studio One stuff.

Everybody has now turned up and the party is in full swing and were all bopping to pop music but as we start to run out of selections I draw out 'the pile' from Carlton. Well in seconds everyone is jumping and after a few more we spend the whole night just playing them over and over!

I am now hooked on this music and 45 years later I am still addicted to it."

YOU CAN GET IT IF YOU REALLY WANT
TROJAN RECORDS TBL 146
Released 1970

DESMOND DEKKER AND THE ACES

Desmond Dacres was born in 1941 in the parish of St Andrew Jamaica, moving to Kingston as a boy. Desmond worked as a welder but always had a passion for music. In time after a couple of failed attempts, being rejected by Dodd then Duke Reid, Desmond eventually got an audition at Beverley's Studio. Following the audition Leslie Kong quickly arranged his first recording at Federal Studios with Honour Your Mother And Father giving Desmond his first hit.

A succession of hits in Jamaica and good sales in England followed including his 1966 rocksteady recording 007, a song about the troubles in Jamaica. The record, with Desmond accompanied by The Aces, reached number 14 in the UK during July 1967 and also charted on the other side of the Atlantic. It was however in 1968 that Desmond's biggest UK hit, one of the early up-and-coming reggae sounds (Poor Mi) Israelites was released, and following steady sales over a long period it eventually entered the UK charts in March 1969, before peaking at number 1 in April.

Israelites was the first reggae record to achieve the number 1 spot on 19th April 1969 where it spent just a week before being replaced with Get Back by The Beatles, a record that came straight into the coveted spot. Israelites remained on the charts for a total of fifteen weeks during 1969 and made several forays back into the charts with subsequent re issues over the next couple of decades.

The Beatles purportedly made reference to Desmond in a song penned by Paul McCartney, Ob-La-Di, Ob-La-Da. Sadly Desmond died of a heart attack in May 2006 at the age of 64 but not before leaving behind a lasting legacy from a plethora of outstanding recordings. Some provided further chart success in the UK before the end of 1972, most notably the Jimmy Cliff penned song You Can Get It If You Really Want, a song that featured as the opening track to Perry Henzell's accomplished 1972 cult film The Harder They Come, although sung by Cliff himself.

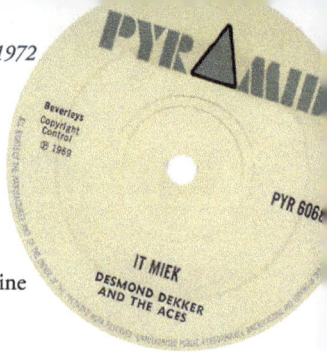

The U.K. singles chart of the 19th April 1969.

1. Desmond Dekker And The Aces - Israelites.
2. Mary Hopkin. - Goodbye
3. Marvin Gaye - I Heard It Through The Grapevine
4. Lulu - Boom Bang -A- Bang
5. Dean Martin - Gentle On My Mind
6. The Who - Pinball Wizard
7. The Hollies - Sorry Suzanne
8. The Foundations - In The Bad Old Days
9. Joe South - Games People Play
10. Noel Harrison - The Windmills Of Your Mind

Israelites riding high in the UK charts signalled the beginning of a period of great success for Desmond who by this time had established a special artist / producer relationship with Leslie Kong. Kong became one of the most successful producers of the late sixties through to the very early seventies creating a distinctive sound, combining an infectious commercial appeal whilst preserving the Jamaican sound that was great to dance to.

Further chart success followed Israelites with a total change of style for It Miek, telling a story about his little sister. The record for the UK market had a slightly different sound to the original Jamaican release PYR-6054, A It Mek, and was issued on the Pyramid label in 1969 under prefix PYR-6068. As with Israelites it was written by Desmond and Lesley Kong. It Miek often spelt It Mek entered the UK charts in 1969 spending eleven weeks in the top 50, peaking at number 7 for two weeks during July. Desmond's fourth chart success Pickney Gal, unlike the previous singles, failed to reach the lofty heights. It entered at number 42 in January 1970, its highest position, spending a mere three weeks in the top 50 but nevertheless a record that ranks amongst his finest, rich with Jamaican patois lyrics. However more chart success would soon come Desmond's way.

On the 22nd July 1969 the British charts looked like this.

1. Thunderclap Newman - Something In The Air
2. Elvis Presley - In The Ghetto
3. The Rolling Stones - Honkey Tonk Woman
4. Plastic Ono Band - Give Peace A Chance
5. Amen Corner - Hello Suzie
6. Family Dog - Way Of Life
7. Desmond Dekker And The Aces - It Miek
8. The Beach Boys - Breakaway
9. Marmalade - Baby Make It Soon
10. Creedence Clearwater Revival - Proud Mary

Pickney Gal was the last of Desmond's recordings to be released on the Pyramid label and the last featuring The Aces. Leslie Kong went on to form an association with the up and coming Trojan, a label that was enjoying considerable chart success with artists such as Jimmy Cliff, Upsetters and The Pioneers to name but a few. Ironically it was Jimmy Cliff who penned Desmond's next success, You Can Get It If You Really Want. Entering the charts at number 46 in August 1970 it spent two weeks at number 2 during October that year.

The British charts looked like this on the 10th October 1970 with only Freda Payne with her Band Of Gold holding Desmond from the top spot.

1. Freda Payne - Band Of Gold
2. **Desmond Dekker - You Can Get It If You Really Want**
3. Deep Purple - Black Night
4. Black Sabbath - Paranoid
5. Bobby Bloom - Montego Bay
6. The Carpenters - (They Long To Be) Close To You
7. Diana Ross - Ain't No Mountain High Enough
8. The Tremeloes - Me And My Life
9. Chairman Of The Board - Give Me Just A Little More Time
10. Poppy Family Featuring Susan Jacks - Which Way You Goin' Billy

After the success of You Can Get It If You Really Want Desmond recorded numerous tracks but only released a couple more singles, none enjoying the previous chart success. Leslie Kong had become Desmond's mentor with unrivalled chart success continuing until his untimely death in 1971 when Kong died of a heart attack at the relatively young age of 38. His death was to have a shattering effect on Desmond and perhaps one that he never fully recovered from in terms of his music.

YOU CAN GET IT IF YOU REALLY WANT
TROJAN RECORDS TBL 146
Released 1970

Side 1
1. YOU CAN GET IT IF YOU REALLY WANT
2. I BELIEVE
3. PERSEVERANCE
4. GET UP LITTLE SUZIE
5. PEACE ON THE LAND
6. CINDY

Side 2
1. PICKNEY GAL
2. YOU GOT SOUL
3. COOMYAH
4. THAT'S THE WAY LIFE GOES
5. PEACE OF MIND
6. POLKADOT

DISCOGRAPHY SINGLES 1968- 1972

PYRAMID

DESMOND DEKKER AND THE ACES

PYR-6020 Sabotage 1968
PYR-6031 Beautiful And Dangerous 1968
PYR-6044 Mother Pepper 1968
PYR-6051 Intensified '68 1968
PYR-6058 Israelites 1968
PYR-6054B (JJ Records) A It Mek 1969
PYR-6068 It Miek 1969
PYR-6078 Pickney Gal 1969

TROJAN

DESMOND DEKKER

TR-7777 You Can Get It If You Really Want 1970
TR-7802 The Song We Used To Sing 1970
TR-7847 Licking Stick 1971
TR-7847 Live And Learn 1971
TR-7876 It Gotta Be So 1972

RHINO

DESMOND DEKKER

RNO-107 Beware 1972

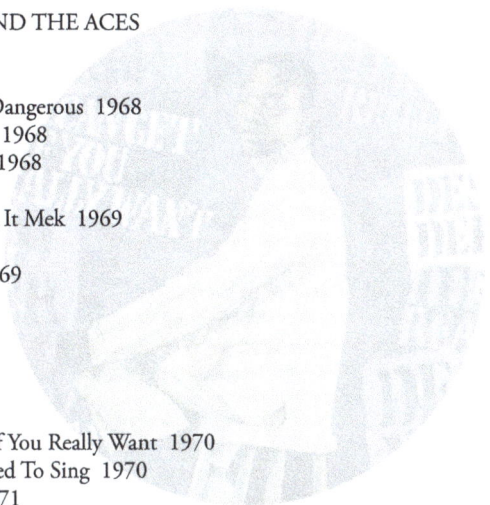

DISCOGRAPHY ALBUMS 1968-1972

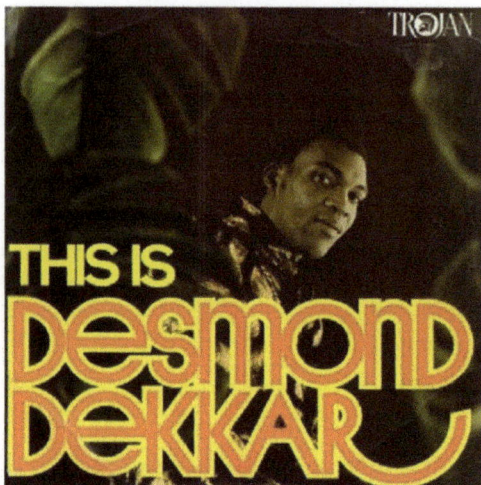

THIS IS DESMOND DEKKAR
TROJAN RECORDS TTL 4 (Leslie Kong) 1969

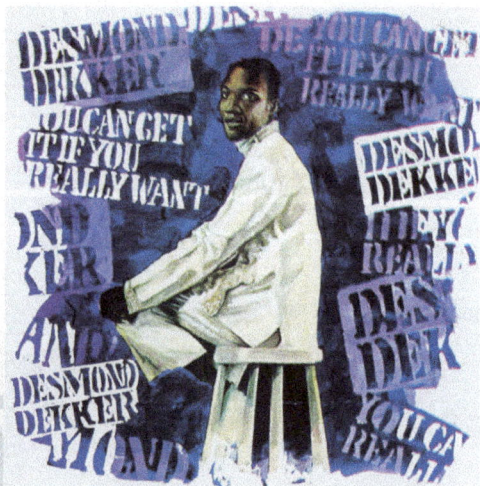

YOU CAN GET IT IF YOU REALLY WANT
TROJAN RECORDS   TBL146 (Leslie Kong) 1970

MAX ROMEO

Max Romeo was born Maxwell Livingstone Smith, in the parish of St Anne, on the north coast of Jamaica in 1944. Max endured hardship in his early years, moving to Kingston at the age of 10, then leaving home to live on the streets at 14. His first introduction to the record industry came after a spell labouring on a sugar plantation finding himself delivering records, always singing as he went. His potential was soon spotted and he was advised to enter a talent contest, a move that prompted him to head back to Kingston in search of fame and fortune.

Max's first record was released in 1967 titled I'll Buy You A Rainbow with a group called The Emotions with Max as the lead singer. The single made number 2 in Jamaica and established Max as a star. A move that eventually brought worldwide fame for Max was an introduction to Derrick Morgan's brother in law, producer Bunny Lee, who was trialling with the new sound evolving as reggae. Bunny 'Striker' Lee would later persuaded Max to go solo.

The name Romeo is said to have come about due to Max spending time with a girl. The story goes that Max was talking to the girl at eight in the morning when her father left for work. Max returned to see the girl later in the day just a short time before her father returned from work. Thinking Max had been there all day, stood in the same spot, the father said to Max, "You must be Romeo". Bunny Lee heard the story and recommended that Max should change his stage name to Max Romeo.

Max began writing songs and Bunny Lee came to Max with a suggestion for doing a rude song, a theme that was becoming popular with some of the other artists at the time. Max penned Wet Dream but history tells that he did not want to perform it. Lee wanted Derrick Morgan to record the song who had previously released Hold You Jack also penned by Max Romeo using the same rhythm. Derrick refused so Bunny, after declines by others including John Holt and Slim Smith persuaded Max to voice the lyrics.

Max has been quoted as saying that he was forced to do that song by Bunny Lee. He claimed he was actually threatened, being told if he didn't do the song he could not stay around. Several versions of this story have been told but what is in no doubt the song became a huge hit in Jamaica. The song was eventually sent over to England with a batch of other recordings to Harry Palmer at Pama who subsequently released it on their Unity label in 1968 and the rest as they say is history, lie dung gal........................

The record managed an airing or two courtesy of Emperor Rosko on Radio One before the hierarchy got wind of the patois content. Max claimed that the song was telling the story of his leaking roof, he was asking his girlfriend to get out of the way as he tried to push a broom up in the hole to stop the leak. The BBC were having none of it, describing it as bawdy, and immediately censored the record. *Give the crumpet to Big Foot Joe - Give the fanny to me* probably didn't help the cause. The ban did however serve to make it more popular with the new skinheads and record buying public with one theory that the youth reacted to an injunction, inhibiting their freedom of choice, thus enhancing sales.

The record took the charts by storm in May 1969 despite having no further air play on the BBC. The record was always referred to as "a record by Max Romeo" during a rundown of the charts. It eventually made it into the top thirty reaching number 10 in August 1969 and was reported to have sold over 250,000 copies, the record spending a very respectful twenty five weeks in the charts. The chart speaks for itself in highlighting what a massive contrast Wet Dream was in comparison to the rest of the top ten, and how the skinheads would have warmed to the incessant, melodic rhythm, a sound they claimed for their own, along that was with their new West Indian friends.

The success of Wet Dream was quickly followed with the release of the album
A DREAM issued by Pama in 1969 PMLP 11

PAMA   **STEREO**   **PMLP- II**

"DREAM" WITH MAX ROMEO

The recipe for a hit, nowadays, seems to be the collection of words that have suggestive meaning against a very rhythmic background, punctuated with heavy breathing. As the theory goes such a record will be banned and the permissive record buying public will react against this injunction that inhibits their freedom of choice, hence a high sales turnover is certain.

MAX ROMEO'S "WET DREAM" falls into this category. Max, twenty-five years old, from Jamaica, made a tremendous impact on the scene recently when "WD", his resounding hit, disrupted the British Charts for more than twenty weeks and was the subject of much controversy. However, that Max is a very talented singer is not a subject for debate. This becomes obvious when one realises the rate at which his fans are growing each day. At the Caribbean Music Festival at Wembley recently, Max received a double standing ovation from the ten thousand capacity crowd. As well as being a fabulous entertainer, Max proved he was truly a top exponent of the Reggae idiom. Due to the general misunderstanding surrounding his chart success, he is now in the unfortunate position of trying to live down an image which is at variance with the genuine warmth and sincerity of Max the person. This long-awaited album is filled with Romeo's versatility, here Max is caught doin' his own thin'- Whatever he is singing or writing, Max is always immaculate. This album is a must for all Reggae-lovers. Well done Max.

SIDE ONE
1. **WET DREAM (Electronically Rebalanced) - (M ROMEO)**
2. **A NO FE ME PICKNEY - (M ROMEO)**
3. **FAR FAR AWAY - (M ROMEO)**
4. **THE HORN - (M ROMEO)**
5. **HEAR MY PLEA - (M ROMEO)**
6. **LOVE - (M ROMEO)**

SIDE TWO
1. **I DON'T WANT TO LOSE YOUR LOVE - (M ROMEO)**
2. **WOOD UNDER CELLAR - (M ROMEO)**
3. **WINE HER GOOSIE - (H DEE)**
4. **CLUB RAID - (M ROMEO)**
5. **YOU CAN'T STOP ME - (M ROMEO)**

Musical Arrangments by: Ranny Williams and Derrick Morgan   Musical Backing: The Rudies   The Hippy Boys
Cover Design: Jeff and Carl Palmer   Produced by: H. LEE / B. LEE / D. MORGAN
A PAMA / UNITY RECORD PRODUCTION

Distributed by - PAMA RECORDS LIMITED, 78 CRAVEN PARK ROAD, LONDON, N.W. IO, ENGLAND

At the top of the pile were the Rolling Stones with quite a variety in between them and Max at number 10.

WET DREAM Max Romeo
Released on UNITY UN-503 1968
Highest chart position 10 16/08/1969

1. Rolling Stones – Honkey Tonk Woman
2. Robin Gibb – Saved By The Bell
3. Joe Dolan – Make Me An Island
4. Plastic Ono Band – Give Peace A Chance
5. Stevie Wonder – My Cherie Amour
6. Clodagh Rodgers – Goodnight Midnight
7. Cilla Black – Conversations
8. Vanity Fare – Early In The Morning
9. Love Affair – Bring Back The Good Times
10. **Max Romeo – Wet Dream**

A tour of the UK followed with the subsequent release of the album, A Dream, issued by Pama. Although Max was banned from performing at several venues many did allow him on stage, with Max remaining in England for eighteen months. A follow up single on Unity, Mini-Skirt Vision, failed to enter the charts but the rude image was destined to stay with him for a long while, however on his return to Jamaica Max was determined to change musical direction.

UN-511, Twelfth Of Never was incorrectly credited to Max Romeo on the label but was in reality by Pat Kelly. Bunny Lee had released Pat Kelly's rocksteady version on Island WI-3124 in 1968 and the vocals were allegedly overdubbed onto a reggae rhythm in 1969 for UN-511, no doubt on the back of the euphoria for Max. Is It Really Over? on Trojan's GG-4535 proved that Max's musical talents went far beyond risqué lyrics.

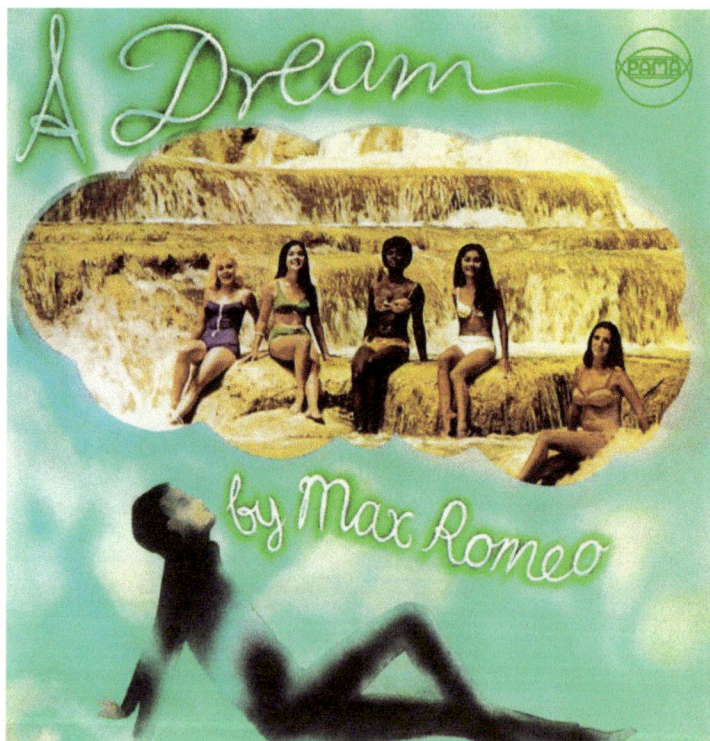

A DREAM
PAMA RECORDS
Released 1969 PAMA PMLP 11

Side 1
1. WET DREAM (Electronically Rebalanced)
2. A NO FEE ME PICKNEY   3. FAR FAR AWAY
4. THE HORN   5. HEAR MY PLEA   6. LOVE

Side 2
1. I DON'T WANT TO LOOSE YOUR LOVE
2. WOOD UNDER CELLAR   3. WHINE HER GOOSIE
4. CLUB RAID   5. YOU CAN'T STOP ME

In 1971 Max released his second album on Pama, PMP-2010 Let The Power Fall produced by Bunny Lee highlighting a complete change of style from the hugely popular album, A Dream. That first album was still selling well according to the sleeve notes. Max became increasingly aware of the social injustices in Jamaica and the huge gulf between the rich and the poor with his music reflecting the restlessness in his homeland with PS-306 Let The Power Fall On I in 1971 and Are You Sure PS-359 released on Pama Supreme in 1972. Another single issued in 1972 was Pray For Me on both the High Note and Pama Supreme labels. it represented the way forward for Max, who has spent much of his career trying to live down the rude image. Notwithstanding Hole Under Cratches was issued in 1973 credited to Henry & Liza, actually Max Romeo & Faye Bennett with a humorous take on the traditional song There's A Hole In My Bucket.

PRAY FOR ME
High Note HS-0581972 and Pama Supreme PS-345 1972

Let The Power Fall was adopted by The Peoples National Party during the Jamaican General Election of 1972, a campaign that saw the late Michael Manley elected Prime Minister.

SINGLES SELECTED DISCOGRAPHY 1968- 1972

UNITY
UN-503 Wet Dream 1968

ISLAND
WI-3111 Walk In The Dawn 1968
WI-3104 Put Me In The Mood 1968

BLUE CAT
BS-161 Me Want Man 1969
BS-163 It's Not The Way 1969

NUBEAT
NB-022 Blowing In The Wind 1969

UNITY
UN-507 Belly Woman 1969
UN-511 Twelfth Of Never 1969 *(Actually Pat Kelly)*
UN-516 Wine Her Goosie 1969
UN-532 Mini-Skirt Vision 1969
UN-547 What A Cute Man 1970
UN-560 Fish In The Pot 1970

CAMEL
CA-82 The Coming Of Jah 1971

PAMA SUPREME
PS-306 Let The Power Fall 1971
PS-318 Don't You Weep 1971
PS-328 Ginal Ship 1971

UNITY
UN-571 Macabee Version 1971

CAMEL
CA-85 Rasta Band Wagon 1972
CA-86 Public Enemy Number One 1972

DYNAMIC
DYN-444 We Love Jamaica 1972

GG RECORDS
GG-4535 Is It Really Over 1972

PAMA SUPREME
PS-345 Pray For Me 1972
PS-359 Are You Sure 1972

THE PIONEERS

The Pioneers roots stem way back in the days of blue-beat by brothers Sydney and Derrick Crooks, with Winston Hewitt making up the trio, and releasing singles in Jamaica on the Caltone label. Glen Adams joined the group replacing Winston Hewitt but their output failed to find success. This led to Sydney concentrating on promoting concerts and the original group disbanding in 1967.

In spite of this it wouldn't be long before Sydney took a job at Joe Gibbs record shop, purchased by Gibbs originally as a TV repair shop, on Beeston Street in Kingston, the record sales proving successful leading to Joe's involvement in the music industry.

The story goes that Sydney wanted to record a duet so promptly enlisted the services of Jackie Robinson who was by trade a welder who just happened to be singing in the street. The song was Gimmie Little Loving and sold well in their native Jamaica. A partnership was duly formed with Jackie taking the role as the lead singer.

Subsequent releases followed including Long Shot Bus Me Bet, a song about a race horse that was destined for fame, with the duo constantly riding high in the islands charts.

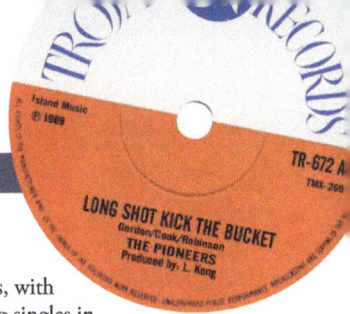

In late 1968 a third member joined to complete the trio, George Agard, who had previously enjoyed a solo career but his attributes worked well, resulting in one of the most popular groups in the history of Jamaican music being born. The Pioneers became a group that had a significant influence on the British charts and the youth of the day, the skinheads.

A change of producer came about with the group working for the up and coming Leslie Kong's Beverley's label. Their second recording was Long Shot Kick De Bucket in 1969, a sequel to the earlier hit telling of the death of the famous race horse at Kingston's Caymanas Park. The song provided yet more chart success in Jamaica. Trojan took a gamble, not intended as a pun, releasing the record as they could see the potential for a hit. The record was however ignored by the BBC who refused to include it on their play list. Long Shot Kick De Bucket was receiving airplay on independent stations and became popular in the clubs but without national exposure very few would hear the record.

The BBC finally gave in and added it to their play list in the autumn of 1969 with it entering the charts in October. The record peaked at a respectful number 21 in November and remained on the charts for eleven weeks. That was the first real introduction to The Pioneers for the skinhead who had by now developed a strong relationship with the music. Included on the Trojan albumTBL103 Long Shot, released in 1969, were tracks in the same vein including Black Bud and Poor Rameses.

Long Shot Kick The Bucket is a tale of the weeping and wailing that ensued after Long Shot was pulled up in the first race at Caymanas Park, Kingston Jamaica. The race was underway with Gayblade and Combat leading Carousel with Long Shot at the rear. It seems that Combat fell then Long Shot fell and as a consequence as they say, all their money they had bet had gone to hell.

Two more chart hits followed for Trojan and The Pioneers, albeit in a different vein to their original recordings with Let Your Yeah Be Yeah reaching number 5 in September 1971 and Give And Take surprisingly only managing number 35 in January 1972. Let Your Yeah Be Yeah became the best selling reggae record of 1971, a celebration not held in high esteem by some who saw it as a diversification from pure reggae. To an extent it was but none the less worked very well allowing the music to interact with the mainstream but retaining its fundamental Jamaican feel, setting it apart from the other records of the day.

Both hits were penned by the up and coming Jimmy Cliff who became a prolific singer, song- writer and actor. Reggae wasn't however all about chart hits, yes it did bring the music to the fore but The Pioneers continued to produce a string of reggae hits over the next couple of years. These were in direct contrast to the more raw down to earth sounds that were still being released by Pama, but still none the less well received including, I Need Your Sweet Inspiration and Roll Muddy River, a track that inspired a further album later in the decade. As a consequence of this change of musical direction, from The Pioneers original sounds to the more pop influenced reggae, further chart success eluded them.

The Pioneers released some thirty singles during the golden age of reggae from 1968 through to the end of 1972.

Stiff competition was running through the UK charts when The Pioneers Let Your Yeah Be Yeah peaked at number 5 in September 1971. The record made it into the top 100 selling singles of 1971 being placed at 75. Reggae was still selling in volumes with Dave & Ansel Collins' Double Barrel and Monkey Spanner at 13 and 68 respectively. Other fellow musicians to feature were Greyhound with Black & White at number 64. To compare with other music genres The Supremes were at 69 with Nathan Jones, Curved Air were at 79 and Elton John was placed at 87 with Your Song.

The British charts of the 11th September 1971 looked like this.

1. Diana Ross - I'm Still Waiting
2. The Tams - Hey Girl Don't Bother Me
3. Dawn - What Are You Doing Sunday
4. The New Seekers - The Never Ending Song Of Love
5. **The Pioneers - Let Your Yeah Be Yeah**
6. Nancy Sinatra And Lee Hazelwood - Did You Ever
7. Buffy Sainte Marie - Soldier Blue
8. The Supremes - Nathan Jones
9. Curved Air - Back Street Luv
10. Carole King - It's Too Late / Feel The Earth Move

GREETINGS FROM THE PIONEERS
Released on Amalgamated AMGLP-2003 1968

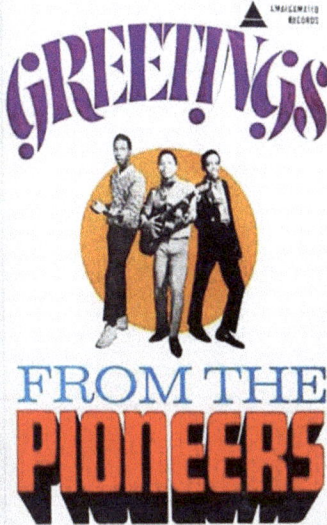

Side 1
1. ME NAW GO A BELIEVE 2. YOU WILL NEVER GET AWAY
3. BABY DON'T BE LATE 4. SHAKE IT UP
5. NO DOPE ME PONY 6. WHIP THEM

Side 2
1. GIMME GIMME GIRL 2. THINGS JUST GOT TO CHANGE
3. SWEET DREAMS 4. TICKLE ME FOR DAYS 5. JACKPOT
6. GIVE ME A LITTLE LOVING

LONG SHOT THE PIONEERS
TROJAN RECORDS TBL103
Released 1969

```
TBL 103

Side 1

1. LONG SHOT (KICK DE BUCKET)
2. CARANAPO
3. BLACK BUD
4. LONG UP YOUR MOUTH
5. BRING HIM COME
6. MOTHER RITTY

Side 2

1. POOR RAMESES
2. SAMFIE MAN
3. BELLY GUT
4. LUCKY SIDE
5. TROUBLE DE A BUSH
6. BOSS FESTIVAL

Produced by - Leslie Kong
All tracks written by Agard, Crooks, Robinson
Licensed from Beverley Records
Published by - Blue Mountain Music
```

LONG SHOT

Produced by: Leslie Kong.
All tracks written by: Agard, Crooks, Robinson

Side 1
1. LONG SHOT KICK DE BUCKET
2. CARANAPO 3. BLACK BUD
4. LONG UP YOUR MOUTH
5. BRING HIM COME 6. MOTHER RITTY

Side 2
1. POOR RAMESES 2. SAMFIE MAN
3. BELLY GUT 4. LUCKY SIDE
5. TROUBLE DE A BUSH 6. BOSS FESTIVAL

RAMESES & LONG SHOT, two of the most colourful horses bred locally both died at last Saturdays Caymanas Park race meeting. Four year old RAMESES, unanimously voted 'Horse of 1968', collapsed and died immediately after finishing un placed in a nine furlong race in which he carried the top weight 9st 7lb and started favourite. LONG SHOT, an 11-year-old gelding, was destroyed after sustaining a fractured shoulder bone when he collided with COMBAT in the 'E' class six Furlongs. He proved himself to be the most durable horse to race in this country with a record number of 202 outings - 37 more than his closest rival.

With Long Shot Kick De Bucket heading up the British charts the trio flew to England to promote the record on an initial six week tour. The Pioneers had by now recorded several of their own penned songs for Leslie Kong back in Jamaica, tracks that featured on their second album Long Shot. Read the personal memories of Jackie Robinson recalling the skinhead years of 68-72 in an exclusive interview with the author up next.

EXCLUSIVE

AN INTERVIEW WITH JACKIE ROBINSON

JB: Jackie, I am really overwhelmed that you would take the time to do an interview for me to discuss what for most of us is the golden era of skinhead reggae, the spirit of 69.

I suppose the best place to start is the beginning, When did you decide you wanted to be a singer?

JR: It was around 1967 when I was sixteen years old.

JB: Jackie, many stories have been told of how you met Sydney, singing in the street was one of them that is detailed in the book, can you recall the time and how the relationship evolved?

JR: I met him at Dynamic Studios in Kingston, Jamaica. We reformed the Pioneers because although the group did some recordings with various members, they did not meet with much success prior to this.

JB: How did the original Long Shot Kick De Bucket record come about, and did you ever put a bet on him?

JR: My late Dad, Ralph Robinson, heard about the incident at Caymanas Park with Long Shot and recalled that we had released a song about him a little while before called Long Shot Bus Me Bet. We took his idea and ran with it. The rest is history. No, I do not and never have bet on horses in my life.

JB: I've also heard tell that Long Shot's death was a personal sadness for the group, but guess those stories are not true.

JR: No, we had not vested interests in horse racing.

JB: Jackie, can you recall the day you came up with Long Shot Kick De Bucket, the record says produced by Leslie Kong but I understand that it was all down to you?

JR: I brought the idea to the group and we produced it along with the musicians. Leslie Kong was in London at the time.

JB: When did you hear that Long Shot Kick De Bucket was taking off in the UK?

JR: Some time in 1969.

JB: Were you aware of the reluctance of the BBC to play reggae on the radio and after some pressure reluctantly added LSKDB to their playlist?

JR: Yes, we were very aware of the situation at the time.

JB: Jackie, the youth, me included, who were the original skinheads (non racist and non political) fell in love with reggae, were you aware that the skinheads were buying the music in volumes along with our new West Indian friends and that LSKDB became an anthem for the skinhead along with DD Israelites?

JR: Yes, we were aware that our music had crossed over and that Long Shot was big and even bigger by the time we arrived in the UK in November of 1969.

JB: Do you have any personal memories putting together the album Long Shot, among one of the first albums I purchased, and still the proud owner today?

JR: Yes, I have a memory of recording the LSKDB song. The musicians had some difficulty accepting the rhythm as we wanted it for LSKDB. They said it would not work but we insisted and it became a massive hit.

JB: We are all aware that Leslie Kong produced some of the iconic reggae sounds the skinheads were buying, what are your memories of him and your time at Beverley's Studio before his untimely death?

JR: He was a decent man and looked after his artistes. From what I hear, this was not happening to the extent in other stables as it was at Beverley's.

JB: Jackie, was there a good camaraderie between yourselves and the other reggae groups who found success in the UK at that time. I have a newspaper cutting in the book 'Pioneers and Upsetters fly in hoping for a White Christmas'. Am I right is saying in the book you came for 6 weeks but stayed?

JR: Yes, those days reggae artistes got on well indeed. We had a contract to do a 6-week tour and it was transformed, thanks to the fans like yourself, into 20 years for me personally. The response from our fan base was tremendous to the point that we were booked /re-booked at most clubs over the country.

JB: Back to the reluctant BBC, I can recall your visit to Top of The Pops for LYYBY, I can't recall, but did you every appear on TOTP with LSKDB?

JR: No, for some strange reason, they did not invite us to perform LSKDB on TOTP. What can I say?

JB: The change in style with Let Your Yeah Be Yeah in 1971 caused some mixed review at the time but still was the most popular reggae record that year in the UK and in the book Emperor Rosko, Radio One DJ at the time, has put it at the top of his ten favourite reggae sounds of the period 68 - 72. Music always evolves but what were you personal thoughts about the change from the distinctive reggae sound of Long Shot Kick De Bucket, it obviously was the right direction to take, but was it a concern at the time?

JR: No, my partners and I were not aware of the Rosko top 10 favs for 1968-1972 and that we headed the list at number one. We were never worried that fans would take issue with strings on our reggae songs; music is always evolving as you know.

JB: Jackie any other thoughts?

JR: I would like to thank you for including the Pioneers as the forefront of your research into the music of the late 60s and early 70s. I am happy to assist in keeping the reggae legacy alive for future generations and to know that I was part of that history-making process among other illustrious performers such as Desmond Dekker as you mentioned.

JB: Jackie thank you for taking the time out to enlighten the book, it has been a real pleasure to hear from one of the true legends of the golden age of reggae.

JR: Again, thank you for your work in the field of reggae music and for personally being a fan of the Pioneers.

Best.

Jackie

Special thanks to Indiana Robinson for arranging the interview.

Jackie Robinson

DISCOGRAPHY SINGLES 1968-1972

AMALGAMATED

AMG-814 Long Shot 1968
AMG-821 Jackpot 1968
AMG-823 No Dope Me Pony 1968
AMG-826 Tickle Me For Days 1968
AMG-828 Catch The Beat 1968
AMG-830 Sweet Dreams 1968
AMG-833 Don't You Know 1968

BLUE CAT

BS-103 Give It To Me 1968

PYRAMID

PYR-6062 Easy Come Easy Go 1968

CALTONE

TONE-119 I Love No Other Girl 1968

BLUE CAT

BS-100 Shake It Up 1968
BS-105 Whip Them 1968

AMALGAMATED

AMG-811 Give Me A Little Loving 1968
AMG-835 Mama Look Deh 1969
AMG-840 Who The Cap Fit 1969
AMG-850 Alli Button 1969

TROJAN

TR-672 Long Shot Kick The Bucket 1969
TR-685 Black Bud 1969
TR-698 Poor Rameses 1969
TR-7710 Samfie Man 1970
TR-7739 Driven Back 1970
TR-7760 Battle Of The Giants 1970
TR-7795 I Need Your Sweet Inspiration 1970
TR-7825 Let Your Yeah Be Yeah 1971
TR-7846 Give And Take 1971

SUMMIT

SUM8511 Starvation 1971

TROJAN

TR-7855 You Don't Know Like I Know 1972
TR-7860 Roll Muddy River 1972
TR-7880 I Believe In Love 1972

DISCOGRAPHY ALBUMS 1968-1972

AMALGAMATED   AMGLP-2003 Greetings From The Pioneers 1968

TROJAN   TBL-103 Long Shot 1969
TROJAN   TRLS-24 Yeah 1971
TROJAN   TRLS-48 I Believe 1972

Let Your Yeah Be Yeah   BBC Top of The Pops 1971

JIMMY CLIFF

Jimmy Cliff (James Chambers) was born on the 1st April 1948 in the Somerton district of St James Jamaica. He began writing songs in primary school. Moving to the capital in 1962 he sought out producers during his time at Kingston Technical School, always trying but without success to get his songs recorded.

He entered many talent contests but his first break came when he met Leslie Kong and they decided to get into the music business. It was his third single, the first two were unsuccessful, that launched him onto the music scene in Jamaica with Hurricane Hattie, a single that became a huge hit for Jimmy in Jamaica at the tender age of 14.

The record was produced by the emerging Leslie Kong who Jimmy would continue to work with right up until Kong's untimely death from a heart attack in 1971. Other hits followed in Jamaica for Jimmy with King Of Kings, Dearest Beverley and Miss Jamaica.

His success led to a contract with Island records and a promising move to the UK, but his career stumbled as Island tried to promote him as a rock star for a time, that was until the release of his first album Hard Road To Travel. The 1968 singles Waterfall WIP-6039 and That's The Way Life Goes WIP-6024 were then followed in 1969 by his international hit Wonderful World Beautiful People. Released on Trojan TR-690 the record rewarded Jimmy and Trojan a respectable number 6 in the UK chart in November that year. Further singles followed including Vietnam and a cover of Cat Stevens Wild World released on Island WIP-6087, reaching number 8 in September 1970.

Singer songwriter Cliff penned numerous hits including Desmond Dekker's massive chart success You Can Get It If You Really Want, Wonderful World Beautiful People and Many Rivers to Cross, all sung by Cliff himself at some time and Give And Take released as a follow up to Let Your Yeah Be Yeah on Trojan by The Pioneers 1n 1971. Jimmy Cliff's first entry on the UK chart during October 1969, Wonderful World, Beautiful People, spent a total of thirteen weeks on the chart. Other reggae to feature the week it peaked at number 6 on the 22nd November were the Upsetters Return Of Django and Harry J All Stars with the skinhead anthem Liquidator, currently at number 46, but destined for the top ten.

The UK chart looked like this on the 22nd November 1969.

1. Archies - Sugar Sugar
2. The Tremeloes - (Call Me) Number One
3. Fleetwood Mac - Oh Well
4. The Beatles - Something / Come Together
5. **Upsetters - Return Of Django / Dollar In The Teeth**
6. **Jimmy Cliff - Wonderful World, Beautiful People**
7. Jethro Tull - Sweet Dream
8. Karen Young - Nobody's Child
9. Kenny Rogers - Ruby Don't Take Your Love To Town
10. Stevie Wonder - Yester-Me Yester-You Yesterday

The Island record release of the Cat Stevens penned song Wild World saw Jimmy Cliff back in the charts with the record peaking at number 8 in September 1970 and spending a total of thirteen weeks on the chart.

Several excellent singles followed over the next couple of years, most notable of these were Struggling Man released on Island, but further chart success eluded him. Vietnam became a second chart entry for Jimmy Cliff in February 1970 albeit only reaching number 46 and spending just three weeks on the chart.

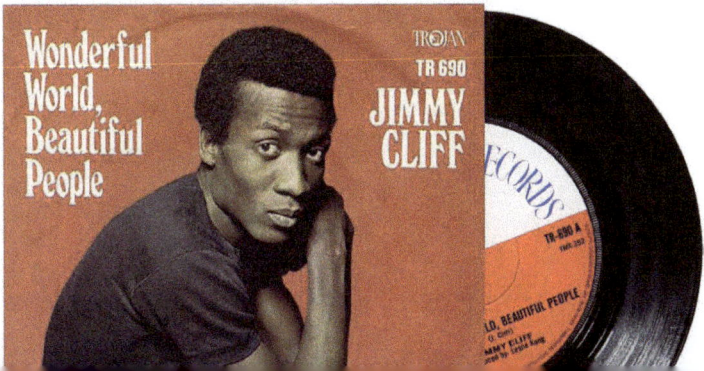

The British chart of the 12th September 1970 featured Jimmy Cliff with Wild World. The track had appeared on Cat Stevens album Tea For The Tillerman, released on Island Records in 1970, but the original version was never released as a single in the UK.

1. Smokey Robinson And The Miracles - Tears Of A Clown
2. Elvis Presley - The Wonder Of You
3. Three Dog Night - Mama Told Me (Not To Come)
4. Chairman Of The Board - Give Me Just A Little More Time
5. Bread - Make It With You
6. Freda Payne - Band Of Gold
7. Chicago - 25 Or 6 To 4
8. **Jimmy Cliff - Wild World**
9. Marmalade - Rainbow
10. Hot Chocolate - Love Is Life

International stardom came the way of Jimmy Cliff in 1972 as he played Ivanhoe 'Ivan' Martin in the film The Harder They Come. Directed by Perry Henzell the film tells the story of a young man drawn to the ghettos of Kingston from the country by the promise of making it big in the record business. Success eludes him and he inevitably turns to a life of crime. The soundtrack elevated reggae to the world stage and still remains one of the most significant works to have come out of Jamaica.

The Bigger They Come The Harder They Fall was the forerunner for the film version single of The Harder They Come, issued on the B side of Sitting In Limbo on Island WIP-6110 in 1971.

Jimmy ended his association with Island Records after the filming of The Harder They Come as he was near broke and asked Chris Blackwell for £50,000 to remain with Island. Chris Blackwell told him that he would soon make that sort of money but Jimmy couldn't wait and left the label. Within a few days of Jimmy leaving the label Island had found a new star in the making.

Having released several singles on Trojan and Pama's subsidiary labels Bob Marley found himself stranded in the UK whilst on tour. The story goes that he walked into Blackwell's office and left with £4,000 to record an album back in Jamaica, and the rest they say is history.

SINGLES DISCOGRAPHY   1968-1972

ISLAND
WIP-6039 Waterfall 1968
   WIP-6024 That's The Way Life Goes 1968

TROJAN
   TR-690 Wonderful World, Beautiful People 1969
   TR-7767 You Can Get It If You Really Want 1969

ISLAND
WIP-6087 Wild World 1970

TROJAN
TR-7722 Vietnam 1970
TR-7745 Sufferin' In The Land 1970
TR- 7845 Those Good Good Old Days 1971

ISLAND
   WIP-6097 Synthetic World 1971
      WIP-6103 Goodbye Yesterday1971
      WIP-6110 Sitting In Limbo 1971
      WIP-6132 Struggling Man 1972

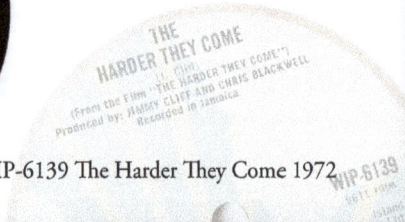

WIP-6139 The Harder They Come 1972

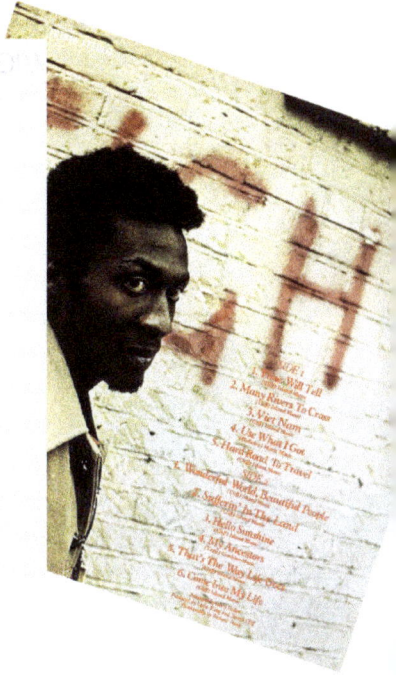

JIMMY CLIFF   JIMMY CLIFF
TROJAN RECORDS TRLS 16 1969

Side 1
1. TIME WILL TELL
2. MANY RIVERS TO CROSS
3. VIETNAM
4. USE WHAT I GOT
5. HARD ROAD TO TRAVEL

Side 2
1. WONDERFUL WORLD, BEAUTIFUL PEOPLE
2. SUFFERIN' IN THE LAND
3. HELLO SUNSHINE
4. MY ANCESTORS
5. THAT'S THE WAY LIFE GOES
6. COME INTO MY LIFE

97

BOB AND MARCIA

Young Gifted And Black - with strings attached. Bob And Marcia's upbeat version of Nina Simone's black power song took the charts by storm and heralded the era of strings attached. The UK version with a vivacious rhythm complete with violins demonstrated the effects of the pop influence from Trojan on the true sound of Jamaica, a sound that can be summed up on the original Jamaican version of the single.

One could argue that if it had not been such an upbeat sweetened version then it would probably have not gained chart success, therefore holding back further interest in reggae music from the mainstream. Crucially the sound was still popular with the skinheads.

The success was followed up with the duos second hit Pied Piper. Young Gifted And Black entered the charts on the 14th March 1970 reaching number 5 in April spending a total of twelve weeks on the chart. Pied Piper followed in 1971 reaching number 11 in July, the duos chart success covering a total of twenty three weeks during 1970 and 1971. Other hits deserted them as reggae was by now beginning to evolve again with Trojan in particular developing a more sophisticated sound, a sound which did bring some initial success for groups such as Greyhound, The Pioneers and Dandy Livingstone but would ultimately disenchant reggae's loyal following of skinheads and the diehard West Indians who shared the love of the true sounds of Jamaica.

The pop influenced sound of Bob And Marcia's hits to the uninitiated of reggae from the early years probably gave a perception that they were just a flash in the pan, however nothing could be further removed from reality. Marcia Griffiths was born in Kingston Jamaica into what was described as a house full of music and love.

Marcia's singing career began in the church choir where her talent was quickly spotted. She soon signed with Coxsone Dodd's Studio One. Her first success came in 1968 with Feel Like Jumping. Further records rapidly followed with Truly, Tell Me Now and a duet with Bob Andy Always Together on the Bamboo label, BAM 40 released in 1970.

A move to Harry Johnson 'Harry J' came in 1969 and after a couple of solos she recorded Young Gifted And Black with Bob Andy, the track later released on Trojan with the strings added in the UK by Johnny Arthey. The duo toured the UK and signed a contract with CBS, a move that eventually hindered more success and the partnership came to an end.

Marcia went on to enjoy great achievements with a solo career and also became a member of Bob Marley's I Threes.

Bob Andy began his career as one of the original members of The Paragons, a group which included John Holt and had a whole string of Jamaican hits during the early sixties, including The Tide Is High. Bob decided to pursue a solo career and joined Coxone Dodd's Studio One where he remained until 1968, producing for Rupie Edwards.

The top ten week commencing the 4th April 1970 saw Young Gifted And Black peak at number 5 surrounded by some very stiff competition from the old heavyweights, while Boris Gardner featured in the charts, currently at number 28 with his skinhead favourite, Elizabethan Reggae. Bob And Marcia's Young Gifted And Black was ranked 59 in the best selling British singles chart of 1970.

The chart for the 4th April 1970 looked like this.

1. Simon And Garfunkel - Bridge Over Troubled Waters
2. Mary Hopkin - Knock Knock Who's There
3. Andy Williams - Can't Help Falling In Love
4. Lee Marvin - Wand'rin' Star
5. **Bob And Marcia - Young Gifted And Black**
6. Pickettywitch -The Same Old feeling
7. The Beatles - Let It Be
8. Kenny Rogers And The First Edition - Something's Burning
9. The Dave Clark Five - Everybody Get Together
10. Elvis Presley - Don't Cry Daddy

Pied Piper peaked at number 11 on 4th July 1971.

9. **Greyhound - Black And White**
10. Mungo Jerry - Lady Rose
11. **Bob And Marcia - Pied Piper**
12. Smokey Robinson And The Miracles - I Don't Blame You At All
13. White Planes - When You Are King
14. Lobo - Me And You And A Dog Named Boo
15. Dawn - Knock Three Times
16. The Supremes And The Four Tops - River Deep Mountain High
17. **Dave And Ansel Collins - Monkey Spanner**

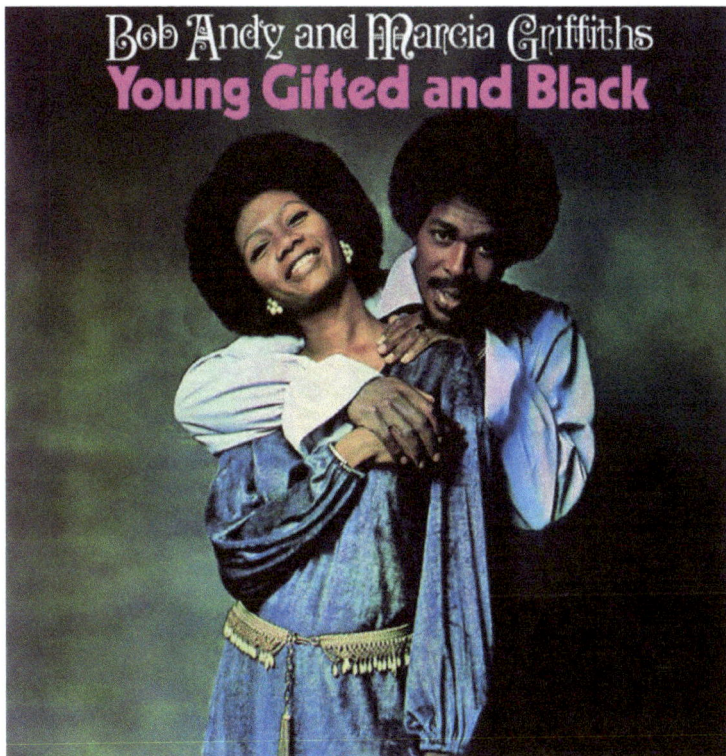

YOUNG GIFTED AND BLACK
TROJAN RECORDS TBL 122
Released 1970

SELECTED SINGLES DISCOGRAPHY 1968-1972

MARCIA GRIFFITHS

COXONE
CS-7035 Mojo Girl 1968
CS-7055 Feel Like Jumping 1968
CS-7062 Hold Me Tight 1968

ESCORT
ES-808 Don't Let Me Down 1969

BAMBOO
BAM-59 Shimmering Star 1970

HARRY J
HJ-6613 Put A Little Love In Your Heart 1970
HJ-6623 Band Of Gold 1970

BOB ANDY

DOCTOR BIRD
DB-119 Games People Play 1969

BOB AND MARCIA

BAMBOO
BAM-40 Always Together 1970

HARRY J
HJ-6605 Young Gifted And Black 1970
HJ-6615 Got To Get Ourselves Together 1970

TROJAN
TR-7818 Pied Piper 1971
TR-7854 But I Do 1972

NICKY THOMAS

Nicky Thomas was born Cecil Nicholas Thomas in Portland Jamaica in 1949. Like some of his future compatriots of the reggae era Nicky began his working life as a labourer where he formed an acquaintance with members of the future group The Gladiators.

His first recording to be a hit at home in Jamaica was Run Nigel Run, the record produced by Derrick Harriott. Soon he started out on his long association with Joe Gibbs, a union that provided Nicky with his most successful recording, Love Of The Common People. Joe Gibbs was a seasoned record producer in Jamaica but Love Of The Common People was his first taste of success in the UK. The UK Trojan release of the record was very pop infused, a version of the Jamaican release with strings added, a successful technique that was used on other singles that made the top thirty. The record allowed Nicky's very distinctive soul-full voice to shine through selling over 175,000 copies and made him an overnight sensation.

A tour of the UK followed prompting him to remain in England where he continued to release other singles and albums. Surprisingly future chart success eluded him despite a string of excellent releases including If I Had A Hammer and Yesterday Man, a record that flirted for a while but just failed to make the charts. Trojan subsequently released the album Love Of The Common People on TBL143 in 1970 produced by Joe Gibbs.

LOVE OF THE COMMON PEOPLE·NICKY THOMAS

By 1971 Nicky was producing for himself and released a single Tell It Like It Is / BBC, a record incidentally that was directing harsh criticism at the BBC for the lack of airplay for reggae. A new album titled Tell It Like It Is was released in 1972 featuring tracks that were self produced.

Many of Trojan's compilation albums featured Nicky's work including the very popular Reggae Chartbusters series. As a consequence of his untimely death in 1990 the world of reggae lost one its famous sons, a very talented performer who had helped elevate reggae to the mainstream in the early 1970s.

Love Of The Common People was ranked 74 in the top 100 singles of 1970, ahead of Ride A White Swan by T.Rex. The British charts looked like this on the 11th July 1970.

1. Mungo Jerry - In The Summertime
2. Free - All Right Now
3. Mr Bloe - Groovin With Mr Bloe
4. Creedence Clearwater Revival - Up Around The Bend
5. The Four Tops - It's All In The Game
6. The Beach Boys - Cottonfields
7. Gerry Monroe - Sally
8. Cliff Richard - Goodbye Sam, Hello Samantha
9. **Nicky Thomas - Love Of The Common People**
10. Fleetwood Mac - The Green Manalishi

SINGLES DISCOGRAPHY 1970-1972

TROJAN

TR-7750 Love Of The Common People 1970
TR-7796 God Bless The Children 1970
TR-7807 If I Had A Hammer 1970
TR-7830 Tell It Like It Is 1971
TR-7850 Yesterday Man 1971
TR-7878 Images Of You 1972

LOVE OF THE COMMON PEOPLE
NICKY THOMAS
TROJAN RECORDS TBL143 Released 1970

Side 1
1. GOD BLESS THE CHILDREN
2. RAINY NIGHT IN GEORGIA
3. IF I HAD A HAMMER
4. TURN BACK THE HANDS OF TIME
5. DOING THE MOON WALK
6. LOVE OF THE COMMON PEOPLE

Side 2
1. MAMA'S SONG
2. HAVE A LITTLE FAITH
3. DON'T TOUCH
4. LONELY FEELIN'
5. I WHO HAVE NOTHING
6. LET IT BE
7. RED EYE

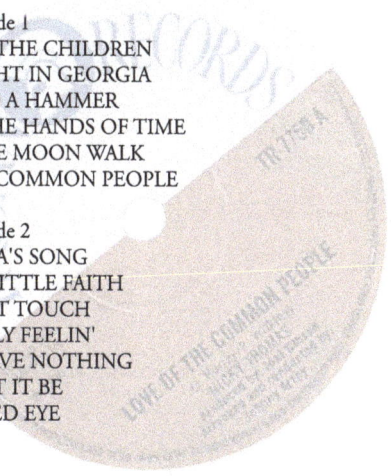

TELL IT LIKE IT IS
NICKY THOMAS
TROJAN RECORDS TRLS 25
Released 1972

Side 1
1. TELL IT LIKE IT IS 2. WATCH THAT LITTLE GIRL
3. DEEP IN THE MORNING 4. YESTERDAY MAN 5. WE PEOPLE
6. LAY LADY LAY IN THE MIDNIGHT HOUR (MEDLEY)

Side 2
1. JUST BECAUSE YOUR LOVE HAS GONE 2. SOUL POWER
3. I CAN'T STAND IT 4. ISN'T IT A PITY 5. BBC
6. LOVE PEACE AND HAPPINESS

DAVE AND ANSEL COLLINS

Dave Barker, born David Crooks in 1948, was raised by his grandmother from the age of four after his parents had emigrated. He soon discovered a talent for singing as a teenager with his musical career unfolding when he formed a group known as The Two Tones, although recording success eluded them.

He then spent some time with Winston Riley's Techniques, forming a duo with Glen Brown. It was while working in the pressing plant at Studio One that he was introduced to Lee 'Scratch' Perry, eventually becoming a regular vocalist. Perry suggested he change his name and record as Dave Barker. He was given every encouragement to develop a style of deejay vocals with the ensuing hit single Shocks Of A Mighty, a track that featured on Tighten Up Volume 3.

double barrel
Dave and Ansel Collins

Ansel Collins, sometimes spelt Ansell or Ansil was also born in Kingston Jamaica in 1949. He began performing with The Invincibles then after a spell working with Lee 'Scratch' Perry he teamed up with Dave Barker where his keyboard playing epitomized the new style of skinhead reggae. The famous reggae double act was often assumed to be brothers. They joined forces in 1971 to release Double Barrel, a track that was penned way back in 1968 but never released. Double Barrel catapulted the duo to the world stage reaching number 22 on the Billboard charts in America, and made it to number 1 in Jamaica.

Perhaps more importantly to the skinheads and a wider audience Double Barrel entered the British charts where it spent two weeks at the top of the pile during May 1971. The record gained the distinction of being the first reggae record to chart on both sides of the Atlantic at the same time.

The follow up release brought further chart success in the UK and international recognition with Monkey Spanner, a record in a similar style reaching a respectful number 7 in July the same year.

The duo were in Jamaica when the news hit that Double Barrel had taken off and were hurriedly flown to England by Winston Riley, that was once a passport could be sorted for Dave Barker.

As soon as the Boeing landed Dave and
Ansel were whisked off to the Top of The
Pops BBC studio to mime for the cameras,
their first taste of a chilly England. The pair spent several weeks
touring the UK for Trojan before returning briefly to Jamaica
to lay down tracks for their forthcoming album, not surprisingly
titled Double Barrel. Ironically the LP ultimately consisted of
previously recorded material written by Winston Riley.

After the release of the album and a handful of singles the pair parted
company with Collins returning to Jamaica to become a session player. The
pinnacle of chart success for Trojan and reggae came in May 1971 when
Double Barrel peaked and spent two weeks at number 1. The chart that
week also featured Bruce Ruffin's Rain making a brief incursion at number
42.

Double Barrel was ranked at 13 and Monkey Spanner at 68 in the top 100
singles of 1971.

The chart on May 1st 1971 looked like this.

1. Dave And Ansil Collins - Double Barrel
2. T.Rex - Hot Love
3. Dawn - Knock Three Times
4. The Rolling Stones - Brown Sugar / Bitch / Let It Rock
5. Waldo de Los Rios - Mozart Symphony No 40
6. Ray Stevens - Bridget The Midget
7. Ringo Starr - It Don't Come Easy
8. Andy Williams - (Where Do I Begin) Love Story
9. Diane Ross - Remember Me
10. CCS - Walkin'

Monkey Spanner came hot on the heels of Double Barrel entering the charts on the 20th June 1971, eventually reaching number 7 on the 11th July where it stayed for three weeks, spending a total of twelve weeks on the charts, ten of those in the top 30.

The chart on July 11th 1971 looked like this.

1. Middle Of The Road - Chirpy Chirpy Cheep Cheep
2. The Sweet - Co-Co
3. Hurricane Smith - Don't Let It Die
4. T.Rex - Get It On
5. Lobo - Me And You And A Dog Named Boo
6. Greyhound - Black And White
7. Dave & Ansel Collins - Monkey Spanner
8. Blue Mink -Banner Man
9. John Kongos - He's Gonna Step On You Again
10. Tami Lynn - I'm Gonna Run Away From You

DISCOGRAPHY SINGLES 1968-1972

DAVE BARKER
PUNCH
PH-20 Prisoner Of Love 1969

ACKEE
ACK-113 Johnny Dollar 1970
ACK-119 Life Of A Millionaire 1970

HIGH NOTE
HI-049 She Want It 1970

JACKPOT
JP-736 The Fastest Man Alive 1970
JP-742 Wet Version 1970
JP-745 Girl Of My Dreams 1970

PUNCH
PH-25 Shock Of Might 1970
PH-42 Reggae Meeting 1970

UPSETTER
US-331 Shocks Of A Mighty (UPSETTERS) 1970
US-358 Shocks 71 1971

SUPRREME
SUP-228 Double Heavy 1971

JACKPOT
JP-803 You'll Be Sorry 1972

ANSEL COLLINS
J-DAN
JDN-4401 Cock Robin 1970

TECHNIQUES
TE-913 Nuclear Weapon 1971

DAVE AND ANSEL COLLINS
TECHNIQUES
TE-901 Double Barrel 1971
TE-914 Monkey Spanner 1971
TE-915 Karate 1971

double barrel

Dave and Ansel Collins

DOUBLE BARREL
DAVE AND ANSEL COLLINS
TROJAN RECORDS TBL 162
(Issued on the TECHNIQUES label) Released 1971

Side 1
1. DOUBLE BARREL 2. WILD BUNCH 3. ELFREGO BACCA
4. MONKEY SPANNER VERSION 5. MY BEST GIRL
6. SECRET WEAPON

Side 2
1. I THE THIRD 2. THAT GIRL 3. IMPOSSIBLE MISSION
4. TEN TO ONE 5. I CAN COUNT THE DAYS
6. TWO FOUR ONE

GREYHOUND

Greyhound launched their musical life as The Rudies in the late 60s, a group formed by Freddie Notes and British based musicians Earl Dunn, Trevor Ardley White and Sonny Binns.

They enjoyed several record releases but by far their most successful was a cover version of Bobby Bloom's Montego Bay a record that achieved a top ten hit for Bobby Bloom in 1970 reaching number 3 in October. The record stayed nineteen weeks in the charts. However Freddie Notes & The Rudies cover version released on Trojan TR-7791 achieved only a modest chart entry, reaching number 45, charting for only two weeks in the same month, a month incidentally that saw Desmond Dekker and Horace Faith riding high.

Additional singles followed including Patches, issued on Trojan TR-7798 which featured on Reggae Chartbusters Volume 2 but further chart success eluded them. Freddie Notes & The Rudies had an album released on Trojan in 1970 titled Unity on TBL 107.

1971 witnessed a parting of the ways for The Rudies, Freddie Notes had left with Glenroy Oakley replacing him so they felt a change of identity was needed, a change that launched a reggae group who would have a relatively successful period over the next couple of years. The name was of course Greyhound.

The first success for Greyhound came with a cover version of a song written in 1955 titled Black And White, a record the group felt suited perfectly a pop-reggae style and sure enough it proved to be a massive hit for Greyhound. The track was released on Trojan TR-7820 on both the orange and white label and the new brown label. The record entered the charts in June 1971 achieving a very respectable two weeks at number 6 during July, spending a total of thirteen weeks on the chart.

The story behind Black And White stemmed from America where in 1954 The Supreme Court outlawed segregation of public schools. It was originally published as a song in 1956, penned by David Arkin with Earl Robinson's music.

Their next success came with another reggae version of a well known song, and one that again suited the pop-reggae idiom superbly. Moon River, a cover of a Henry Mancini number, this time released as a Trojan Maxi single TR-7848 C/W I've Been Trying and Keep The Pressure On. It achieved a top 12 for Greyhound in February 1972 and everything seemed to be going well, including a new album release on Trojan, Black And White TRL-27.

Greyhound however only achieved one more chart success following on the heels of Moon River. Just as Moon River was dropping out of the charts I Am What I Am entered peaking at number 20 in April 1972. Released on Trojan TR-7853 it was their last recording for the label and within a year the group had broken up.

MONTEGO BAY
Freddie Notes & the Rudies

FREDDIE NOTES AND THE RUDIES Montego Bay was released as a single in 1970 on Trojan TR-7791 and an album of the same title on TBL 152.

BLACK AND WHITE

The British charts looked good for reggae during July 1971 with two records in the top 10, Greyhound had peaked at number 6 and Monkey Spanner was riding high at number 7.

1. T.Rex - Get It On
2. Middle Of The Road - Chirpy Chirpy Cheep Cheep
3. The Sweet - Co-Co
4. Lobo - Me And You And A Dog Named Boo
5. Hurricane Smith - Don't Let It Die
6. **Greyhound - Black And White**
7. **Dave & Ansel Collins - Monkey Spanner**
8. New World - Tom Tom Turnaround
9. Blue Mink - Banner Man
10. The Temptations - Just My Imagination

Trojan released Moon River as a Maxi single on TR-7848 in 1971 with the B side featuring two tracks, I've Been Trying and Keep The Pressure On. It peaked at number 12 on both the 5th and 19th of February, spending a total of eleven weeks on the charts. Moon River was the second of a hat-trick of hits for Greyhound. The single released on the traditional TR label as well as the colourful Trojan Maxi label also came with an additional picture sleeve option.

1. Chickory Tip - Son Of My Father
2. T.Rex - Telegram Sam
3. The Chi-Lites - Have You Seen Her
4. Slade - Look Wot You Dun
5. Neil Reid - Mother Of Mine
6. Don McLean - American Pie
7. The New Seekers - I'd Like To Teach The World To Sing
8. Sonny And Cher - All I Ever Need Is You
9. Fortunes - Storm In A Teacup
10. Al Green - Let's Stay Together
11. America - Horse With No Name
12. **Greyhound - Moon River**

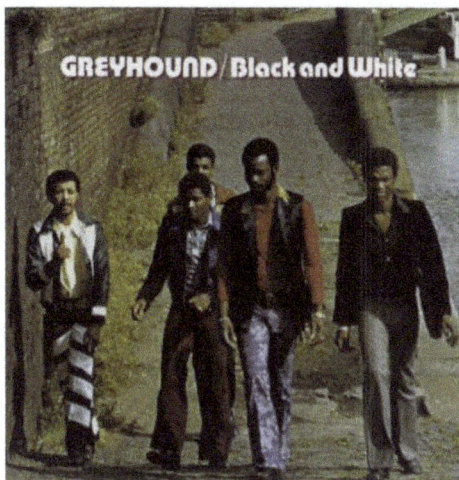

BLACK AND WHITE
Released 1972 on TROJAN TRL 27

Side1.
1. BLACK AND WHITE 2. LOVE IS BLUE
3. SAND IN YOUR SHOES 4. THE CHANGE
5. BE LOVING TO ME 6. YOU'RE THE ONE

Side 2
1.YESTERDAY'S LOVE 2. PEACE AND LOVE 3. MOON RIVER
4. FUNKY JAMAICA 5. HIGH AND DRY

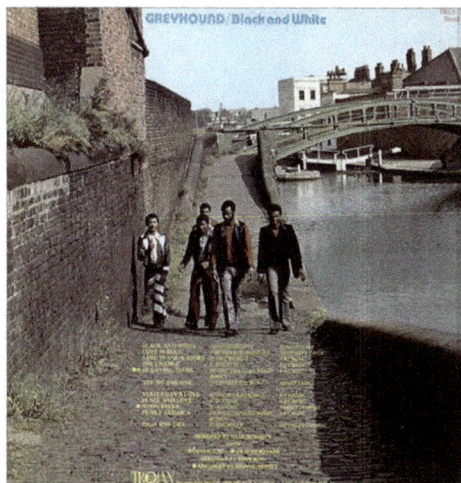

Moon River was composed by Johnny Mercer (lyrics) and Henry Mancini (music) in 1961, the same year that Andy Williams first recorded the song.

DISCOGRAPHY SINGLES 1968-1972

FREDDIE NOTES & THE RUDIES

GRAPE
GR-3010 Guns Of Navarone 1969

TROJAN
TR-7713 Shanghi 1969
TR-7734 Down On The Farm 1970
TR-7791 Montego Bay 1970
TR-7798 Patches 1970

GRAPE
GR-3011 Babylon 1970

B&C
CB-125 It Came From Out Of The Sky 1970

I Am What I Am peaked at number 20 during April 1972 spending nine weeks on the chart. The chart of April 1972 also saw Johnny Nash with Stir It Up and Paul Simon's Mother And Child Reunion feature.

GREYHOUND

TROJAN
TR-7820 Black And White 1971
TR-7848 Moon River 1971
TR-7853 I Am What I Am 1972

BLUE MOUNTAIN
BM-1016 Dream Lover 1972

TOOTS AND THE MAYTALS

Originally just The Maytals their distinctive style of reggae combined with Frederick 'Toots' Hibbert's voice gave them a distinctive sound all of their own. Frederick grew up singing Gospel music with the church choir in the parish of Clarendon, Jamaica; he was one of seven children.

At the age of 16 he moved to Kingston where he meet Henry 'Raleigh' Gordon and Nathaniel 'Jerry' McCarthy, and the trio was born. Their first album Never Grow Old was released in Jamaica during 1964 with great success. Their second album, produced by the legendry Byron Lee titled The Sensational Maytals, was released just a year later in 1965.

1966, a legendary year in England, saw Frederick arrested and imprisoned for possession of marijuana in his native Jamaica, an incident that inspired one of his best loved tracks, 54-46 That's My Number.

Toots was arrested for possession of marijuana in 66 but has always declared his innocence. "*They frame me; they put something in my bag. It was a very cruel thin*". The story goes that on the night he was arrested Hibbert says, he was on his way to a show and had stopped to bail a friend out of jail. He was carrying a bag containing his stage suit but neglected to bring his driver's licence. "*The police told me I needed a licence to bail the person out, so I left my bag there and went back to get it. When I came back, they say they find ganja in it*". It was while in prison that he penned the hit 54-46 That's My Number, the title of which was inspired by his prison identification number.

1967 saw him released from the custodial sentence with the band changing their name to Toots And The Maytals. Their next three albums were all produced by the legendary Leslie Kong.

In 1968 a record was released on Pyramid PYR-6057 that was claimed to have had a great influence on the name of the new beat that was upping the pace from rocksteady with the title Do The Reggay.

The first reggae record! When Toots was asked about Do The Reggay being the first to evolve from rocksteady into reggae his response was, "*People tell me that, but when I did it, I didn't know. There was the beat in Jamaica; reggae was played long before I started singing. And there was a slang, like a nickname for someone who don't dress properly - like if you are barefoot, people would call you streggae. They say hey, that guy is streggae, don't talk to him. If a girl don't dress properly, like don't have on any top, they call her streggae. So one morning, one Tuesday morning, we just said Let's go along and do some reggae. Those days we'd just make stuff up, anything. A bird flies around the corner, you write a song about it. So we just say Do the reggay, do the reggay, and that's it. A few words, y'know? And nobody paid it any mind until it started to go all over the world. I saw it in the Guinness Book of Records. So I thank God that I did something good, and I didn't even plan it*".

1968 saw the release in the UK of 54-46 That's My Number on the Pyramid label, utilising the rhythm track from Marcia Griffith's Feel Like Jumping. A follow up single, 54-46 Was My Number, having a slight change of title and pace was issued on Trojan TR-7808 in late 1970. The lyrics to the record describing Toots time in prison and quoting his prison ID number was one of the first to achieve popularity outside of Jamaica and a true favourite with the skinheads. Between the two 54-46 numbers they released Monkey Man, a song about a girl choosing another man over Toots, surprisingly The Maytals only British chart entry. The track also featured on Trojan's highly successful Reggae Chartbusters Volume 2 in 1970. Monkey Man reached number 47 in the UK Singles chart during that year, astonishingly only spending four weeks on the chart.

SWEET AND DANDY
BEVERLEY'S RECORDS 1969
Produced by Leslie Kong

Side 1
1. MONKEY MAN 2. PRESSURE DROP 3. I SHALL BE FREE
4. BLA BLA BLA 5. JUST TELL ME 6. WE SHALL OVER COME

Side 2
1. SWEET AND DANDY 2. SCARE HIM 3. ALIDINA
4. I NEED YOUR LOVE 5. 54-46 THAT'S MY NUMBER
6. OH YEAH

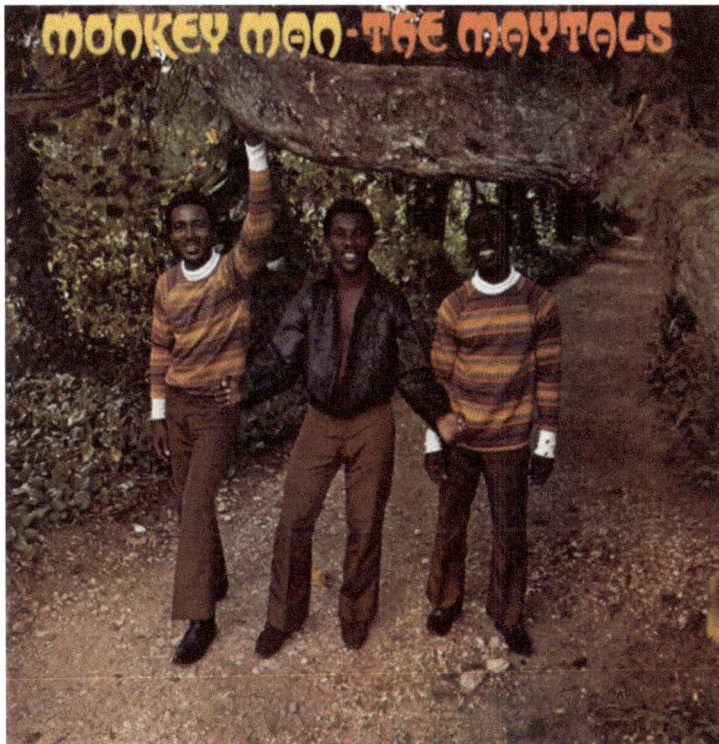

MONKEY MAN
TROJAN TBL 107 1970
Produced by Leslie Kong

Side 1
1. PEEPING TOM 2. REVIVAL REGGAE
3. GIVE PEACE A CHANCE 4. GOLD AND SILVER
5. THE PREACHER 6. BLA BLA BLA

Side 2
1. AFRICAN DOCTOR 2. MONKEY MAN
3. SUN MOON AND STAR 4. PRESSURE DROP
5. SHE'S MY SCORCHER 6. I SHALL BE FREE

SELECTED DISCOGRAPHY SINGLES 1968-1972

PYRAMID
PYR-6043 Struggle 1968
PYR-6048 Just Tell Me 1968
PYR-6055 School Days 1968
PYR-6057 Do The Reggay 1968
PYR-6030 54-46 That's My Number 1968

NUBEAT
NB-031 My Testimony 1969

PYRAMID
PYR-6066 Don't Trouble Trouble 1969
PYR-6070 Alidina 1969
PYR-6073 Pressure Drop 1969
PYR-6074 Sweet And Dandy 1969

TROJAN
TR-7711 Monkey Man 1969
TR-7726 Sweet And Dandy 1970
TR-7741 Bla Bla Bla 1970
TR-7757 Water Melon 1970
TR-7786 Dr. Lester 1970
TR-7808 54-46 Was My Number 1970

SUMMIT
SUM-8510 Peeping Tom 1970
SUM-8513 Monkey Girl 1971
SUM-8520 One Eye Enos 1971
SUM-8527 It's You 1971

TROJAN
TR-7849 Johnny Cool Man 1971

HILLCREST
HCT-4 Hey Rasta Man 1972

SUMMIT
SUM-8533 Never You Change 1972
SUM-8537 It Must Be True love 1972

TROJAN
TR-7865 Louie Louie / Pressure Drop 72 1972
TR-7874 Pomps And Pride 1972

PRESSURE DROP was re-worked in 1972 and released by Trojan as the B side of TR-7865 LOUIE LOUIE.

The Maytals enjoyed a cameo role in the 1972 film The Harder They Come. Both the original 1969 version of Pressure Drop and Sweet And Dandy in the studio under the ever watchful eye of Leslie Kong featured on the sound track. Sweet And Dandy tells the story of Ettie and Johnson, a young couple about to get married having last minute nerves. They are both pacified and encouraged on by their older relatives while all the while the guests are eager to celebrate the occasion and get a slice of the wedding cake. The conclusion sees the happy couple dancing.

JUDGE DREAD

Alexander Hughes was born on the 2nd May 1945 in Kent, although he will always be remembered as Judge Dread. Perhaps his biggest tribute was becoming the first white recording artist to have a hit in Jamaica with Big Six. The Judge had several other accolades to his name including the greatest number of banned records by the BBC, running to a staggering total of eleven, coincidently the number of chart hits to his name.

He could also boast the greatest number of reggae records to enter the UK chart, no mean feat when you consider the competition from the likes of Desmond Dekker and Bob Marley to name just two.

During his teenage years he lodged with a West Indian family in Brixton where he had his first introduction to Jamaican music. His early career was to some extent determined by his size, first a bouncer at a local club then spending time as a bodyguard for Prince Buster, Coxone Dodd and Duke Reid while they were touring Britain. Next up came a stint at wrestling, AKA The Masked Executioner, and then a stint with Trojan as a debt collector.

A man of many talents he also had a session as a DJ on a local radio station and had his own sound system, but his BIG break was about to come. Alex was infatuated by Prince Buster's ribald Big Five so he went into the Trojan studio to record his own follow up using the rhythm track of Verne & Sons Little Boy Blue. The lyrics were a rude version of nursery rhymes and by out-and-out luck Trojan's Lee Gopthal came in during the recording. The story goes that he was so impressed that he signed the DJ to the company and decided to release Big Six. Alex chose to issue the record under his stage name of Judge Dread in honour of a character from Prince Buster. The record was released appropriately on Trojan's subsidiary Big Shot label BI-608.

The record sold well locally but a deal was then struck with EMI for distribution that saw the record take the charts by storm despite no air play as the BBC had banned the record. Trojan's devious attempts to convince otherwise that the record was not rude fell on the same deaf ears that had banned Wet Dream some three years earlier.

Despite the ban the record became a hit following as it did in the footsteps of Max Romeo's chart success of 1969 with Big Six reaching number 11 in October 1972. The record spent some six months on the chart selling a very creditable 300,000 copies.

BI-608 A

Big Six was ranked 45 in the top selling UK singles of that year, a great achievement for a record despite the ban by the BBC. To put it into context Elton John was at number 52 with Crocodile Rock, Slade were placed at 56 with Gudby T'Jane, Paul Simon was at 59 with his reggae song Mother And Child Reunion and T. Rex were at 90 with Jeepster.

For several years the sounds emanating from Jamaica were finding their way to these shores so it was somewhat of a coup that Big Six became a huge hit in Jamaica, with Judge Dread finding himself in Kingston to perform before a live audience. No one had seen Judge Dread and it was reported that the crowd thought that the big guy roaming around on stage was in fact his bodyguard, until that was he grabbed the microphone and began to sing. The crowd were said to have been amazed as no one considered that the Judge could be white.

The follow up in the UK also on Big Shot BI-613 was understandably titled Big Seven. The new single continued in the same vein only this time using the rhythm from My Conversation, originally released in 1968 by The Uniques. Big Seven did even better despite its inevitable ban reaching number 18 in December 1972, before peaking at number 8 on the 13th January 1973. The Judge enjoyed further chart success over the coming years and continued touring, with his last appearance coming on the 13th March 1998 at The Penny Theatre in Canterbury. Judge Dread died of a heart attack as he was leaving the stage at the end of his performance. Initially the audience thought it was part of his act before they realised the seriousness of the situation.

Judge Dread with The Pioneers, The Cimarons, Nicky Thomas,
Tito Simon, Buster Pearson and Danny Ray

CHARTBUSTERS – THE SINGLES THAT MADE THE TOP 30

The vinyl 45 or 7 inch was named after its play speed with the first single produced in 1949 by RCA in America. The format soon took off with the young record buying public who preferred the smaller and cheaper 45 to the more expensive 12 inch LP. In Britain the sales of records increased providing competition for the USA but it was a tiny Island in the Caribbean that was witnessing a new revolution.

The sound system operators in Jamaica were turning their hand to record production, releasing an outpouring of ska, replacing the imported American R&B that had previously been the only source of music. The first recording studio to open in Jamaica was Ken Khouri Federal Records, recording mento music. 1954 saw Jamaica's first record label Federal Records launched by Khouri with Coxone Dodd and Duke Reid following suit. The music produced was a fusion of Caribbean and rhythm and blues and led to the development of bluebeat. The bass evolved to a more prominent feature and ska was born, the forerunner of rocksteady and reggae. The singles that made the charts come next, kicking off with perhaps the most icon reggae sound, even for the uninitiated.

ISRAELITES   DESMOND DEKKER AND THE ACES
Released on PYRAMID PYR 6058 1968
Highest chart position 1 19/04/1969

Desmond Dekker was already a superstar in his native Jamaica courtesy of his hit song Music Like Dirt winning the 1968 Jamaican Festival. The inaugural festival was set up in 1962 to showcase performing artists by the Minister of Community Development, Edward Seaga, who eventually became the Prime Minister. Desmond found favour in Britain where the mods embraced his music. In 1968 he released Israelites. However the record remained largely overlooked for many months. Nevertheless it did eventually catch on and entered the charts on the 22nd of March 1969 and within four weeks it was at the top of the pile Albeit for just one week Israelites spent seven weeks in the top 10. The record also found success across the Atlantic becoming the first true reggae sound to chart in America.

PYR 6058 A

Beverley's
Bird Music
℗ 1968

ISRAELITES
DESMOND DEKKER
and THE ACES

4. ELVIS PRESLEY – IN THE GHETTO
5. ROBIN GIBB – SAVED BY THE BELL
6. AMEN CORNER – HELLO SUZIE
7. DESMOND DEKKER AND THE ACES – IT MIEK
8. CLODAGH RODGERS – GOODNIGHT MIDNIGHT
MARMALADE – SAVED BY THE BELL
FAMILY DOGG – WAY OF LIFE

IT MIEK   DESMOND DEKKER AND THE ACES
Released on PYRAMID PRY 6068 1969
Highest chart position 7 26/07/1969

It Miek, appearing on some labels as It Mek was released in June 1969 and entered the charts in July, issued as the follow to up Israelites by Desmond Dekker and The Aces. The song was written by Desmond and produced by Leslie Kong. The Aces became Desmond's backing group back in Jamaica as early as 1965 but when international recognition arrived the two members, Wilson James and Easton Barrington Howard, refused to travel to England, leaving Desmond's future recording career as a solo artist. The track was laid down in Jamaica with the brass section added in the UK. It Miek charted for eleven weeks and sold globally over a million copies. The song is telling of Desmond's little sister with the title Mek being Jamaican patois for let us do it or even make up your mind, with many references telling of the song titles meaning as that's the reason. The last track released featuring The Aces was Pickney Gal, a record that surprisingly only made number 46, charting for just three weeks in January 1970.

WET DREAM   MAX ROMEO
Released on UNITY UN-503 1968
Highest chart position 10 16/08/1969

The well documented single from Max Romeo was an up-tempo number with a very strong melody, almost unique at the time, and had already made a name for Max in his native Jamaica, receiving plenty of air play.

Max wrote lyrics using the rhythm track of Derrick Morgan's Hold You Jack and I Love You. Derrick was scheduled to add his vocals to the track but refused as did many other artists including John Holt and Slim Smith. Although the single was released in 1968 it didn't start to sell until 1969. Already a hit in Jamaica, the single entered the UK charts in May that year reaching the top ten in August 1969. Although early sales of the record were slow when it started to take off it was banned by the BBC with their DJ's Tony Blackburn and Alan Freeman instructed to make reference to the record only as a record by Max Romeo.

The record sold over 250,000 copies remaining on the chart for almost six months. In an interview in 2007 when asked why he'd recorded it Max suggested the devil made him do it.

RETURN OF DJANGO UPSETTERS
Released on UPSETTER US-301 1969
Highest chart position 5 08/11/1969

The popularity of the music the skinheads had endeared themselves to was highlighted here when the instrumental Return Of Django entered the charts on the 4th of October 1969, attaining the number 5 slot in November, where it stayed for two weeks. Return Of Django spent a total of fifteen weeks on the chart, no doubt assisted by the B side featuring Dollar In The Teeth. The Upsetters were a studio band and the record was written and produced by Lee 'Scratch' Perry. The title track was a reference to the spaghetti western Django, released in 1966.

An album of the same name was released by Trojan in 1970 on the Upsetter label TRLS19.

LONG SHOT KICK THE BUCKET   THE PIONEERS
Released on TROJAN TR-672 1969
Highest chart position 21 15/11/1969

Long Shot Kick The Bucket is a true classic skinhead reggae sound, being the sequel to the Jamaican hit Long Shot Bus Me Bet released in 1968 on the Joe Gibbs Amalgamated label. The song related to the death of a horse at Jamaica's famous Caymanas Park race course in Kingston. An instant hit in Jamaica, the record was released in the UK by Trojan and appeared on both the orange and orange and white labels. It was picked up by the independent radio stations but blatantly ignored by the BBC who did eventually yield and added it to their playlist.

The record entered the charts in October reaching number 21 and featured for eleven weeks. Chart success prompted Sidney, Jackie and George to fly to London to promote the record. Trojan released Long Shot an album produced by Lesley Kong that including the single in late 1969.

WONDERFUL WORLD BEAUTIFUL PEOPLE JIMMY CLIFF
Released on TROJAN TR-690 1969
Highest chart position 6 22/11/1969

Jimmy Cliff became an established star in Jamaica in 1962 at the tender age of 14. Wonderful World Beautiful People was released in the UK on Trojan in 1969 and featured as the opening track on Trojan's first Reggae Chartbuster album released in 1970. The song, very though provoking, takes a look at the state of the world, and with an excellent beat, entered the charts in October 1969 where it remained for thirteen weeks. Jimmy's next recording, his own penned song, You Can Get It If You Really Want issued on Trojan never made the chart, although Desmond Dekker's version also released by Trojan a month later went onto become a massive international hit.

Jimmy's next release Vietnam, a protest song, sold well in America but only made the top 50 in the UK for three weeks during spring 1970, peaking at number 46. The track featured on Trojan's 1970 album Reggae Chartbusters Volume 2.

LIQUIDATOR HARRY J ALL STARS
Released on HARRY J TR-675 1969
Highest chart position 9 29/11/1969

Harry J All Stars included bassist 'Family Man' Aston Barrett, drummer Carlton Barrett and guitarist Alva Lewis who were originally The Hippy Boys. Aston 'Family Man' and his brother Carlton went on to form the core of The Wailers. The original version of the rhythm was taken from What Am I To Do by Tony Scott. Harry Johnson acquired the rights to the tune and released it as The Harry J All Stars.

The tune found instant popularity with the skinheads and was adopted as an anthem at several football grounds throughout England during the early 70s. Accusations that the record fuelled violence amongst rival gangs eventually lead to its ban at many grounds. The Staple Singers used the introduction and bass line for their 1972 hit, I'll Take You There. Liquidator entered the charts during October 1969 reaching number 9 in November and featured in the chart for twenty weeks.

ELIZABETHAN REGGAE BORIS GARDNER
Released on DUKE DU-39 1969
Highest chart position 14 07/03/1970

The reggae version of the English composer Ronald Binge's Elizabethan Serenade written in 1951 was released on the Duke label DU-39 in 1969. It immediately became a popular instrumental with the skinheads, and soon gained international recognition. The provenance to the record though was in some doubt as the first pressings credited production of Elizabethan Reggae to Byron Lee and the artist as being Byron Lee & The Dragonaires (spelt Dragonairs on the label) with the track appearing on the B side of DU-39. The original A side featured Soul Serenade by Byron Lee & The Dragonaires.

Elizabethan Reggae entered the chart at number 48 on the 17th January 1970 but dropped out only to re-enter on the 31st of January. The record remained on the chart roller coasting for the next twelve weeks, peaking at number 14. The chart from the 28th of February onward attributed Elizabethan Reggae to Boris Gardner with production of the record credited to Junior Chung, the pressing now having Elizabethan Reggae on the A side and Soul Serenade by Byron Lee & The Dragonaires on the B side, nevertheless still under the same prefix DU-39.

YOUNG GIFTED AND BLACK   BOB AND MARCIA
Released on HARRY J HJ-6605 1970
Highest chart position 5 04/04/1970

Young Gifted And Black was a UK release of a Jamaican single with strings attached, and an upbeat version of Nina Simone's black power song. The strings were added in the UK for the release on Trojan's Harry J label. The original Jamaican version was sweetened for the general UK record buying public with violins enhancing the vivacious rhythm. The record was a popular choice with the skinheads but a change in direction from the raw sounds of reggae. However had it been the genuine Jamaican article it may not have found favour outside the skinheads collection. The record entered the charts in March 1970 peaking at number 5 before falling back out in May.

The B side of HJ-6605 featured an instrumental version by The Jay Boys which was a boss tune with the skinheads and constantly requested at a stomp, The instrumental seen by many to be more popular than the A side.

The Jamaican version was released on Pama's Escort label ES-824 but was hastily replaced with a version from Denzil & Jennifer.

4. MR BLOE – GROOVIN WITH MR BLOE
5. CREEDENCE CLEARWATER REVIVAL - UP AROUND THE BEND
6. THE FOUR TOPS - IT'S ALL IN THE GAME
7. THE BEACH BOYS - COTTONFIELDS
8. GERRY MONROE - SALLY
9. NICKY THOMAS – LOVE OF THE COMMON PEOPLE
10. FLEETWOOD MAC – THE GREEN MANALISHI
CLIFF RICHARD – GOODBYE SAM HELLO SAMANTHA

LOVE OF THE COMMON PEOPLE NICKY THOMAS
Released on TROJAN TR-7750 1970
Highest chart position 9 11/07/1970

Nicky Thomas will always be remembered for this wonderful adaptation of Love Of The Common People, a true reggae infused pop sound reaching number 9 in the UK and spending fourteen weeks on the chart during the summer of 1970.

The song was originally penned by John Hurley and Ronnie Wilkins with The Everley Brothers releasing it as a single in 1967. The song tells of poverty and unemployment for USA families with mention of the USA governments free food tickets. It describes how their clothes were less than new and the lyrics were interpreted by many as a protest to life for the poor in the USA at that time.

It was the only chart success for Nicky although he would produce and release many excellent recordings including BBC, the record taking a swipe at the lack of air play for reggae on the nation's number one station. The world of reggae lost one of its famous sons due to his untimely death in 1990.

WILD WORLD JIMMY CLIFF
Released on ISLAND WIP-6087
Highest chart position 8 12/09/1970

A reunion with Island records in 1970 saw Jimmy Cliff's rendering of the Cat Stevens penned Wild World released, some three months before Stevens' own version was released in America. Ironically Cat Stevens original single was never released in the UK, the song featuring only as a track on an Island album. Jimmy Cliff's version remained on the chart for twelve weeks. Wild World has been covered many times most notably by Maxi Priest who enjoyed chart success with his reggae version in the 80s.

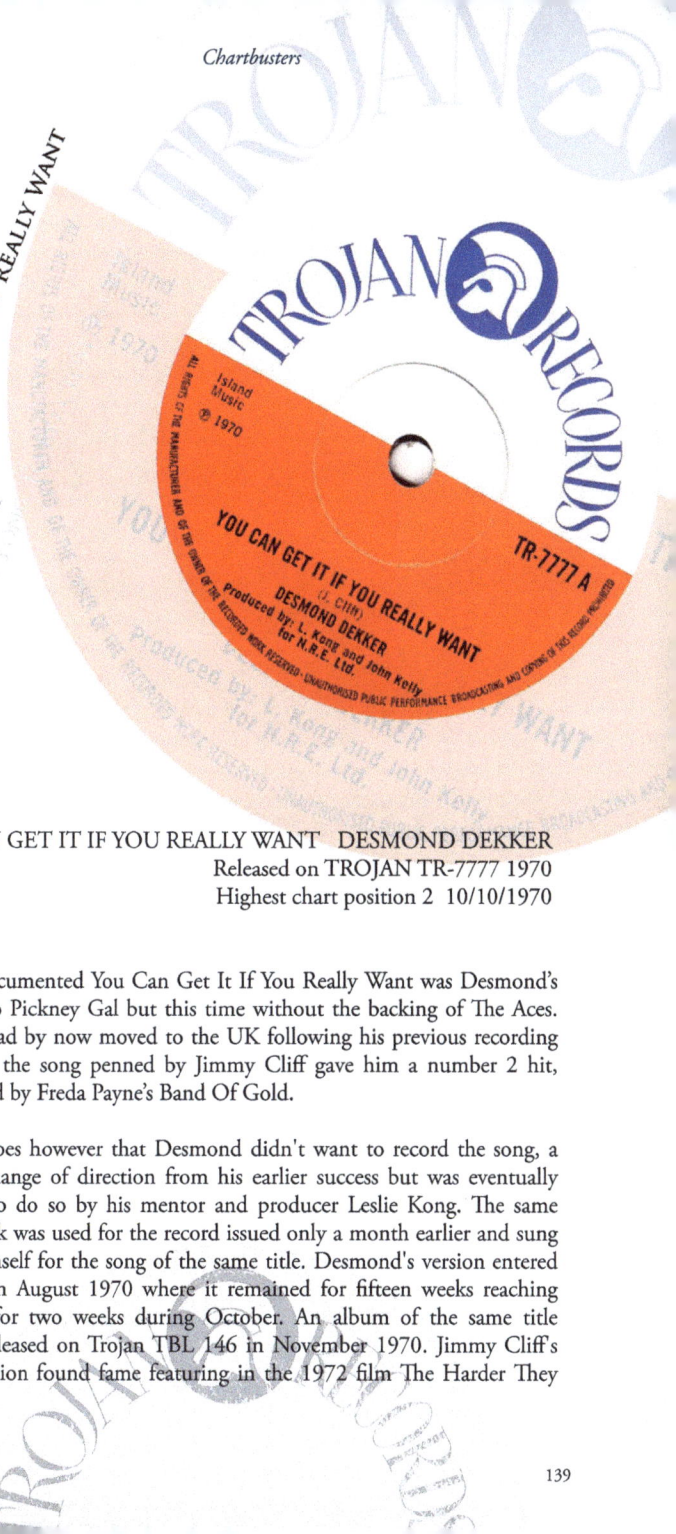

YOU CAN GET IT IF YOU REALLY WANT   DESMOND DEKKER
Released on TROJAN TR-7777 1970
Highest chart position 2 10/10/1970

The well documented You Can Get It If You Really Want was Desmond's follow up to Pickney Gal but this time without the backing of The Aces. Desmond had by now moved to the UK following his previous recording success and the song penned by Jimmy Cliff gave him a number 2 hit, only eclipsed by Freda Payne's Band Of Gold.

The story goes however that Desmond didn't want to record the song, a complete change of direction from his earlier success but was eventually persuaded to do so by his mentor and producer Leslie Kong. The same rhythm track was used for the record issued only a month earlier and sung by Cliff himself for the song of the same title. Desmond's version entered the charts in August 1970 where it remained for fifteen weeks reaching number 2 for two weeks during October. An album of the same title followed, released on Trojan TBL 146 in November 1970. Jimmy Cliff's original version found fame featuring in the 1972 film The Harder They Come.

139

10. THE TEMPTATIONS – BALL OF CO
11. MATTHEW'S SOUTHERN COMFORT – W
12. THE FAMILY – STRANGE BAND
13. HORACE FAITH – BLACK PEARL
14. CLARENCE CARTER – PATCHES
15. DES O'CONNOR – THE TIP OF MY FINGERS
16. SMOKEY ROBINSON AND THE MIRACLES – TEARS OF A CLOWN

BLACK PEARL HORACE FAITH
Released on TROJAN TR-7790 1970
Highest chart position 13 17/10/1970

This Johnny Arthey strings added version of a record by Sonny Charles &
The Checkmates made it to number 13 in the UK on the 17th October
1970. The record was to some extent over cooked, and a far cry from the
pure reggae that endeared the skinheads amongst others, but it sold well
and gained the only hit for Horace. It was described at the time as
swamped with pop hooks, nevertheless it was a huge hit spending some
ten weeks on the chart. Black Pearle featured on Reggae Chartbusters
Volume 2.

DOUBLE BARREL DAVE AND ANSIL COLLINS
Released on TECHNIQUES TE-901 1971
Highest chart position 1 01/05/1971

The number one hit was produced by Winston Riley and released both in Jamaica and the UK in 1970, Double Barrel with its distinctive beat and Dave Barkers bellowing vocals were a recipe for success with the skinheads, declaring that he was the magnificent! The UK release was issued on Trojan's Winston Riley's Techniques label and soon became an instant hit with both Collins and Barker whisked off to Britain, once passports were sorted, with the duo taking the top spot on Top of The Pops. Although the new release seemed ahead of its time the track had been laid down some three years earlier in Jamaica, with Riley bringing in Barker to overdub the rhythm track.

The record featured Dave Barker vocals, Ansil Collins keyboard and a 15-year-old Lowell 'Sly' Dunbar. A tour of the UK followed but the duo have always maintained that although the song was big they didn't get a great reward in monetary terms, now where has that been said before!

17. TONY CHRISTIE – I DID WHAT I DID FOR A...
18. PERRY COMO – I THINK OF YOU
19. BRUCE RUFFIN – RAIN
20. PETER NOONE – OH YOU PRETTY THING
21. T. REX – HOT LOVE
...AND WILLIAMS – (WHERE DO I BEGIN) LOVE STORY
...LITTLE ONE

RAIN BRUCE RUFFIN
Released on TROJAN TR-7814 1971
Highest chart position 19 29/05/1971

Rain, a far cry from the genuine skinhead article, was released on Trojan
TR-7814. The record enjoyed mediocre chart success featuring for eleven
weeks in the early summer of 1971, the top spot being a very respectable
number 19. The song was a cover of Jose' Feliciano's 1969 American hit.

The B side featured Geronimo and although the label credits Bruce Ruffin
as the artist it was in fact the Pryamids, the track originally released in
1970 on Duke DU-80.

Following the chart success of Rain Bruce moved to London. The track
had an outing on the third and final collection in the series of Trojan's
Reggae Chartbusters albums in 1971.

PIED PIPER BOB AND MARCIA
Released on TROJAN TR-7818 1971
Highest chart position 11 10/07/1971

The second follow up to Young Gifted And Black marked a return to chart success for the duo of Bob Andy and Marcia Griffiths. Pied Piper continued the pop-reggae idiom, with this up-tempo number in a similar vein to the previous success entering the charts on the 5th of June 1971. Pied Piper charted for thirteen weeks, peaking at number 11 during July.

Pied Piper was the last chart success for the duo who then signed with CBS, a move that hindered their progress and the pair parted musical company.

TROJAN RECORDS
TR-7820 A
Arranged by: Tony King
Made In England
Essex Music
℗ 1971
BLACK AND WHITE
(Arkin/Robinson)
GREYHOUND
Produced by: Dave Bloxham

1. MIDDLE OF THE ROAD - CHIRPY CHIRPY CHEEP CHEEP
2.
3. THE SWEET - CO-CO
4. LOBO - ME AND YOU AND A DOG NAMED BOO
5. HURRICANE SMITH - DON'T LET IT DIE
6. GREYHOUND - BLACK AND WHITE
7. DAVE AND ANSEL COLLINS - MONKEY SP
8. NEW WORLD - TOM TOM TURNAROU
9. BLUE MINK - BANNER MAN
10. THE TEMPTATIONS - JUST MY IM

BLACK AND WHITE   GREYHOUND
Released on TROJAN TR-7820 1971
Highest chart position 6 17/07/1971

The first success for Greyhound came with a cover version of a song written in 1955 titled Black And White, a record the group felt suited perfectly a pop-reggae style and sure enough it proved to be a massive hit for Greyhound. Released on both the orange and white Trojan label and the brown shield label the record entered the charts in June 1971 achieving a respectable two weeks at number 6 during July spending a total of thirteen weeks on the chart.

The story behind Black And White stemmed from from America where in 1954 The Supreme Court outlawed segregation of public schools. It was originally published as a song in 1956, penned by David Arkin with Earl Robinson's music.

4. T REX – GET IT ON
5. LOBO – ME AND YOU AND A DOG NAMED BOO
6. GREYHOUND – BLACK AND WHITE
7. **DAVE AND ANSEL COLLINS – MONKEY SPANNER**
8. BLUE MINK – BANNER MAN
9. JOHN KONGOS – HE'S GONNA STEP ON YOU AGAIN
10. TAMI LYNN – I'M GONNA RUN AWAY FROM YOU

MONKEY SPANNER   DAVE & ANSEL COLLINS
Released on TECHNIQUES TE-914 1971
Highest chart position 7 17/07/1971

Monkey Spanner was the follow up to the massive number one hit Double Barrel and once again took the charts by storm, becoming a summer sensation and an anthem for the skinheads. Monkey Spanner, now credited to Ansel, entered the chart on the 26th of June 1971 where it remained for twelve weeks, its pinnacle of success at number 7 attained for three weeks during July. Like its predecessor Monkey Spanner featured Version 2 on the B side.

Chart success was not what the reggae sound was all about but by attaining the chart it presented a rare opportunity for its followers. We could hear reggae on national radio but perhaps more importantly see out idols on the television through the media of Top of The Pops, remember this was before video and decades before DVD became a part of everyday life.

LET YOUR YEAH BE YEAH THE PIONEERS
Released on TROJAN TR-7825 1971
Highest chart position 5 11/09/1971

Let Your Yeah Be Yeah was a song penned by Jimmy Cliff and became the second of a hat-trick of hits for the Pioneers. Featuring on the chart for twelve weeks it rewarded the trio with appearances on BBC Top of The Pops. Although not held in high esteem by some the record became one of the best selling reggae 45s of 1971. It peaked at number 5 the same month producer Leslie Kong suffered a fatal heart attack. Although by now his involvement in the Pioneers music had decreased significantly his death was still a sad loss to the trio.

6. DON MCLEAN - AMERICAN PIE
7. THE NEW SEEKERS - I'D LIKE TO TEACH THE WORLD TO SING
8. SONNY AND CHER - ALL I EVER NEED IS YOU
9. FORTUNES - STORM IN A TEACUP
10. AL GREEN - LET'S STAY TOGETHER
11. AMERICA - HORSE WITH NO NAME
12. GREYHOUND - MOON RIVER

MOON RIVER GREYHOUND
Released on TROJAN MAXI TR-7848 1971
Highest chart position 12 05/02/1972

Moon River was the second of Greyhound's chart successes during the twilight years of skinhead reggae. The pop infused record was a hit for the group in early 1972. Moon River enjoyed eleven weeks of charting reaching a respectable number 12, no mean feat given that the love affair was almost over with the reducing ranks of skinheads.

Released as a Trojan Maxi single the B side featured two tracks, I've Been Trying and Keep The Pressure On. As well as the colourful Trojan Maxi label an additional picture sleeve option was available.

MOTHER AND CHILD REUNION PAUL SIMON
Released on CBS CBSS7793 1972
Highest chart position 5 18/03/1972

Paul Simon travelled to Jamaica to cut a ska track, Mother And Child Reunion, but when he arrived in the studio the musicians told him that ska was out, it's now reggae, so the song was recorded in reggae, apparently the first time Paul Simon had heard the term. Paul Simon had wanted to get the authentic feel for the song using Jamaican musicians and recorded it at Dynamic studios in Kingston. It has been well documented that recording sessions would be held up when goats roamed through the studio and that the equipment was a far cry from what he was accustomed to in America, but it did manage to create an authentic track.

1. NILSSON - WITHOUT YOU
2. DON MACLEAN - AMERICAN PIE
3. THE NEW SEEKERS - BEG STEAL OR BORROW
4. CHICORY TIP - SON OF MY FATHER
5. PAUL SIMON - MOTHER AND CHILD REUNION
6. GILBERT O'SULLIVAN - HOME AGAIN (NATURALLY)
7. MICHAEL JACKSON - GOT TO BE THERE

The infectious upbeat sound of Mother And Child Reunion was one of the very first reggae songs by a white American musician. Released in the UK on the CBS label it entered the charts on the 19th February 1972 peaking at number 5 four weeks later. It only spent twelve weeks on the chart but ten of those were in the top 30. Trojan released their own up-tempo reggae version on TR-7852 recorded by The Uniques, a group who had enjoyed considerable success during the rocksteady era. Although TR-7852 failed to share the chart success of the original Paul Simon single it was a popular release finding its way onto Club Reggae Volume 3 and is included here as Sony Music Entertainment in America were unable to grant permission for inclusion of the original label of the Paul Simon version.

STIR IT UP JOHNNY NASH
Released on CBS CBSS7800 1972
Highest chart position 13 29/04/1972

Stir It Up was written by Bob Marley in 1967 and issued on Trojan TR-617 by The Wailers in 1968. It was later re-worked and featured on the legendary Catch A Fire album released in 1973. CBS released Stir It Up in the UK and it became a hit for Johnny Nash. The record spent twelve weeks on the chart but surprisingly only reached the moderate heights of number 13. Johnny Nash had enjoyed earlier chart success in the UK and America in 1968 with Hold Me Tight reaching number 5 in the UK, a record that charted for sixteen weeks. You Got Soul followed by Cupid both gained the number 6 slot and coincidently both charted for twelve weeks in early 1969. Conceivably if Stir It Up had been released earlier in the skinhead era it may well have topped the charts.

I AM WHAT I AM   GREYHOUND
Released on TROJAN TR-7853 1972
Highest chart position 20 29/04/1972

Greyhound's third success remained on the chart for nine weeks during the spring of 1972 but it only achieved a mediocre top 20 position. This was an indication of things to come as a year or so earlier this would surely have been a top ten hit, continuing in the pop-reggae idiom. It was one of the last before a complete change in style to what has already been described as string laden and watered down. It was a direction that saw the remaining skinheads, who by now were some of a new generation of the traditional skinheads, some following on from their brothers, becoming disillusioned with the sound. Some hanging onto the lasting hope for a resurgence of the original skinhead era which never came.

150

MAD ABOUT YOU BRUCE RUFFIN
Released on RHINO RNO 101 1972
Highest chart position 9 29/07/1972

Mad About You featured for twelve weeks on the chart although this was pure pop reggae, a far cry from the familiar reggae-pop infused sounds of Greyhound and the Pioneers. Mad About You achieved the lofty heights of number 9 but it was a very polished-sweetened reggae sound that the ebbing band of followers could no longer empathise with. Gone were the raw sounds and incessant rhythms, setting it apart from the mainstream.

6. ALICE COOPER – SCHOOL'S OUT
7. JOHNNY NASH – I CAN SEE CLEARLY NOW
8. THE NEW SEEKERS – CIRCLES
9. BRUCE RUFFIN – MAD ABOUT YOU
10. DAVID BOWIE – STAR MAN
11. THE SWEET – LITTLE WILLY
HAWKWIND – SILVER MACHINE

151

2. GARY GLITTER – ROCK AND ROLL PARTS 1 AND 2
3. DR HOOK AND THE MEDICINE SHOW – SYLVIA'S MOTHER
4. THE NEW SEEKERS – CIRCLES
5. JOHNNY NASH – I CAN SEE CLEARLY NOW
6. THE SWEET – LITTLE WILLY

I CAN SEE CLEARLY NOW JOHNNY NASH
Released on CBS CBSS8113 1972
Highest chart position 5 29/07/1972

Johnny Nash was back in the charts in June 1972 with his own penned
song I Can See Clearly Now taken from his album of the same name,
recorded in London the same year. The record featured on the charts for
fifteen weeks reaching the lofty height of number 5.

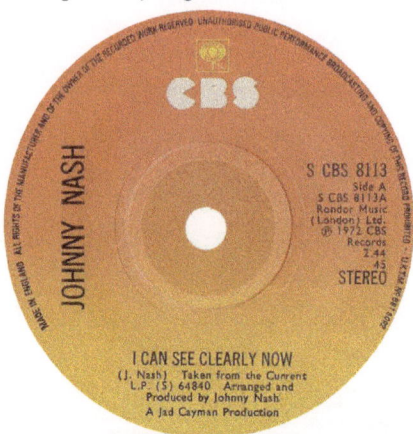

12. F DRIFTERS – COM...
12. ELVIS PRESLEY – BURNING LOVE
13. JUDGE DREAD – BIG SIX
14. MICHAEL JACKSON – AIN'T NO SUNSHINE
14. DANDY LIVINGSTONE – SUZANNE BEWARE OF THE DEVIL
15. ROXY MUSIC – VIRGINIA PLAIN
16. CLIFF RICHARD – LIVING IN HARMONY

SUZANNE BEWARE OF THE DEVIL DANDY LIVINGSTONE
Released on HORSE HOSS 16 1972
Highest chart position 14 07/10/1972

No stranger to the reggae scene but surprisingly it had taken the entire era of skinhead reggae before producer and singer Dandy Livingstone, AKA Dandy enjoyed top thirty chart success. It was achieved with Suzanne Beware Of The Devil. Nicky Thomas had recorded a similar version on Trojan TR-7862 the same year. The track was originally issued as a B side to What Do You Wanna Make Those Eyes At Me For on TR-7857 however once the potential was spotted for a hit it was hastily removed and replaced with Talking About Sally with the single subsequently released on Trojan's Horse label. The record first charted in September 1972, where it remained for eleven weeks. Much of Dandy's work featured on Trojan's successful compilation albums.

9. PYTHON LEE JACKSON – IN A B...
10. 10CC – DONNA
11. JUDGE DREAD – BIG SIX
12. DAVID BOWIE – JOHN I'M ONLY DANCING
13. FARON YOUNG – IT'S FOUR IN THE MORNING
14. DANDY LIVINGSTONE – SUZANNE BEWARE OF THE DEVIL

BIG SIX JUDGE DREAD
Released on BIG SHOT BI-608 1972
Highest chart position 11 14/10/1972

Alex Hughes was infatuated by Prince Buster's ribald Big Five and recorded his own follow up using the rhythm track of Verne & Sons Little Boy Blue. The record was released under the name of Judge Dread in honour of a character from Prince Buster. The record eventually took the charts by storm despite no air play as the BBC had banned the record. Trojan's devious attempts to convince otherwise that the record was not rude fell on the same deaf ears that had banned Wet Dream some three years earlier. The ban didn't prevent the record becoming a chart hit with Big Six peaking at number 11 and featuring on the chart for some six months, selling a very laudable 300,000 copies.

THERE ARE MORE QUESTIONS THAN ANSWERS
JOHNNY NASH
Released on CBS CBSS8351 1972
Highest chart position 9 28/10/1972

The third of Johnny Nash hits coming at the end of the golden era of reggae, mirroring his early success during the later end of the rocksteady period, His last offering featured on the chart for nine weeks as 1972 was drawing to a close.

6. GARY GLITTER – I DIDN'T KNOW I LOVED YOU (TILL I SAW YO
7. PETER SKELLERN – YOUR'E A LADY
8. ELVIS PRESLEY – BURNING LOVE
9. JOHNNY NASH – THERE ARE MORE QUESTIONS THAN ANSWER
10. THE SWEET WIG-WAM BAM
11. THE CARPENTERS – GOODBYE TO LOVE

BIG SEVEN JUDGE DREAD
Released on BIG SHOT BI-613 1972
Highest chart position 18 30/12/1972 *

As night follows day Big Seven followed Big Six with another massive hit
in the same vein, this time achieving greater chart success. Big Seven was
co-written with Rupie Edwards who purchased a rhythm track from
Bunny Lee. The track was previously released by The Uniques in 1968
titled My Conversation. The backing track also featured as the rhythm for
President Mash Up The Resident by Shorty, a track that featured on
Tighten Up Volume 6.

Big Seven entered the charts while Big Six was still selling well, with the
Judge enjoying two chart entries for twelve weeks. Despite the inevitable
ban the record sold well reaching number 8 in the following January,
having first entered the charts on the 9th of December 1972. Big Seven
featured on the chart for eighteen weeks with predictably Eight, Nine, Ten
and One continuing the theme of risqué lyrics dubbed over a classic reggae
track.

* Big Seven peaked at number 8 13/01/1973

Looking back on the chart hits of 1968-1972 it was a remarkable period for reggae, and Trojan in particular, as they had issued twenty four of the twenty nine reggae records that made it into the top 30. If we had counted Johnny Reggae from The Piglets that would have completed a top 30, thirty. The record released on BELL-1180 with the arrangement provided courtesy of Johnny Arthey reached the lofty heights of number 3 on the 20th November 1971.

Following the launch of BBC Radio One in September 1967 the chart was compiled from a combination of data from record shops collated by four music magazines including Record Mirror and Melody Maker. Concerns arose over the fixing of the charts, in the main by record promoters buying large quantities of a record at the targeted shops. This method was withdrawn in 1969. The British Market Research Bureau used a new method where every sale from 300 shops was recorded, the chart then compiled from a random selection of 150 of the outlets.

It seemed that the hierarchy and the mainstream DJ's at the BBC refused to play the new Jamaican music on their shows, reluctantly doing so when a song had made head way towards the charts. Accusations of patois lyrics making the records indiscernible to the mainstream and the skinhead connection were said to have been reasons to shelve the music. The emerging Radio One had launched in the autumn of 67 and appeared hostile to reggae from the outset, all that was except for the main man, Emperor Rosko, who had fallen in love with and championed Jamaican music from the earlier days of ska.

Emperor Rosko, born Michael Pasternak, in Los Angeles had arrived at the BBC following stints with Radio Caroline and Radio Luxembourg. The Emperor produced his own shows and did not comply with the hits that were happening and was able to feature a wider spectrum of music, including of course reggae. He built up a tremendous following with his Saturday slot always a programme awaited with anticipation by the skinheads and other music lovers of Motown and the new rock. Rosko became a reggae legend when he appeared on the cover of Club Reggae Volume 4 released on Trojan TBL 188 in late 1972 and cut his own version of Prince Buster's Alcapone released on Trojan TR-7758 in 1970.

"I control this business, I make hits, not the public, I tell the DJs what to play".

It must be the producer up next!

LESLIE KONG

The legendary producer Leslie Kong is credited to bringing reggae to the fore in the UK and without his influence the UK reggae scene would have been much poorer. He began his working life with his brothers running an ice cream parlour and record shop called Beverley's on Orange Street in Kingston.

It was on Orange Street he had a chance meeting with Jimmy Cliff for the first time in 1962. Leslie had heard Jimmy singing Dearest Beverley outside his shop and sent him to Derek Morgan to see if his songs would make the grade. Derek then brought Jimmy to Leslie, a meeting incidentally that led to Kong launching his own record label aptly named Beverley's. Jimmy Cliff's first record, the song he had been singing, was issued on Beverley's titled Dearest Beverley, a song that launched his distinguished career.

That same year Leslie Kong also recorded Bob Marley's first ever singles One Cup Of Coffee and Judge Not and Jimmy Cliff's massive Jamaican hit Miss Jamaica. Leslie Kong soon built himself a reputation as Jamaica's foremost producer. He became known as the Chinaman and through the evolvement of ska to rocksteady then reggae he worked with some of the best artists including Desmond Dekker and Toots & The Maytals. A shrewd businessman he set up a deal with Island's Chris Blackwell in 1963 to issue work on the Black Swan label.

When Blackwell eventually bought out Kong's shares in Island Kong established a new partnership with Graeme Goodall's Pyramid label. When Pyramid closed down in 1969 Kong set up a licensing agreement with Trojan Records. Leslie Kong was the first Jamaican producer to achieve an international hit in 1967 with Desmond Dekker's 007 (Shanty Town) reaching number 14 on the UK chart. It would however be the 1968 release originally titled (Poor Mi) Israelites but shortened to Israelites for the UK market that brought him truly international acclaim.

It hit the number one spot on the British chart during April 1969, a massively popular record with the up-and-coming skinheads and the West Indians, selling over two million copies worldwide and for many their first introduction to reggae. Many other quality recordings have originated from Beverley's studios including The Pioneers Long Shot Kick De Bucket, although Leslie was in London when the Pioneers cut the track, The Maytals 54-46 That's My Number and their popular hit Monkey Man, a record that incidentally gained a UK chart entry at number 47 in 1970.

Leslie Kong was a talented producer who would only employ the best musicians with his session band known as The Beverley All Stars. Artists who recorded at Beverley's include Peter Tosh, Ken Boothe, Bruce Ruffin and The Gaylads. The acclaimed film released in 1972, The Harder They Come, saw Leslie Kong in a cameo appearance as the producer overseeing a recording session with Toots & The Maytals with Ivan (Jimmy Cliff) watching on in awe.

It is well documented that Leslie Kong died of a heart attack in August 1971 prior to the release of the film in the UK. His death had a devastating effect of the future work of many artists. One fact that has come out again and again is that he was a fair man, a man who looked after his recording stars, paying salaries to some and finding them work on the hotel circuits of the north coast and Kingston between recording sessions.

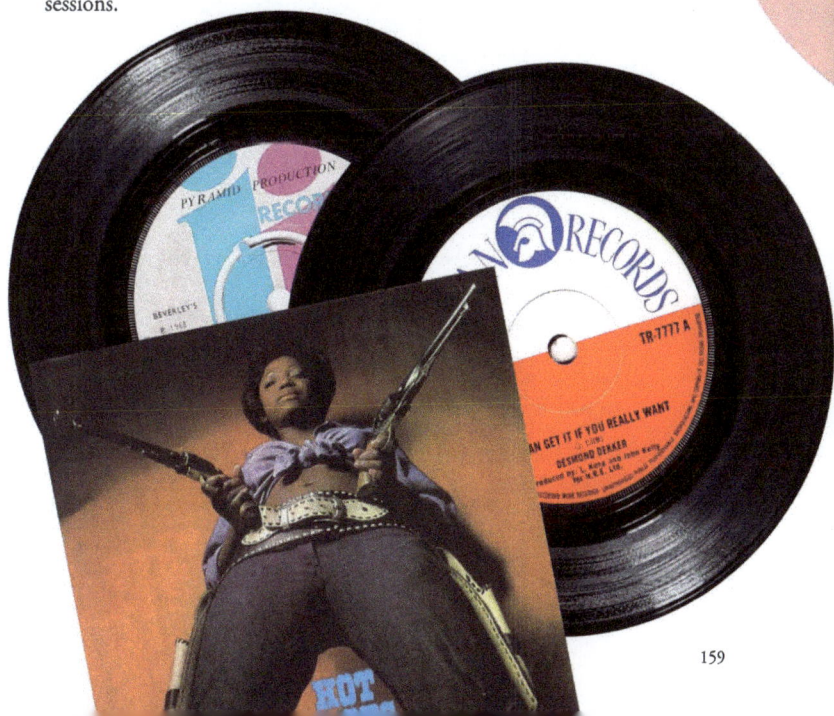

Leslie Kong's legendary talents as a record producer came to the fore when the budget label, Music For Pleasure, a company at the time well known for bargain priced albums, licensed an LP from Trojan. The record became popular with the skinheads and was available on the high Street at that well known record outlet Woolworths, how do I know, well that's where I purchased my copy. Very little has been written about Leslie Kong's contribution to reggae, in particular the skinhead years, over the last 40 years and it is difficult to understand why.

REGGAE PARTY
MFP 5176 1970
Various Artists
Produced by Leslie Kong

Side 1
1. PICKNEY GAL - Desmond Dekker
2. SOUL SHAKEDOWN PARTY - Bob Marley & The Wailers
3. SIMMER DOWN QUASHIE - The Pioneers
4. PRESSURE DROP - The Maytals 5. ABC REGGAE - Rockstones
6. SAMFIE MAN - The Pioneers

Side 2
1. DOUBLE SHOT - Beverley All Stars 2. WHY BABY WHY - Ken Boothe
3. I'M THE ONE - Bruce Ruffin 4. WATER MELON - The Maytals
5. SOUL SISTER - Gaylads 6. SAY DARLING SAY - Melodians

Produced by Leslie Kong and released courtesy of Trojan Records

SELECTED DISCOGRAPHY   LESLIE KONG   1968 - 1972

SINGLES

PYRAMID

PRY 6030 54-46 That's My Number - Toots And The Maytals 1968
PRY 6058 Israelites - Desmond Dekker And The Aces 1968
PRY 6078 Pickney Gal - Desmond Dekker And The Aces 1969

TROJAN

TR 672 Long Shot Kick De Bucket - The Pioneers 1969
TR 690 Wonderful World Beautiful People - Jimmy Cliff 1969
TR 695 Sweet Sensation - The Melodians 1969
TR 7710 Samfie Man - The Pioneers 1970
TR 7711 Monkey Man - Toots And The Maytals 1970
TR 7716 Why Baby Why - Ken Boothe 1969
TR 7720 A Day Seems So Long - The Melodians 1969
TR7722 Vietnam - Jimmy Cliff 1969
TR7757 Water Melon - The Maytals 1970
TR7777 You Can Get It If You Really Want - Desmond Dekker 1970
TR7795 I Need Your Sweet Inspiration - The Pioneers 1970
TR7808 54-46 Was My Number - Toots And The Maytals 1970

SUMMIT

SUM-8508 Rivers Of Babylon - The Melodians 1970

ALBUMS

TROJAN

TRLS 16 Jimmy Cliff - Jimmy Cliff 1969
TBL 103 Long Shot - The Pioneers 1969
TBL 107 Monkey Man - Toots And The Maytals 1970
TBL 128 Hot Shots Of Reggae - Various Artists 1970
TBL 146 You Can Get It If You Really Want - Desmond Dekker 1970

MUSIC FOR PLEASURE

MFP 5176 Reggae Party - Various Artists 1970

BUNNY 'STRIKER' LEE

In 1968 Bunny 'Striker' Lee became one of the first Jamaican producers to come to England for a meeting with Island Records boss Chris Blackwell. Blackwell was looking for material aiming at capturing the new sounds the emerging skinheads were beginning to embrace.

Bunny Lee born on 21st August 1941 was one of six children and was brought up in the Greenwich Farm district of Kingston. It has been documented that he would often walk barefoot to school. A man of great self-belief with a determination to make it, forcing his way into the music business first as a radio plugger for Coxsone Dodd and Duke Reid.

Impressed with Bunny Duke Reid offered him recording time at his legendary Treasure Isle studios and began his career as a producer.

Striker was instrumental in the slowed down rocksteady rhythm upping the tempo to reggae with the famous organ shuffle coming to the fore on Bangarang. Bangarang means woman don't want no problem, anyone don't want no problem.

During his first visit to England in 1968 to see Chris Blackwell he had a chance meeting with the Palmer brothers. That meeting led to a deal being struck to produce singles in Jamaica and send over to England to be released on his Unity label, one of the Pama subsidiaries. Jackpot was set up to release material by Trojan.

Everything changed with Max Romeo's Wet Dream, the well documented hit based on a bawdy conversation Lee had overheard. Originally sent over as a B side the record became a hit, spending six months in the charts, partly thanks to being banned by the BBC, and made his name in England.

In Jamaica Bunny is credited with bringing home the term reggae after one of his trips to England. He came up with the John Crow Skank dance to accompany Delroy Wilson's Better Must Come. The People's National Party in Jamaica adopted Better Must Come for their election campaign in 1972.

The previous year he released the winning entry in the Festival Song Competition with Eric Donaldson's Cherry Oh Baby.

SELECTED DISCOGRAPHY PRODUCED BY BUNNY LEE 68-72

BIG SHOT
BI-507 Raving Ravers - Lester Stirling 1969

BULLET
BU-520 Hear Come The Heartaches -Delroy Wilson 1972

DYNAMIC
DYN-420 Cherry Oh Baby - Eric Donaldson 1971
DYN-428 Just A Dream - Slim Smith 1970

GAS
GAS-103 Blowing In The Wind - Max Romeo 1968
GAS-115 How Long Will It Take - Pat Kelly 1968
GAS-125 If It Don't Work Out - Pat Kelly 1969

ISLAND
WI-3121 Please Don't Leave Me - Pat Kelly 1968
WI-3122 My Conversation - Uniques / Slim Smith 1968
WI-3124 Twelfth Of Never - Pat Kelly 1968
WI-3146 The Russians Are Coming - Val Bennett 1968
WI-3159 Hold You Jack - Derek Morgan 1968

JACKPOT
JP-736 The Fastest Man Alive - Dave Barker 1970
JP-742 Wet Version - Dave Barker 1970
JP-763 Better Must Come-Version - Bunny Lee's All Stars 1971
JP-772 Stick By Me - John Holt 1970
JP-773 Jumping Jack - Dennis Alcapone And The Agrovators 1971
JP-787 Come On - The Cables 1971
JP-789 Rain From The Sky - Slim Smith 1972
JP-797 Me Naw Run - Derrick Morgan 1972
JP-805 Guilty - Ken Parker 1972

PAMA
PM-856 Good Hearted Woman - Cornell Campbell 1972

SMASH
SMA-2301 My Boy Lollipop - Maxine 1970

TROJAN
TR-613 Tighten Up - Untouchables 1968
TR-7884 Hat Trick - U Roy 1972

UNITY
UN-502 Bangarang - Lester Stirling & Stranger Cole 1968
UN-503 Wet Dream - Max Romeo 1968

EXCLUSIVE

AN INTERVIEW WITH BUNNY 'STRIKER' LEE

JB: Bunny or should I call you Striker, it's a great honour to speak with you. Let me start if I may with your memories of the early soundsytems?

BSL: There was Goodie's, Count Nick the Champ, Count Smith the Blues Blaster, then Sir Coxsone came in, King Edwards the Giant, Duke Reid, Prince Buster. Merritone is one of the surviving sounds that's still there now, 50 years on, the oldest surviving one. It's a nice quality hifi.

JB: Bunny, You started out as a record plugger. What did that involve and was it a way to get into the music business.

BSL: Yes I worked for Coxson, Duke Reid and Leslie Kong. When I finished work I go straight to the record shop and you collect the records before you go to the radio station, carry it in the radio station and plug it, get it played. Them days you'd have two radio stations, RLR and JBC. We buy time to get the records played yunno. Duke Reid was a man that give me the first studio time to start.

JB: Bunny, you worked alongside the greats of reggae, like Derrick Morgan, Max Romeo, Pat Kelly, the list is endless you must have very fond memories of those days. Did you all have dreams of making it big.

BSL: Slim Smith was another, one of Jamaica's greatest singers. You will never have a next Slim Smith - him irreplaceable. Some men just born great. Look how many years him dead now and you put on a Slim Smith record. Look at My Conversation, The riddim just go on and go on. Every time you hear Conversation it come like you just make it. Cornel Campbell good too. Dave Barker! Lloyd Parks. But, as I say, Slim Smith stand up in that group, as a singer. Pat Kelly, what about that falsetto like Sam Cooke or Curtis Mayfield. When Curtis Mayfield heard Slim Smith sing his tune, man, Curtis said, "Damn, this guy is good! This guy sounds like me". Making it big? I have to do what I have to do just follow my own thing.

JB: Bunny anyone else we should mention here?

BSL: Horace Andy a good singer, too. I see 'him the other day, good singer. All the singer them good. Errol Dunkley, I find Errol Dunkley as a youth and carry him go to Joe Gibbs. You have many good singers. Alton was good, great in him class. John Holt have a voice you cannot hide. Ken Boothe - you name them, man. Jackie Wilfred Edwards, one of the greatest singer to come out a Jamaica. Owen Gray is like a blues blaster from the olden days, like Rosco Gordon.

Owen Gray, him is still around. You have Winston Francis, you have some great singers come out a Jamaica. But as I say, Derrick Morgan come up, him was like me teacher, yunno, when me just start my session, me and him used to walk. Derrick an' Prince Buster. And I say "Bwoy, me a go come like Buster when I start produce".. Prince Buster know what him want! Him start a whole heap a trend too. Lascelles Perkins, one of the first superstar from Trench Town. Bob Marley, everybody look up to him.

JB: Anyone we have missed?

BSL: Yes, Val Bennett! Roland Alphonso and all those cats in his band too, yunno. Val Bennett is the man who was, like, the father of all them guys. Val Bennett now, is him play all 'Alcapone Don't Talk' (simply 'Al Capone (Guns Don't Argue)' by Buster All Stars) for Prince Buster, you know that?

JB: We must discuss what was perhaps the most iconic skinhead record Max's Wet Dream. So many stories surround Max not wanting to record it, can you set the record straight and tell how it came about.

BSL: Wet Dream was a tune I sent to Pama as a B-side to make up numbers. They called me. I tried to ask about seven different people to sing it and they wouldn't sing it. Maxy was a salesman at the time, so Maxy would always sing on a b-side, so I said 'Maxy go sing this tune', so Glen Adams told him to do it. The rest is history. Maxy, Glen and Coxsone went in the studio, one cut and it was done. Then Maxy was one of the first big artists to come to England, the thing hit. Six weeks in the chart. It was in the top ten. But it couldn't get airplay. It was one of the first reggae tunes that hit up here, in 67. Along with Train to Skaville' by The Ethiopians. They were the first set that came up to tour.

JB: Seven Letters, produced by you, is cited as the first true reggae record, along with others like Nanny Goat by Larry Marshall and your Bangarang by Lester Sterling. What can you recall of the cross over from rocksteady to reggae. There has always been some dispute about who invented what and when it comes to Jamaican music, do you feel like you never got the credit for certain things?

BSL: Rocksteady was a beautiful music. Up to now, you still have the rock steady. But, you see, the reggae - you know what 'reggae' is? Reggae is the organ shuffle in the rock steady. It carries up back the beat a little. Carry up back the beat and make it in-between. Because you take out the organ shuffle out of the reggae... you take the organ shuffle out of the business. It was started by us in '68 upstairs in Duke Reid's studio, (Bunny sings) Woman No Want Bangarang............, and the same with the version thing. I don't want to blow my own horn, my records speak for themselves.

JB: Bunny this brings me onto the years when reggae emerged from rock steady, a period often referred to as skinhead reggae in the UK and really what the book is all about. Were you aware of the skinheads buying reggae in volumes in the UK at the time?

BSL: Yes very much and I came to England in 1969 with Derrick Morgan.

JB: Bunny is it correct you came to England in 68 to meet with Chris Blackwell and had a chance meeting with the Palmer Brothers who set up a deal for your Jamaican production to be sent to England and issued by Pama on your Unity label. You must have had a good relationship with Pama, tell me about it and did you have a good relationship with Trojan?

BSL: I was there when Trojan formed, I took Dandy round there, he was working with Rita King, and Pama gave Dandy some money to make an album. Everybody wanted Duke Reid's product, but Duke Reid is a man who carries around like 6 guns, no-one wanted to pirate his thing cos if they went to Jamaica they'd have to deal with him. He was an ex-policeman. but a very nice person. So they got together, Blue Cat and Island and formed the Trojan label. Island and Trojan put out the same tunes, even now.

They first put out Dandy Returns, the album sold 15,000, and then Trojan set up a shop named Music City. When I come up I started Pama records, in the late 60s, The three brother them come and see me and them give me about 700 pound. I go back to Jamaica and start to make some music and the rest is history. They became as big as Trojan. At one point bigger. Island were putting my stuff out here first.

JB: Any recollections of the BBC at the time and their reluctance to play any reggae?

BSL: Yes the BBC never played reggae music in the old days. You take it to them and they put it in the bin.

JB: Bunny perhaps a message for all those original skinheads of 69, me included who embraced the music all those years ago, and many thanks for sharing your thoughts with me.

BSL: As long as you have music you will always have skinheads, long may they rein. boys, girls, ladies and men, you will always have skinheads, they are great!

Striker Lee, is a true pioneer of reggae music but a very humble man. I had the great honour to speak with him and he tells it as it was but not a man to brag or boast. Many thanks to Young Striker for arranging the interview.

Edward O'Sullivan Lee OD, better known as Bunny 'Striker' Lee

Bangarang is known in Jamaica to be the first reggae song with the introduction of the organ shuffle. Bunny 'Striker' Lee set up the Unity label for his productions with a black hand and a white hand shaking over a mountain.

LEE 'SCRATCH' PERRY

Lee 'Scratch' Perry was born Rainford Hugh Perry on the 20th March 1936 in Kendal, a small town close to the centre of Jamaica. One of the major influential figures in the emerging world of reggae producer 'Scratch' is best known as The Upsetter. His musical career can be traced as far back as 1959 when he formed an association with Clement 'Coxone' Dodd's sound system, initially as a record seller.

He progressed to supervising auditions at Dodd's shop located on Orange Street in Kingston, although his relationship with Dodd was described as sometimes turbulent. During his time as a producer in the early sixties, although he was never credited on the records, he also recorded some work of his own.

The situation worsened with Dodd, due it was said to personal and financial problems, so he moved to Joe Gibbs Amalgamated Records. Perry continued recording but problems soon surfaced again and he left Gibbs to form his own Upsetter label.

His first single People Funny Boy credited to Lee 'King' Perry was released on Doctor Bird DB-1146 aimed as an insult to Gibbs, selling a remarkable 60,000 copies in Jamaica. The record carried what was described as a fast chugging beat, a change from the slower rocksteady, a beat that soon became identifiable as reggae.

The record was popular with the emerging skinheads who had bought previous Lee Perry recordings from 1968 including David Isaacs Place In The Sun and The Untouchables Tighten Up. Both tracks appeared later on Trojan's early compilation series Tighten Up, an album that retailed for just 14/6d. The album became an integral part of the skinheads collection and the forerunner for Trojan's Club Reggae and Reggae Chartbusters.

From 1968 through to 1972 Perry continued to release numerous recordings on several different labels including the UK Upsetter label, a subsidiary of Trojan that brought chart success for the Upsetters in 1969 with Return Of Django. The record peaked at number 5 in the top 30 where it remained for three weeks during November that year, spending a creditable fifteen weeks on the chart. One of the follow up releases Clint Eastwood flirted just outside but never quite made the charts, released on Pama's Punch label.

The UK charts looked like this on the 15th November 1969.

1. Archies- Sugar Sugar
2. Fleetwood Mac - Oh Well
3. The Tremoloes - (Call Me) Number One
4. The Hollies - He Ain't Heavy He's My Brother
5. **Upsetters - Return Of Django / Dollar In The Teeth**
6. The Beatles - Something / Come Together
7. **Jimmy Cliff - Wonderful World, Beautiful People**
8. Frank Sinatra - Love's Been Good To Me
9. Karen Young - Nobody's Child
10. Lou Christie - I'm Gonna Make You Mine

Between 1968 and 1972 no fewer than six albums were produced by Perry. Without doubt the most famous group ever to emerge from Jamaica was Bob Marley And The Wailers who had worked with Perry and released several tracks during 1970 through to 1972. Most notable of these were, Duppy Conqueror released on Upsetter UPS-348, My Cup released on Upsetter UPS-340, Down Presser released on Punch PH-77, Small Axe on Upsetter UPS-357 and Keep On Moving on Upsetter UPS-392.

DUPPY CONQUEROR

Produced by Lee Perry during 1970 and released on UPSETTER US-348 Duppy Conqueror was said to have been written by Bob Marley as a consequence of Bob complaining to Lee that he was too successful and was being plagued by hangers on, referring to them as Duppies. A Duppy in Jamaican folklore is a ghost / a wicked supernatural being. The story goes that Lee said to Bob that he could sort it out as they are Duppy Conquerors, with Bob proceeding to write the song.

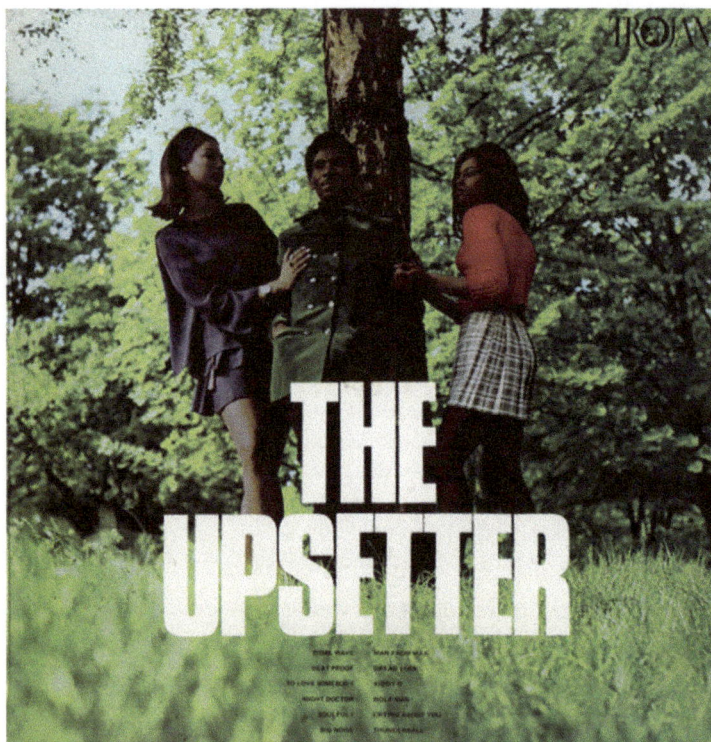

THE UPSETTER
TROJAN RECORDS TTL 13
Released 1969

Side 1
1. TIDAL WAVE 2. HEAT PROOF 3. TO LOVE SOMEBODY
4. NIGHT DOCTOR 5. SOULFUL I 6. BIG NOISE

Side 2
1. MAN FROM MI5 2. DREAD LUCK 3. KIDDY O
4. WOLF MAN 5. CRYING ABOUT YOU 6. THUNDERBALL

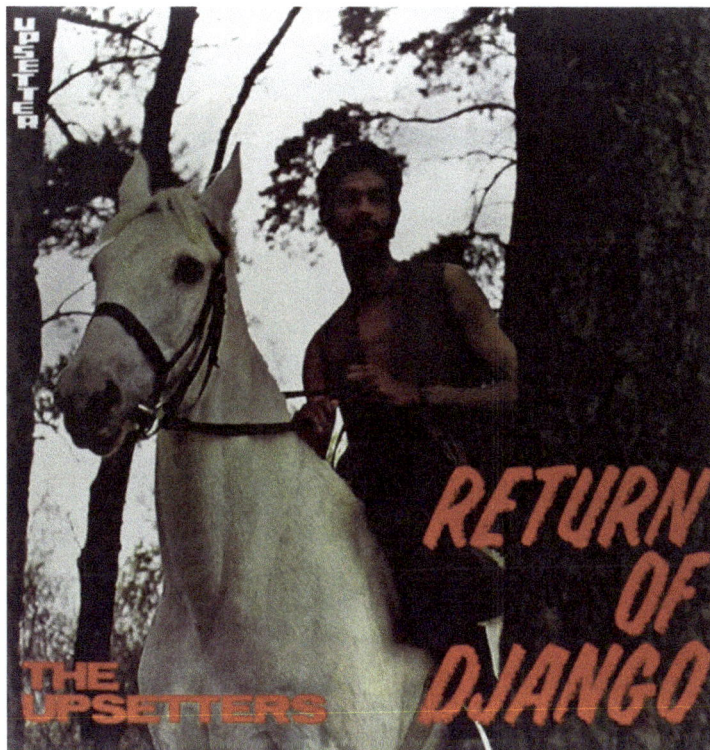

RETURN OF DJANGO
TROJAN (UPSETTERS) TRLS 19
Released 1970

Side 1
1. RETURN OF DJANGO 2. TOUCH OF FIRE 3. COLD SWEAT
4. DRUGS AND POISON 5. SOULFUL I 6. NIGHT DOCTOR

Side 2
1. ONE PUNCH 2. EIGHT FOR EIGHT 3. LIVE INJECTION
4. MAN FROM MI5 5. TEN TO TWELVE 6. MEDICAL

14'6

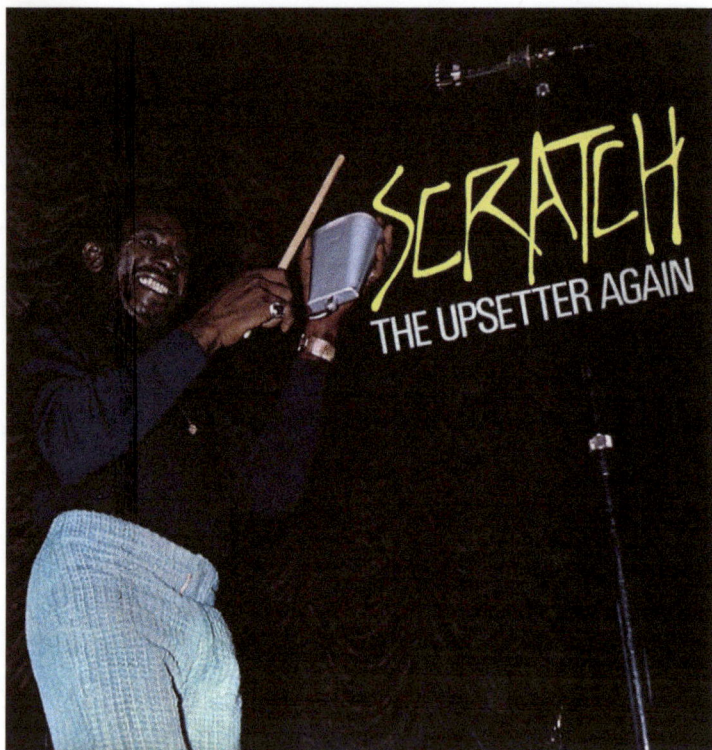

SCRATCH THE UPSETTER AGAIN
TROJAN RECORDS TTL 28
Released 1970

Side 1
1. BAD TOOTH 2. THE DENTIS' (AKA THE DENTIST)
3. OUTER SPACE 4. ONE PUNCH
5. WILL YOU STILL LOVE ME
6. TAKE ONE

Side 2
1. SOUL WALK   2. I WANT TO THANK YOU
3. MULE TRAIN Count Prince Miller
4. TOUCH OF FIRE 5. SHE IS GONE AGAIN Alva Lewis
6. THE RESULT

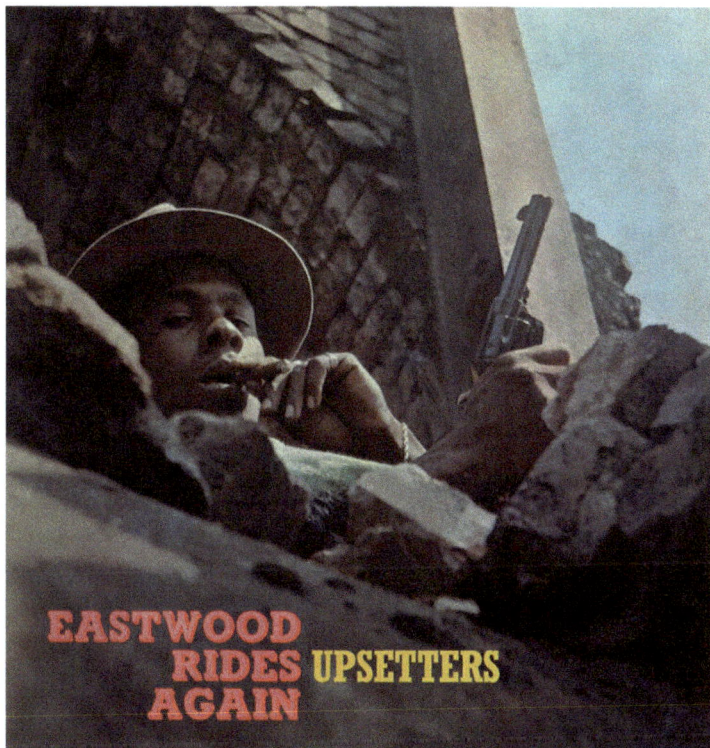

EASTWOOD RIDES AGAIN
TROJAN RECORDS TBL 125
Released 1970

Side 1
1. EASTWOOD RIDES AGAIN 2. HIT ME
3. KNOCK ON WOOD The Untouchables
4. POP CORN 5. CATCH THIS 6. YOU ARE ADORABLE
7. CAPSOL

Side 2
1. POWER PACK 2. DOLLAR IN THE TEETH
3. BABY BABY Val Bennett 4. DJANGO
5. RED HOT 6. SALT AND PEPPER 7. TIGHT SPOT

The Upsetters had two albums released on the PAMA label during 1970.

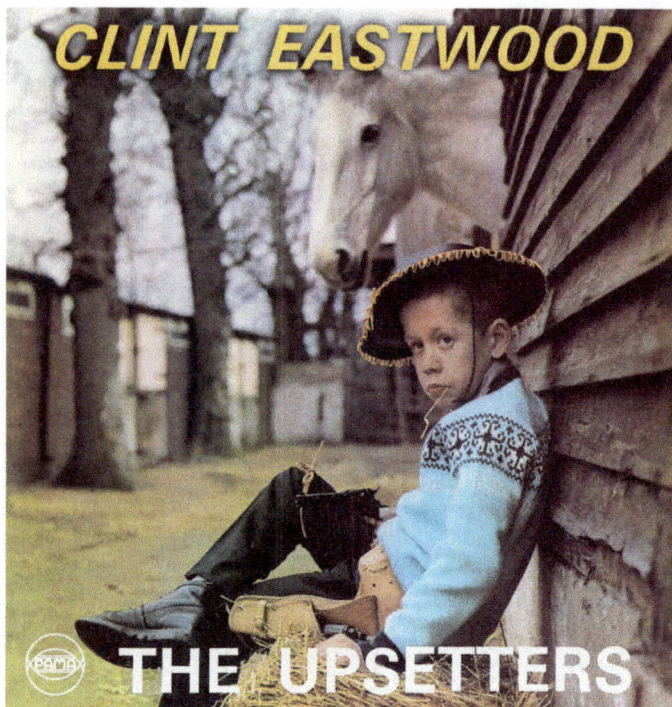

CLINT EASTWOOD
PAMA RECORDS PSP 1014 1970

Side 1
1. RETURN OF THE UGLY 2. FOR A FEW DOLLARS MORE
3. PRISONER OF LOVE 4. DRY ACID
5. RIGHTFUL RULER 6. CLINT EASTWOOD

Side 2
1. TASTE OF KILLING 2. SELASSIE 3. WHAT IS THIS?
4. NEVER FOUND ME A GIRL 5. MY MOB 6. CAUGHT YOU

MANY MOODS OF THE UPSETTERS
PAMA RECORDS SECO 24 1970

Side 1
1. EX - RAY VISION 2. CAN'T TAKE IT ANY MORE
3. SOUL STEW 4. LOW LIGHT 5. CLOUD NINE 6. BEWARE

Side 2
1. SERIOUS JOKE 2. GOOSEY 3. PROVE IT 4. BOSS SOCIETY
5. MEAN AND DANGEROUS 6. GAMES PEOPLE PLAY

HARRY JOHNSON (HARRY J)

Harry Zephaniah Johnson, better known as Harry J, was born on July 6th 1945 in Westmoreland, Jamaica. His early success as a producer came with the golden age of reggae.

His first introduction to the music business was playing the bass with a group called The Virtues but he soon moved on to a stint as an insurance salesman. On returning to the music industry his first work as a record producer came in 1968 when he launched his own record label, Harry J. The first release was The Beltones No More Heartaches, considered by many to be one of the first reggae songs ever recorded at the same time as Studio One produced Nanny Goat by Larry & Alvin. Coxone Dodd had allowed Johnson to use the facilities at Studio One.

1969 brought success with his internationally acclaimed hit Liquidator TR-675 reaching number 9 in the UK chart in November, a very popular tune and a record that became an anthem with the emerging skinheads. The provenance starts out with Tony Scott's What Am I To Do released on Pama's Escort label ES-805 in 1969. With the help of Winston Wright Harry Johnson created a legendary piece of music with its distinctive organ melody. The track was later used as the introduction on a hit for the Staple Singers, I'll Take You There. An album followed aptly titled Liquidator by Harry J All Stars issued on the Harry J label with a Trojan prefix TBL 104 in 1969. The song soon became a favourite anthem on the football terraces and remains so half a century later.

Further chart success followed in 1970 with the massive hit for the vocal duo Bob And Marcia with Young Gifted And Black on HJ-6605 reaching a commendable number 5 in the UK in April 1970. The UK hit was a strings added version of their original Jamaican recording.

In 1972 he sold his record shop to set up his own studio on Roosevelt Avenue in Kingston Jamaica. The Harry J Studio later became a recording Mecca for many artists including Bob Marley And The Wailers and The Rolling Stones. Chris Blackwell the founder of Island Records spent a great deal of time at Harry J's before moving to England and it was to here that Blackwell sent Bob Marley to record the classic album Catch A Fire. The studio also featured in the reggae movie Rockers.

The UK chart of the 29th November 1969 was a high spot in the golden age of skinhead reggae and quite a money spinner for Trojan with three records riding high in the top ten. Liquidator at number 9 spent a total of twenty weeks on the chart roller coasting then enjoying somewhat of a brief resurgence rising back up the chart to reach number 10 in January 1970.

1. Archies - Sugar Sugar
2. The Tremeloes - (Call Me) Number One
3. Stevie Wonder - Yester-Me Yester-You Yesterday
4. Fleetwood Mac - Oh Well
5. Kenny Rogers - Ruby Don't Take Your Love To Town
6. The Beatles - Something / Come Together
7. **Jimmy Cliff - Wonderful World, Beautiful People**
8. **Upsetters - Return Of Django / Dollar In The Teeth**
9. **Harry J All Stars - Liquidator**
10. Jethro Tull - Sweet Dream

SINGLES PRODUCED BY HARRY J 1968–1972

TROJAN (ISSUED ON HARRY J LABEL)

HJ-675 Liquidator - Harry J All Stars 1969
HJ-693 Put A Little Love In Your Heart - Marcia Griffiths 1969
HJ-694 Spyrone - Harry J All Stars 1969

HARRY J

HJ-6600 The Big Three - Harry J All Stars 1970
HJ-6602 The Dog - Harry J All Stars 1970
HJ-6603 Feel A Little Better - Lloyd Parks 1970
HJ-6604 Fire Fire -The Jamaicans 1970
HJ-6605 Young Gifted And Black - Bob And Marcia 1970
HJ-6607 Jack The Ripper - The Jay Boys 1970

SINGLES PRODUCED BY HARRY J 1968–1972 (continued)

HJ-6608 Reach For The Sky - Harry J All Stars 1970
HJ-6609 Jay Moon Walk - The Jay Boys 1970
HJ-6610 Je T'Aime - The Jay Boys 1970
HJ-6611 Hang My Head - Bob Andy 1970
HJ-6612 Peace Of Mind - Bob Andy 1970
HJ-6613 Put A Little Love In Your Heart - Marcia Griffiths 1970
HJ-6614 Didn't I - The Cables 1970
HJ-6615 Got To Get Ourselves Together - Bob And Marcia 1970
HJ-6616 Salt Of The Earth -The Cables 1970
HJ-6617 Del Gago - The Jay Boys 1970
HJ-6618 I Can't Get Next To You - The Jay Boys 1970
HJ-6619 Cambodia - The Blake Boys 1970
HJ-6620 Feel Alright - The Cables 1970
HJ-6621 Return Of The Liquidator - Harry J All Stars 1970
HJ-6623 Band Of Gold - Marcia Griffiths 1970
HJ-6624 The Same Old Life - Roy Panton 1970
HJ-6625 More Heartaches - Lizzie 1970
HJ-6626 Holy Moses - The Jay Boys 1970
HJ-6628 The Arcade Walk - The Jay Boys 1971
HJ-6631 United We Stand - Bob Andy And Marcia Griffiths 1971
HJ-6634 Set Me Free - Uriel Aldridge 1971
HJ-6640 Come Back And Stay - The Fabulous Five 1972
HJ-6641 Down Side Up - Carey & Lloyd 1972
HJ-6642 Skank In Bed - Bongo Herman & Les 1972

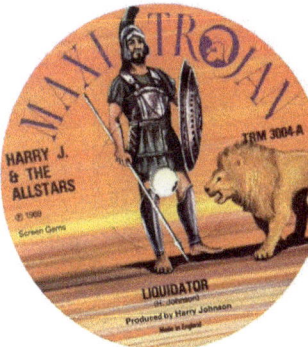

In 1972 Liquidator was re-released on Trojan's colourful Maxi label. TRM-3004 featured on the B side My Cherie Amour and Je T'aime, both tracks previously had an outing on the 1969 album Liquidator.

177

LIQUIDATOR
HARRY J ALL STARS
HARRY J TBL 104 Released 1969

Side 1
1. JACK THE RIPPER 2. BIG THREE 3. MY CHERIE AMOUR
4. DON'T LET ME DOWN 5. LIQUIDATOR 6. SPYRONE

Side 2
1. REACH FOR THE SKY 2. INTERROGATOR 3. JAY MOON WALK
4. EL CONG 5. JE T'AIME 6. THE DOG

DANDY LIVINGSTONE SINGER / PRODUCER

Dandy Livingstone was born Robert Livingstone Thompson in Kingston, Jamaica on the 14th December 1943. He moved to England at the age of 15 at a time when many West Indians first came to Britain, seeking opportunities to better themselves and their children. Many had been recruited to overcome the shortage of workers particularly in transport and hospitals. Some were soldiers from the war that had only ceased a decade or so earlier, brave men who had fought for Britain during the 1939-1945 campaign.

Dandy's first record was somewhat of a surprise, being issued without his knowledge. The record released on the Planetone label in 1963 resulted from of a jamming session with a friend. While Livingstone was working in a record shop owned by Lee Gopthal, who later launched Trojan Records, he discovered that a local record company, Carnival Records, were looking for a Jamaican vocal duo. Livingstone filled both roles by double taking his own voice and the records were issued with the credit going to the artist Sugar & Dandy. One single, What A Life, released in 1964 on the Carnival label CV-7015 sold over 25,000 copies. Live performances featured Tito Simon as the other half of the duo.

The story goes that Dandy took an album worth of material to Pama but Lee Gopthal from the up and coming Trojan signed Livingstone in 1968 under their noses, releasing their first two albums, Follow That Donkey on TRL 1 and Dandy Returns on TRL 2. The single Engine 59 released on Nu Beat NB-005 in 1968 credits The Rudies with the composer R. Thompson, and the vocals sounding suspiciously like Dandy. Robert Thomson being a man of many talents moved into production in 1968, a year that saw him team up with Audrey Hall, recording as Dandy & Audrey. As with other producers Trojan set up a subsidiary label, Downtown, to release Livingstone's work as singer and producer. The label was superseded by J-Dan from early 1970.

His productions included work for The Marvels and a single for Nicky Thomas, ironically titled Suzanne Beware Of The Devil, a song that brought Thompson chart success towards the end of 1972. He also produced Red Red Wine for Tony Tribe, a hugely popular single with the growing band of skinheads in 1969. Livingstone also worked with Rico Rodriguez who featured on the hit Rudy A Message To You and produced several singles for Rodriguez under the name of Rico & The Rudies.

The single Reggae In Your Jeggae was released on the Downtown label DT-410 in 1969 and became a popular record with the skinheads. Version Girl, credited on the label to Boy Friday and produced by Dandy, was a classic remake of Jackie Edwards What's Your Name and was released on Downtown DT-470.

An album by Dandy & Audrey, Morning Side Of The Mountain, was issued on the Downtown label bearing the Trojan prefix TBL 118 during 1970.

Several singles followed most notably recording as Boy Friday as the notes on Club Reggae Volume 2 mentioned, *The last year has seen the emergence of the 'Version' either being the instrumental of a vocal, or a record brought up to date by dubbing the voice of a D.J. over the old tape. Examples of the latter are any U-Roy or Dennis Alcapone records, both noted for their fast talking rhymes using local slang and dialect, and thus quite often making the words completely unintelligible to an English audience. Producer Dandy gently satirizes the situation with his Version Girl sung by Boy Friday, a relatively unknown singer whose voice sounds suspiciously familiar!*

By 1971 Thompson was becoming disillusioned with the music business and seemed to be losing direction so he moved to Jamaica as he said at the time to recharge his musical batteries. A year later he returned with new material and Trojan issued an album, but more important he had a new identity, he was now known as Dandy Livingstone.

SUZANNE BEWARE OF THE DEVIL

Dandy Livingstone eventually found chart Success in 1972 with Suzanne Beware Of The Devil. The track, originally issued as a B side to What Do You Wanna Make Those Eyes At Me For on TR-7857. Nicky Thomas' version was also issued the same year as an A side on TR-7862. Once the potential was spotted for a hit it was hastily removed and replaced with Talking About Sally, with the track released as a single on Trojan's Horse label.

HOSS-16 climbed to number 14 during October and was one of the last four reggae records to feature in the charts during the skinhead years of 68-72. An album followed titled Dandy Livingstone and was released on the more expensive Trojan prefix TRLS 45, although Suzanne Beware Of The Devil never made it onto the album.

The UK chart of the 7th October 1972 looked like this and included Judge Dread with Big Six at number 12 and Johnny Nash with his hit More Questions Than Answers featuring at number 26.

1. Davis Cassidy - How Can I Be Sure
2. T Rex - Children Of The Revolution
3. Lieutenant Pigeon - Mouldy Old Dough
4. Sweet - Wig-Wam Bam
5. Donny Osmond - Too Young
6. Peter Skellern - Your A Lady
7. Slade - Mama Weer All Crazee Now
8. Gary Glitter - I Didn't Know You Loved Me (Till I Saw You Rock And Roll)
9. Faron Young - Four In The Morning
10. The Drifters - Come On Over To My Place (1972)
11. Elvis Presley - Burning Love
12. **Judge Dread - Big Six**
13. Michael Jackson - Ain't No Sunshine
14. **Dandy Livingstone - Suzanne Beware Of The Devil**

SINGLES DISCOGRAPHY 1968–1972

TROJAN

TR-601 Donkey Returns *Brother Dan All-stars* 1968
TR-607 Read Up *Brother Dan All-stars* 1968
TR-608 Another Saturday Night *Brother Dan All-stars* 1968
TR-618 The Toast *Dandy* 1968

DOWNTOWN

DT-401 Move Your Mule *Dandy* 1968
DT-402 Come Back Girl *Dandy* 1968
DT-404 Tell Me Darling *Brother Dan* 1968
DT-405 Copy Your Rhythm *Brother Dan All-stars* 1968
DT-406 Doctor Sure Shot *Dandy* 1969
DT-410 Reggae In Your Jeggae *Dandy* 1969
DT-413 Moma Moma *The Israelites* 1969
DT-415 Rock Steady Gone *Dandy* 1969
DT-416 I'm Your Puppet *Dandy* 1969
DT-421 Games People Play *Dandy & Audrey* 1969
DT-426 Everybody Feel Good *Downtown All-stars* 1969
DT-429 People Get Ready *Dandy /The Rudies* 1969
DT-433 Seven Books *The Israelites* 1969
DT-434 Be Natural Be Proud *Dandy* 1969
DT-437 Come On Home *Dandy* 1969
DT-441 Burial Of Long Shot (Part 1) *Prince Of Darkness* 1969
DT-442 Everybody Loves A Winner *Dandy* 1969
DT-445 Come Together *The Israelites* 1969
DT-447 Music Doctor *The Music Doctors* 1969
DT-448 Meeting Over Yonder *Prince Of Darkness* 1969
DT-450 Skinheads A Message To You *Desmond Riley* 1969
DT-456 Raining In My Heart *Dandy* 1970
DT-458 Build Your Heart On A Solid Foundation *Dandy* 1970
DT-462 Morning Side Of The Mountain *Dandy & Audrey* 1970
DT-470 Version Girl *Boy Friday* 1970
DT-471 Music So Good *Boy Friday* 1970
DT-473 Take A Message Rudy *Boy Friday* 1970

J-DAN

JDN-4403 Bush Doctor *The Music Doctors* 1970
JDN-4404 Preaching Love *The Music Doctors* 1970
JDN-4410 Can't Help From Crying *The Israelites* 1970
JDN-4411 The Wild Bunch *The Music Doctors* 1970
JDN-4414 In The Summertime *The Music Doctors* 1970

TROJAN

TR-7800 Take A Letter Maria *Dandy* 1970
TR-7816 Same Old Fashioned Way *Dandy* 1971

J-DAN

JDN-4416 I Don't Want No War *Boy Friday* 1971
JDN-4417 Discretion Version *The Music Doctors* 1971
JDN-4418 Situation Version *Boy Friday* 1971

DOWNTOWN

DT-476 There'll Always Be Sunshine *Boy Friday* 1971
DT-477 Hot Pants *Boy Friday* 1971

TROJAN

TR-7828 Salt Of The Earth *Dandy* 1971

DOWNTOWN

DT-480 The Pliers *The Music Doctors* 1971
DT-481 El Raunchy *Boy Friday* 1971
DT-483 Could It Be True *Dandy & Jackie* 1971
DT-484 Daddy's Home *Dandy* 1971
DT-489 Give Me Some More *Studio Sound* 1972

TROJAN

TR-7857 What Do You Wanna Make Those Eyes At Me For?
Dandy Livingstone 1972
(B side originally featured Suzanne Beware Of The Devil)

HORSE

HOSS-16 Suzanne Beware Of The Devil
Dandy Livingstone 1972

HOSS-25 Big City / Think About That
Dandy Livingstone 1972

183

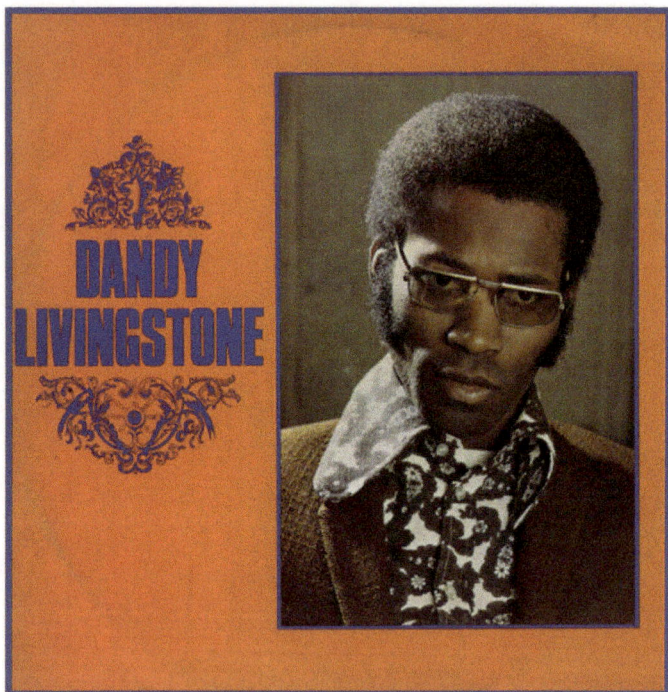

DANDY LIVINGSTONE
TROJAN RECORDS TRLS 45
Released 1972

Side 1
1. BIG CITY 2. MAKE ME YOUR NUMBER ONE
3. WAR ACROSS THE NATION
4. WHAT DO YOU WANNA MAKE THOSE EYES AT ME FOR
5. THINK ABOUT THAT 6. SUNSHINE GIRL

Side 2
1. JAMAICA IS FUN 2. BRAND NEW DAY
3. AT THE CLUB 4. CONFIDENTIAL
5. DON'T BREAK YOUR PROMISE

CLANCY ECCLES PRODUCER AND ARTIST

Clancy Eccles was brought up in the Parish of Saint Mary in Jamaica, the son of a tailor and builder. Early in his life he was influenced by spiritual music in church and grew to love singing. Clancy's musical career began with a stint working on the north coast hotel circuit, eventually moving to Ocho Rios. His big musical break like many of his contemporaries came when he moved to Kingston and took part in a talent show, this one organized by Coxone Dodd. Clancy's early success featured several ska hits including River Jordon and Sammy No Dead.

Clancy then launched a series of talent shows of his own and began to organise concerts including amongst many The Wailers in the mid sixties. He left the music industry in 1965 to follow his father's profession as a tailor for a short time before returning to the music business in 1967. This time around though saw Clancy producing his own recordings as well as other artists.

Clancy Eccles was influential during the period of the hardening of rocksteady into reggae and has been credited as being the originator of the word reggae, derived from streggae, a word used in Kingston to describe a woman of the streets. The claim is emphasized in Bag A Boo (Don't You Brag And Don't You Boast), a B side of The Slickers Auntie Lulu released in 1969 on the Duke label.

However before Bag A Boo his first hit in the UK was What Will Your Mama Say released on Pama PM-701 in 1968. Clancy's Fattie Fattie released on Trojan TR-658 became a classic skinhead track, although the lyrics to this day remain somewhat of a mystery. As with Fattie Fattie and Fire Corner on DU-30 released through Trojan on the Duke label much of his other production work also found favour with the skinheads, including Herbman Shuffle from the legendary DJ King Stitt, pronounced Stitch.

Clancy's session band, The Dynamites, recorded numerous instrumentals with many featuring as the B side to Clancy's singles. Clandisc a subsidiary of Trojan was launched in 1969 for the UK production of Clancy's own and his artists work. The label soon grew a reputation for quality releases including, Holly Holy by The Fabulous Flames and Sweet Jamaica sung admirably by Clancy, both outstanding tracks.

Both tracks featured on Trojan's Club Reggae Volume 1 and Volume 2 respectively. Clancy had built a reputation of fairness and a sense of equality and helped fellow musicians including Lee 'Scratch' Perry set up his own label in 1968. Clancy Eccles died on the 30th June 2005 in Spanish Town Hospital Jamaica after suffering a heart attack.

SELECTED DISCOGRAPHY SINGLES 1968-1972

DOCTOR BIRD
DB-1156 Feel The Rhythm 1968

PAMA
PM-701 What Will Your Mama Say 1968

CLANDISC
CLA-201 The World Needs Loving 1969
CLA-202(B) Mount Zion 1969
CLA-220(B) Dance Beat 1969

DUKE
DU-9(B) Bag A Boo 1969
DU-30 Fire Corner 1969

TROJAN
TR-639 Sweet Africa 1969
TR-647 Bangarang Crash 1969
TR-658 Fattie Fattie 1969

CLANDISC
CLA-214 Africa 1970
CLA-221 Unite Tonight 1970
CLA-235 John Crow Skank 1971

TROJAN
TR-7815(B) Credit Squeeze 1971

CLANDISC
CLA-239 Hallelujah Free At Last 1972

FREEDOM
TROJAN RECORDS TTL 22
Issued on CLANDISC Released 1969

Side 1
1. FREEDOM 2. WHAT WILL YOUR MOTHER SAY
3. TWO OF A KIND 4. THE WORLD NEEDS LOVING
5. DOLLAR TRAIN 6. CONSTANTINOPLE

Side 2
1. FATTIE FATTIE 2. AUNTIE LULU
3. SHU BE DU 4. MY GIRL
5. I NEED YOU
6. MOUNTZION

ERIC DONALDSON

The very successful singer-songwriter Eric Donaldson was born in St. Catherine Jamaica on the 11th June 1947. He attended school in Spanish Town before taking a job as a painter. Known for always singing in his spare time he cut some un-released tracks for Studio One during his late teens. In the mid-sixties he formed a vocal group, The West Indians, with their first Jamaican hit coming in 1968 with Right Time, a track produced by JJ Johnson.

The group also recorded for Lee 'Scratch' Perry, changing their name to The Killowatts. However no real success came and the group broke up in 1970. Donaldson then cut some tracks for Alvin Ranglin's GG Label including Lonely Nights then for Dynamic Studios a track called Never Gonna Give You Up, but neither found favour at the time.

In 1971 as a last stand Eric entered the Festival Song Competition with Cherry Oh Baby. It was said by many at the time from the first rehearsals that those present knew they were listening to the winner. From that day Eric Donaldson will forever be associated with the Jamaican Festival Song Competition and in particular for his winning entry, a song recorded by many since but never equalled. The song was sung in his trademark falsetto voice, a triumph that launched his career.

It has been reported that when he first came out on stage at the famous State Theatre for the final competition shouts of go away country man could be heard. Then he began to sing and before the first line was completed it was bedlam. People in the front rows rushed on stage lifted him to their shoulders and proclaimed him even then as one of the biggest super stars to hit Jamaica in a long while.

An album was recorded at Dynamic Studios and released toward the end of 1971 on Byron Lee's subsidiary label Jaguar. The album Eric Donaldson sold an extraordinary 50,000 copies. Seven of the tracks were Donaldson' original compositions, including of course Cherry Oh Baby and Miserable Woman with a cover of Love Of The Common People included. Trojan in due course released the album in the UK during 1972 on TRLS 42.

Eric soon became a household name in Jamaica although chart success in the UK eluded him, nonetheless outstanding reggae singles should not and never were measured on chart success alone.

ERIC DONALDSON
JAGUAR RECORDS Jamaican release 1971
TROJAN RECORDS TRLS 42 Released 1972

Side 1
1. CHERRY OH BABY 2. MISERABLE WOMAN
3. GOT TO GET YOU OFF MY MIND
4. PLEASE LET ME LOVE YOU
5. GO AWAY

Side 2
1. LOVE OF THE COMMON PEOPLE 2. NEVER ON A SUNDAY
3. JUST CAN'T HAPPEN THIS WAY 4. BUILD MY WORLD
5. THE LION SLEEPS

CHERRY OH BABY featured as the opening track on the successful
Trojan Club Reggae Volume 2 TBL 164 released in 1971.

SINGLES DISCOGRAPHY 1968-1972

PUNCH

PH-9 (B) Never Get Away 1970

DYNAMIC

DYN-420 Cherry, Oh Baby / Sir Charmers Special 1971
DYN-423 Love Of The Common People 1971
DYN-425 Just Can't (Happen This Way) 1971
DYN-431 I'm Indebted 1971
DYN-439 Miserable Woman 1972
DYN-445 Blue Boot 1972
DYN-452 Little Did You Know 1972

DERRICK MORGAN

Derrick Morgan was born on the 27th March 1940 in the parish of Clarendon, Jamaica. At the age of 17 he entered a talent show which he won, receiving a rousing reception. Two years later he began recording for Duke Reid who at the time was resourcing new talent for his Treasure Isle label. One of Morgan's early records gave him a popular hit in Jamaica. Fat Man was released on the Blue Beat label, then later re worked in 1970 and issued as the flip side of Return Of Jack Slade on Pama's Unity label, UN-546. During the early years of ska Derrick worked alongside Desmond Dekker, Bob Marley and Jimmy Cliff and it was a meeting with Jimmy Cliff that led to a fruitful relationship with producer Leslie Kong.

Morgan created a different record in 1960 being the only artist to hold the top seven positions in the Jamaican chart simultaneously. 1961 saw a massive hit for him in his homeland with the release of You Don't Know, a Leslie Kong production later re titled Housewife's Choice, a track now synonymous with the name Derrick Morgan. The record launched a rivalry between him and Prince Buster who accused Derrick of stealing his ideas. Buster released Blackhead Chiney Man taking a swipe at Kong. A counter release was quick to come from Derrick Morgan titled Blazing Fire. Listen to the tracks and you will see how intense the rivalry was. Further releases and counter releases followed including Thirty Pieces Of Silver from Buster with Morgan responding with No Raise No Praise. Clashes often erupted amongst the respective followers to such an extent the government of the day had to step in. A photo shoot was arranged appearing in the Jamaican Daily Gleaner portraying the rivals as friends.

Derrick continued to release first class quality material including Tougher Than Tough, The Conqueror and Seven Letters cited by some as the first true reggae record, although a fact disputed by others. By this time Island records in the UK had picked up on Derrick's records releasing tracks like Gimme Back on WI-3101 in 1968.

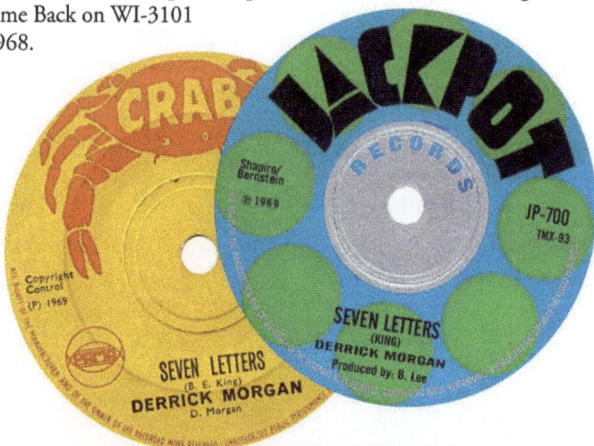

Derrick's brother in law Bunny 'Striker' Lee, who Derrick had helped start up in the music industry released Derrick's song Hold You Jack in the UK on Island WI-3159 in 1968. The record became a huge hit for Derrick in Jamaica and with a fast moving melodic rhythm the track was utilised for Wet Dream.

Another track produced by Bunny 'Striker' Lee was Seven Letters, released during 1969 in the UK on the Crab label, CRAB-8. With the popularity of reggae in the UK taking off due to the skinheads indulgence Derrick moved to England with Bunny Lee and 1969 saw their release of the skinhead anthem Moon Hop on Crab CRAB-32, with backing provided by The Rudies.

A great rivalry existed between Pama and Trojan, one that had been fuelled by Bunny Lee's licensing of Derrick Morgan's Seven Letters to both Trojan and Pama. The single Seven Letters was issued on both Trojan's Jackpot label JP-700 and Pama's Crab label prefix CRAB-8 in 1969. Seven Letters the album was issued by Trojan on TTL 5 in 1969.

SEVEN LETTERS
TROJAN RECORDS TTL 5 1969

Side 1
1. SEVEN LETTERS 2. BLAZING FIRE 3. GYPSY WOMAN
4. TEARS ON MY PILLOW 5. HOLD YOU JACK
6. GIMME BACK 7. CONQUERING RULER

Side 2
1. FAT MAN 2. SHOWER OF RAIN 3. FORWARD MARCH
4. HOUSEWIFES' CHOICE 5. IT'S ALL RIGHT
6. NO RAISE NO PRAISE 7. ONE MORNING IN MAY

MAN ON THE MOON was the headline of 21 July 1969 and launched a succession of reggae hits. One being Derrick Morgan's Man Pon Moon on Pama's Crab label, CRAB-30 in the UK. The Jamaican Unity label released a single with Moon Hop on the B side. Moon Hop was later issued on the Crab label in the UK as an A side on CRAB-32.

Derrick's Morgan's Moon Hop sold well and made a brief entry in the British Chart at number 49 in January 1970, albeit for just one week. Trojan countered with their own version, Skinhead Moonstomp, and that seemed to hold back any further chart progress for the original Moon Hop.

Pama released an album Moon Hop on Pama Special PSP 1006 in early 1970 featuring of course Moon Hop, Man Pon Moon and Derrick Top The Pop. Failing eyesight eventually forced Derrick to give up making regular stage appearances.

ALBUM DISCOGRAPHY 1968-1972

PAMA
ECO-10 Derrick Morgan In London 1969

TROJAN
TTL-5 Seven Letters   1969

PAMA
PSP-1006 Moon Hop   1970

MOON HOP
DERRICK MORGAN
PSP 1006   1970

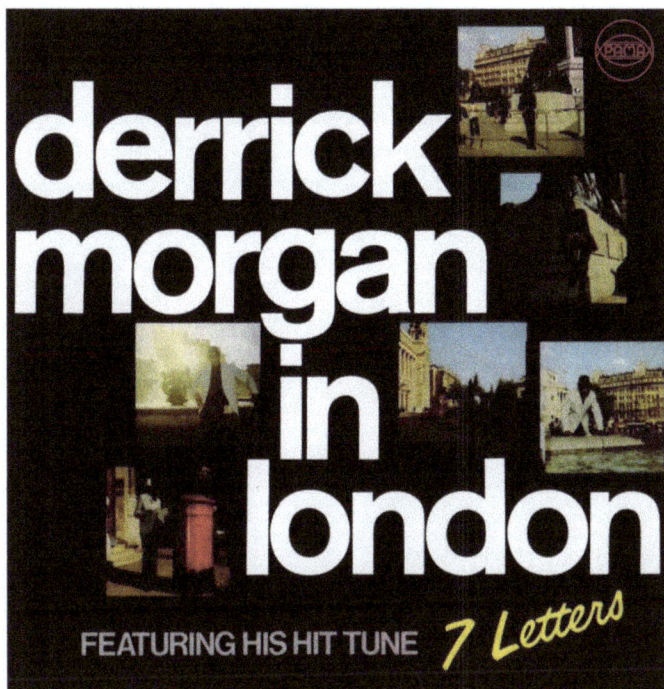

DERRICK MORGAN IN LONDON   PAMA ECO-10 1969
Side 1
1. SEVEN LETTERS 2. FIRST TASTE OF LOVE 3. HOW CAN I FORGET
4. STAND BY ME 5. DON'T PLAY THAT SONG 6. TOO BAD

Side 2
1. ONE MORNING IN MAY 2. COME WHAT MAY 3. SEND ME SOME LOVING
4. MAKE IT TAN DEAY 5. GIVE ME BACK 6. RIVER TO THE BANK

SELECTED SINGLES DISCOGRAPHY 1968-1972

CRAB
CRAB-3 River To The Bank 1968
CRAB-8 Seven Letters 1969
CRAB-22 Make It Tand Deay 1969
CRAB-30 Man Pon Moon 1969
CRAB-32 Moon Hop 1969

ISLAND
WI-3094 Conquering Ruler 1968
WI-3101 Gimme Back 1968
WI-3159 Hold You Jack 1968

JACKPOT
JP-700 Seven Letters 1969
JP-797 Me Naw Run 1972

JJ RECORDS
PRY-6061 What's Your Grouse 1968
PRY-6063 Johnny Pram Pram 1968

NU BEAT
NB-008 Hey Boy Hey Girl * 1968
NB-016 I Love You 1968

PAMA SUPREME
PS-321 John Crow Skank 1971

PUNCH
PH-107 Forward March 1972

PYRAMID
PRY-6024 No Dice 1968
PRY-6025 Do The Beng Beng 1968
PRY-6029 I Am The Ruler 1968
PRY-6040 Want More 1968

TROJAN
TR-626 Fat Man 1968

UNITY
UN-540 Derrick Top The Pop 1969
UN-546 Return Of Jack Slade / Fat Man 1969
UN-569 The Conqueror 1969
* With Patsy Morgan, Derrick's sister.

GUNS DON'T ARGUE
DENNIS ALCAPONE   TROJAN TBL 187
Released 1972

DENNIS ALCAPONE

Dennis Alcapone was born Dennis Smith on the 6th August 1947 in Clarendon Jamaica but moved to Kingston from a very early age. Dennis began his working life as a welder for the Jamaican Public Services by day, but his nights were spent at the various sound systems of the time, including those run by Coxone Dodd, Duke Reid and Prince Buster.

He set up his own small Hi Fi sound system El Paso with two friends and was soon spotted by producer Keith Hudson who liked his sharp talking over the records of the day. The founder of the Deejay or Toaster was Ewart Beckford, better known as Hugh Roy who began talking over Duke Reid rocksteady tracks and was seen as the Daddy of talk over, but Dennis Alcapone came very close. His first recording was under the title of Dennis Smith. He joined Clement Dodd's Studio One as the legendary Hugh Roy or U.Roy was well established with Duke Reid as his number one deejay.

His debut single for Dodd was Nanny Version and became an instant hit in Jamaica with his talk over revamping an old song, it was also the first record to be credited to Dennis Alcapone. That first record had many convinced that it was in fact U.Roy but it soon became apparent that Alcapone's voice was clearer and more distinct and became the sound the youth wanted to hear.

Dennis found considerable chart success in Jamaica and topped the charts with several singles including Guns Don't Argue AKA Alcapone Guns Don't Bark and Ripe Cherry, both using backing tracks of fellow studio artist Eric Donaldson's Love Of The Common People and Cherry, Oh Baby respectively. Guns Don't Bark featured on Trojan's Club Reggae Volume 3 and Ripe Cherry found its way onto the popular Tighten Up Volume 5.

During 1971 Dennis joined forces with his old friend Bunny Lee releasing It Must Come utilising Better Must Come as the backing track and Cherry Oh Baby featured again on another track this time produced by Lee 'Scratch' Perry. Well Dread was originally scheduled to be voiced by Lizzy but Perry decided that Dennis should voice it himself.

An inevitable album followed, originally released in Jamaica in 1971on the Jaguar label. The same album was released in the UK on Trojan in 1972, appropriately titled Guns Don't Argue on TBL187.

GUNS DON'T ARGUE
DENNIS ALCAPONE   TROJAN TBL 187 1972

Side 1
1. ALCAPONE GUNS DON'T ARGUE 2. IT MUST COME
3. AIN'T TOO PROUD TO BEG 4. EVERYBODY NEEDS LOVE
5. IF IT DON'T WORK OUT

Side 2
1. TEACHER TEACHER 2. LEFT WITH A BROKEN HEART
3. YOU GOT WHAT IT TAKES 4. WORLD WIDE LOVE
5. SOMEONE DANCING WITH MY GIRL

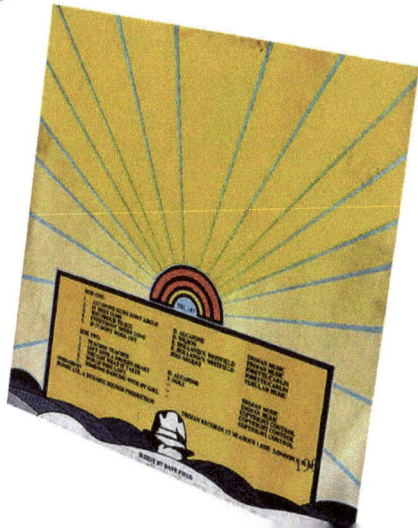

SINGLES DISCOGRAPHY 1970-1972

ACKEE
ACK-114 Happy Go Lucky Girl 1970

BANANA
BA-324 Nanny Version 1970

CAMEL
CA-56 Everybody Bawlin 1970

SUPREME
SUP-214 You Must Believe Me 1970

BANANA
BA-326 Home Version 1971
BA-328 Duppy Serenade 1971
BA-341 Forever Version 1971

BIG SHOT
BI-565 Shades Of Hudson 1971
BI-572 Out De Light Baby 1971

CAMEL
CA-74 This A Butter 1971

DUKE
DU-125 Medley Version 1971

DYNAMIC
DYN-421 Horse And Buggy 1971
DYN-422 Ripe Cherry 1971
DYN-427 Alcapone Guns Don't Bark 1971

EXPLOSION
EX-2039 Revelation Version 1971

G.G.
GG-4526 King Of Kings 1971

JACKPOT
JP-773 Jumping Jack 1971
JP-775 Togetherness 1971
JP-776 Tell It Like It Is 1971

PUNCH
PH-61 Mosquito One 1971

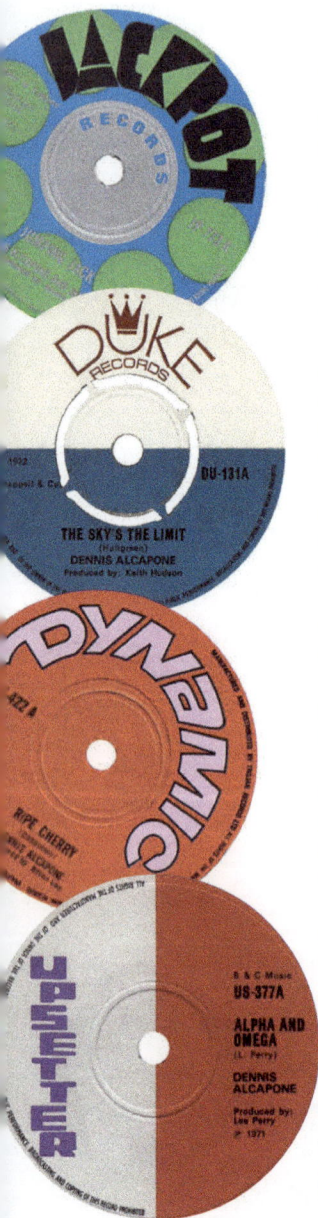

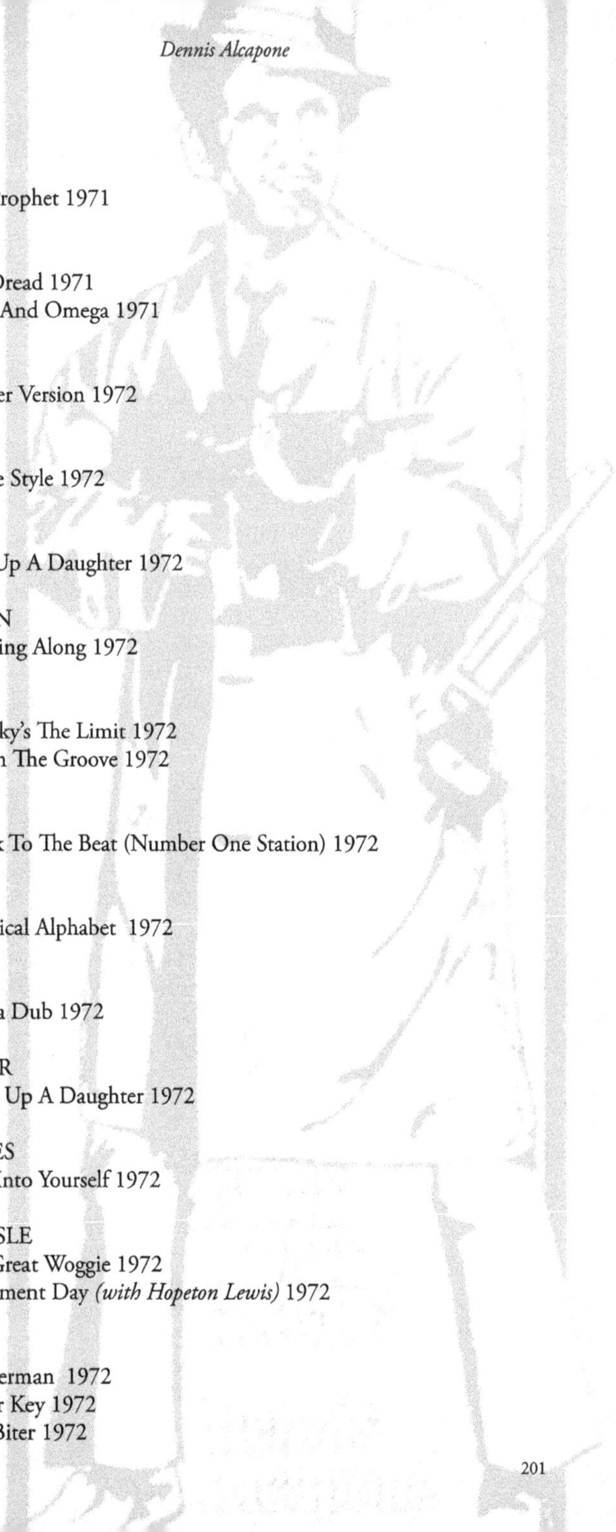

TROPICAL
AL-003 False Prophet 1971

UPSETTER
US-373 Well Dread 1971
US-377 Alpha And Omega 1971

ACKEE
ACK-146 Power Version 1972

ATTACK
ATT-8027 Fine Style 1972

BULLET
BU-509 Dup-Up A Daughter 1972

DOWNTOWN
DT-496 Swinging Along 1972

DUKE
DU-131 The Sky's The Limit 1972
DU-147 Get In The Groove 1972

DUKE REID
DR-2520 Rock To The Beat (Number One Station) 1972

G.G.
GG-4538 Musical Alphabet 1972

GRAPE
GR-3035 Rasta Dub 1972

GREENDOOR
GD-4041 Rub Up A Daughter 1972

TECHNIQUES
TE-918 Look Into Yourself 1972

TREASURE ISLE
TI-7069 The Great Woggie 1972
TI-7071 Judgement Day *(with Hopeton Lewis)* 1972

UPSETTER
US-381 Wonderman 1972
US-388 Master Key 1972
US-389 Back Biter 1972

U ROY or HUGH ROY

U Roy also known as Hugh Roy was born Ewart Beckford in Jones Town, Jamaica on the 21st September 1942. Reggae's greatest deejay also known as 'The Originator' found recognition in the late 60s and early 70s with a string of hits. He is famed as the inventor of toasting, using vocal improvisation and rapping over previously released popular songs.

His musical career began back in 1961 as a deejay at several of the sound systems of the day including Coxone Dodd's number two set whilst King Stitt known as 'The Ugly One' ran his number one station; sounds a familiar lyric. Working with Duke Reid gave Hugh Roy access to Treasure Isles vast back catalogue of hits to experiment with and although not the first deejay to talk over an old hit he was the first to find fame through his recording techniques, he didn't just talk over he wrote a riddim from start to finish ending up with a polished track.

Working alongside Duke Reid they created Wear You To The Ball, a record previously a hit for The Paragons in the 60s now getting a new lease of life and a huge hit in Jamaica for Hugh Roy and John Holt. John Holt was the lead singer with The Paragons and had become a huge fan of Hugh Roy as he was known at that time.

The hits began to come with Wear You To The Ball released on Duke Reid DR-2513 in 1970 kicking it all off. Next up was You'll Never Get Away Duke Reid DR-2514 and Version Galore, also released on the Duke Reid label DR-2515. U.Roy worked with most of the top Jamaican producers including Bunny Lee, Lee 'Scratch' Perry, Sonia Pottinger and Alvin Ranglin. An album was released in the UK in 1971 on Trojan TBL161 titled Version Galore.

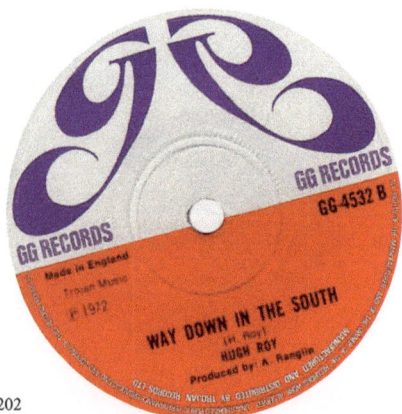

Included on the album were several re workings of the classic hits from The Paragons. On The Beach and the popular The Tide Is High featured, a track incidentally that provided a huge number one hit for Blondie in 1980 on both side of the Atlantic, although many at the time did not realise its provenance. Other tracks attributed to the Paragons on the album were Happy Go Lucky Girl and of course Wear You To The Ball, a record that featured on Trojan's first in the series of Club Reggae issued the same year.

1972 saw the release on Pama prefix PM-835 of Way Down South. Produced by Alvin Ranglin the track was a version of Take Warning by Billy Dyce and also featured as the B side on Trojan's GG label prefix GG-4532 as Way Down In The South. The track also made it onto Pama's Straighten Up Volume 3 album, both released the same year.

1972 heralded the release on Trojan of a second album in the Version series Version Galore volume 2 on TBL 175. Although this time the album also featured tracks by one of his deejay compatriots, the up and coming Dennis Alcapone, of whom it has already been said had a clearer style that endeared him greatly to the youth and in particular the remaining skinheads.

VERSION GALORE TROJAN RECORDS TBL 161 Released 1971

SELECTED SINGLES DISCOGRAPHY 1970-1972

DUKE REID
DR-2513 Wear You To The Ball - Hugh Roy And John Holt 1970
DR-2514 You'll Never Get Away - Hugh Roy 1970
DR-2515 Version Galore - Hugh Roy 1970

DUKE
DU-105 Love I Tender - Hugh Roy 1970

UNITY
UN-568(B) Wake The Nation - Jeff Barnes & Hugh Roy 1970

DUKE REID
DR-2509 Wake The Town - Hugh Roy 1970
DR-2510 Rule The Nation - Hugh Roy 1970
DR-2517 Tom Drunk - U-Roy & Hopeton Lewis 1971
DR-2518 True True - Hugh Roy 1971
DR-2519 Flashing My Whip - Hugh Roy 1971
DR 2520 Rock To The Beat - U.Roy 1972

DYNAMIC
DYN-488 Festival Wise - Hugh Roy 1972

GRAPE
GR-3026 On Top Of The Peak - U.Roy 1972

TROJAN
TR-7884 Hat Trick C/W Wet Vision - U.Roy 1972

GG
GG-4532 B Way Down In The South - Hugh Roy 1972

PAMA
PM-835 Way Down South - Hugh Roy 1972

BOB MARLEY AND THE WAILERS

The renowned group was lead by Bob Marley who was born Nesta Robert Marley in the village of Nine Mile in the parish of St. Anne, Jamaica on 6th February 1945. His father was a white Jamaican of English descent. It is understood that a Jamaican passport official inadvertently swapped his first and middle names.

Bob Marley passed away on the 11th May 1981 having become the first truly international reggae super star. The Wailers had begun life in 1963 formed by Bob Marley, Peter Tosh and Bunny Wailer. Their original recordings were under the guise of The Wailing Wailers, later changing their name to The Wailers.

Their early recordings were of an exceptional standard; just listen if you can to Simmer Down and Shame And Scandal. In 1967 The Wailers started their own record label and released their first singles including Nice Time and Stir It Up a track penned by Bob for his wife Rita. The label soon folded and Bob began writing songs for Johnny Nash including amongst many Guava Jelly.

1970 through to 1972 saw the groups recordings produced by Lee 'Scratch' Perry with their most notable tracks released on a variety of labels including Guava Jelly on Trojan's Green Door GD-4025 and Small Axe on Perry's Trojan subsidiaries Upsetter label US-357 with Lively Up Yourself issued on the charismatic Pama Punch label, PH-102. Stir It Up was first popularised by the American singer Johnny Nash reaching number 13 on the UK charts in 1972.

The emerging reggae years in the UK of 1968–1972 were dominated by and will always be remembered and rightly so for groups like The Pioneers, Greyhound, Toots And The Maytals, the Upsetters alongside Desmond Dekker, Jimmy Cliff, Nicky Thomas, Dave And Ansel Collins and Bob And Marcia. Bob Marley And The Wailers had already enjoyed considerable success in Jamaica but in the UK were to some extent during this period in the shadows to the main stream and never broke into the charts. During 1971 they were described as a group with fine harmonizing and controversial lyrics and their singles Small Axe and Duppy Conqueror featured on Trojan's Club Reggae Volume 2 and Tighten Up Volume 5 respectively. Their time would come and it was somewhat ironic that the break came with the departure of Jimmy Cliff from Island Records leaving Chris Blackwell looking for a talented replacement.

By 1972 The Wailers had already released three albums and several singles. They were signed to CBS Records and arrived in the UK to work with Johnny Nash on the soundtrack for a film.

However when financing for the film ran short they found themselves stranded in the UK, without the cash to return home. Bob Marley, Bunny Wailer, and Peter Tosh had to find a way to return to Jamaica.

Chris Blackwell was an admirer of the group and had previously released Wailers material in the UK including Bend Down Low on WI-3043 in 1967 and Hooligan C/W Maga Dog on WI-212 as early as 1965. A meeting was arranged and Bob walked into Blackwell's office.

Chris Blackwell has been quoted as saying *"They were like the real life characters from The Harder They Come. They weren't actors, they were real rebels trying to get a fair deal in a rotten system."*

Chris Blackwell eventually offered them £4,000 to record an album for Island back in Jamaica. Catch A Fire was released later in 1973 and the rest they say is history. The album included Stir It Up and established the band and in particular Bob Marley as international superstars who began a new transformation, resurrecting the incessant sounds of Jamaica during the mid seventies, a sound they could truly call their own.

SINGLES DISCOGRAPHY 1968-1972

FAB
FAB-34 Pound Get A Blow 1968
FAB-36 Thank You Lord 1968
FAB-37 Nice Time 1968

TROJAN
TR-617 Stir It Up 1968

ESCORT
ERT- 842 To The Rescue 1970

UPSETTER
US-340 My Cup 1970
US-348 Duppy Conqueror 1970

BULLET
BU-486 Maga Dog 1971 (Peter Tosh)
BU-493 Lick Samba 1971

GREENDOOR
GD- 4005 Trench Town Rock 1971

PUNCH
PH-77 Down Presser 1971

UPSETTER
US-357 Small Axe 1971
US-371 Dreamland 1971
US-372 More Axe 1971

SUMMIT
SUM-8526 Stop The Train 1971

GREENDOOR
GD-4025 Guava Jelly 1972

PUNCH
PH-101 Screw Face
PH-102 Lively Up Yourself 1972

UPSETTER
US-392 Keep On Moving 1972

ALBUM DISCOGRAPHY 1968-1972

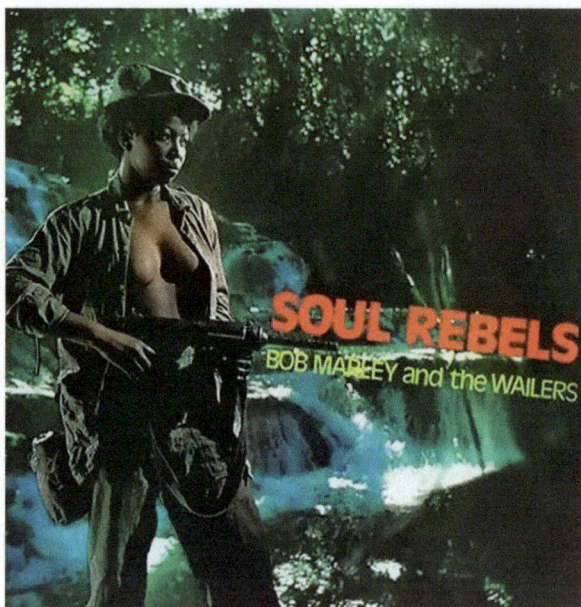

SOUL REBEL
TROJAN RECORDS TBL 126 1970

Side 1
1. SOUL REBEL 2. TRY ME
3. IT'S ALRIGHT 4. NO SYMPATHY
5. MY CUP 6. SOUL ALMIGHTY

Side 2
1. REBEL'SHOP 2. CORNER STONE
3. 400 YEARS 4. NO WATER
5. REACTION 6. MY SYMPATHY

SOUL REVOLUTION PART II
UPSETTER TBL 65 1971

Side 1
1. KEEP ON MOVING 2. DON'T ROCK MY BOAT
3. PUT IT ON 4. FUSSING AND FIGHTING
5. DUPPY CONQUEROR
6. MEMPHIS

Side 2
1. RIDING HIGH 2. KAYA
3. AFRICAN HERBSMAN 4. STAND ALONE
5. SUN IS SHINING 6. BRAIN WASHING

SOUL REVOLUTION was the second Wailers album produced by Lee 'Scratch' Perry and originally released as a very limited edition on the Jamaican Maroon label. SOUL REVOLUTION PART II was an interesting sequel, an album of pure rhythm tracks thought to be a first in Jamaican music.

JOHNNY NASH

Johnny Nash began his musical career as a pop singer in the late 1950s. He was born John Lester Nash Jr. in Houston, Texas, USA in 1940. As early as 1965 Johnny Nash had formed the JAD Record label in New York.

The reggae connection began during 1968 when Nash travelled to Jamaica and recorded several hits encouraged by the fact that his girlfriend had close family connections with the local radio and television host Neville Willoughby. His aim was to bring the rocksteady sound to America from Jamaica.

To help with this task Nash was introduced to a relatively young local group who were at the time struggling to make it in the music business called The Wailers. Bob Marley, Peter Tosh and Bunny Wailer introduced Nash to the local scene and all three were signed to an exclusive publishing deal with JAD, Nash financing some of their early work with Byron Lee's Dragonairies.

Johnny Nash enjoyed early success in the UK chart with the rocksteady releases Hold Me Tight reaching number 5 in 1968 and You Got Soul number 6 in January 1969. His follow up release Cupid matched the previous achievement in April the same year. Further chart success followed with Stir It Up, written by Bob Marley, released on CBS Records CBS-7800 peaking at number 13 in April 1972 and therefore popularising the song.

The single was taken from the album I Can See Clearly Now recorded in London the same year, an album that included a further three tracks penned by Marley, Guava Jelly, Comma Comma and You Poured Sugar On Me.

The album sold over a million copies, and was awarded a gold disc in November 1972. The album yielded two further chart hits for Nash; the title track peaked at number 5 in June 1972 with a follow up There Are More Questions Than Answers gaining a chart position the same year. Johnny Nash continued to find chart success in the coming years.

Although not seen by all as pure skinhead reggae his influence on the charts before the skinhead era had dawned and as it was drawing to a close should not be regarded lightly, nor should his close association with The Wailers.

The UK chart of the 29th April 1972 featured Johnny Nash with Stir It Up, Greyhound's I Am What I Am peaking at number 20 the same week and Paul Simon's Mother And Child Reunion heading down the charts having achieved a creditable number 5 position during March.

13. Johnny Nash - Stir It Up
20. Greyhound - I Am What I Am
48. Paul Simon - Mother And Child Reunion

The UK chart of the 22nd July 1972 looked like this;

1. Donny Osmond - Puppy Love
2. Gary Glitter - Rock And Roll Parts 1 And 2
3. Dr Hook And The Medicine Show - Sylvia's Mother
4. The New Seekers - Circles
5. Johnny Nash - I Can See Clearly Now
6. The Sweet - Little Willy
7. The Partridge Family - Breaking Up Is Hard To Do
8. Slade - Take Me Back 'Ome
9. The Who - Join Together
10. Elvis Presley - American Trilogy

Johnny Nash's next release There Are More Questions Than Answers achieved number 9 on the 28th October 1972, a chart that also saw Judge Dread feature with his Big Six at number 15 on its way down from the lofty position of number 11 the previous week.

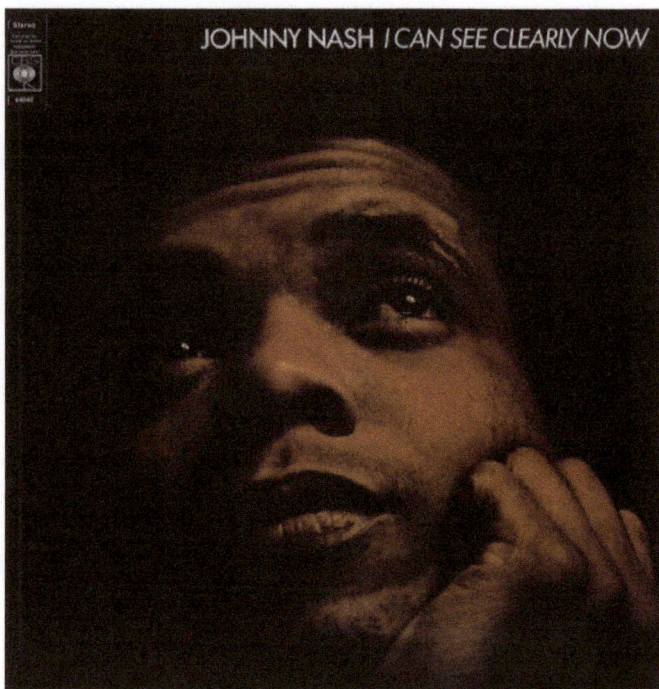

I CAN SEE CLEARLY NOW
JOHNNY NASH
CBS RECORDS CBSS 64840 Released 1972

Side1
1. STIR IT UP (R. Marley) 2. THAT'S THE WAY WE GET BY
3. GUAVA JELLY (R. Marley) 4. SO NICE WHILE IT LASTED
5. OOH BABY YOU'VE BEEN SO GOOD TO ME
6. YOU POURED SUGAR ON ME (R. Marley)

Side 2
1. I CAN SEE CLEARLY NOW 2. COMMA COMMA (R. Marley)
3. WE'RE ALL ALIKE 4. HOW GOOD IT IS
5. CREAM PUFF
(Original pressing featured
THE FISH AND THE ALLEY OF DESTRUCTION)
6. THERE ARE MORE QUESTIONS THAN ANSWERS

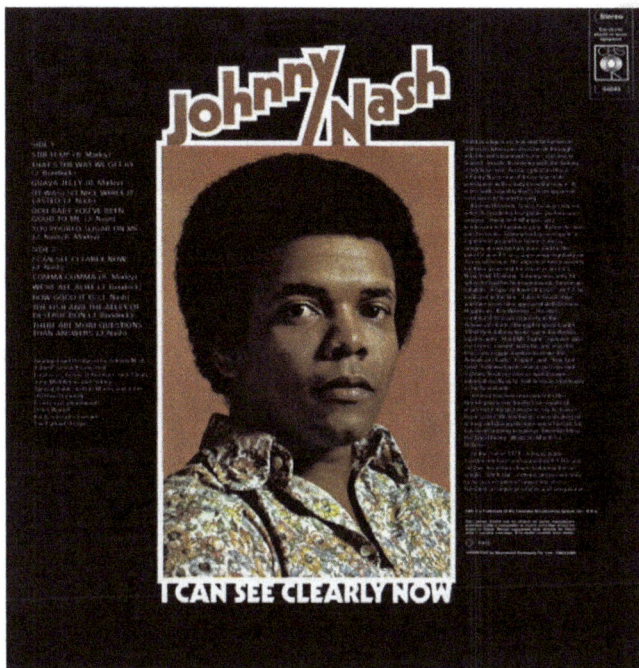

SELECTED SINGLES DISCOGRAPHY 1968-1972

MAJOR MINOR
MM-586 You Got Soul 1968

REGAL ZONAPHONE
RZ-3010 Hold Me Tight 1968

MAJOR MINOR
MM-603 Cupid 1969
MM-701 (What A) Groovy Feeling 1970

CBS
CBS-7800 Stir It Up 1972
CBSS-8113 I Can See Clearly Now 1972
CBSS-8351 There Are More Questions Than Answers 1972

THE VARIOUS ARTISTS

BORIS GARDNER

Boris Gardner or (Boris Gardiner) was born in Kingston, Jamaica on the 13th January 1943. He spent much of his early years in the music business performing on the hotel circuit during the 1960s. During the emerging years of reggae he worked exclusively as a session musician with the Upsetters, The Aggrovaters and The Chrystallites.

He enjoyed a solo hit in 1970 releasing his own version of Elizabethan Serenade on the Duke label in the UK, DU-39 titled Elizabethan Reggae. The record reached a respectable number 14 in the UK spending over three months on the chart. The record was a popular choice with the skinheads who could dance to the catchy instrumental that featured on Trojan's first Chartbuster series TBL105 also released in 1970.

The story goes though that he nearly missed out on the recognition for the single as the label on the original pressings in the UK had credited Byron Lee as the artist, who was the instrumentals record producer. The UK singles chart for the first week on the 17th January and the subsequent re-entry on the 31st and the next four weeks all used Byron Lee as the artist. However all record and chart data after the 28th February gave Boris Gardner the credit he deserved. Trojan released a debut album the same year titled Reggae Happening on TBL 121. Boris continued to release other material but it only gained success in his native Jamaica until 1986 when he found chart success again with his massive number one hit, a vocal rendition, I Want To Wake Up With You.

BRUCE RUFFIN

Bruce Ruffin was born Bernardo Constantine Balderamus on the 17th February 1952 in the parish of St. Catherine, Jamaica. He joined The Techniques in 1967 performing as a talented singer and writing material for the group who had enjoyed a string of rocksteady hits in the 1960s. He recorded as a soloist in 1969 a track titled Long About Now. Rain was released on Trojan TR-7814 with the B side featuring the popular Geronimo, The record reached number 19 in May 1971 and featured on Trojan's extremely popular Reggae Chartbusters Volume 3 TBL 169. 1972 saw the release of Mad About You this time on Rhino RNO-101, earning further chart success reaching a commendable number 9 in July. By this time the unpretentious sound of reggae had moved on, in most cases to a more polished sweetened pop orientated string laden affair, a sound the ebbing ranks of skinheads could no longer empathise with.

TONY TRIBE

A popular choice with the skinheads was Red Red
Wine by Tony Tribe with the original release on the
Downtown label DT-419, in 1969, having some copies
miss credited to Tony Tripe. Despite its popularity and an appearance on
top of the pops dressed as a skinhead it only made it to number 46.
Another record followed on Downtown, DT-439 I'm Gonna Give You All
The Love I've Got the same year but tragically the singer was killed in a car
crash in 1970.

KING STITT

Winston Sparkes was born in Kingston in 1940 although he became
known as King Stitt (pronounced Stitch). The name Stitt is said to have
come about due to a nickname he picked up because of a stammer as a
boy. What is in no doubt is how he became a legendary DJ when he came
to the attention of Coxone, who soon elevated him to his number one set
with U Roy behind running number two. King Stitt had arrived when
crowned king of the DJ's as early as 1963. He created some of the first
deejay records when he began recording over reggae rhythms in 1969.
Taking advantage of the facial distortion he was born with Winston nick
named himself The Ugly One, taking reference from the spaghetti western
The Good, The Bad And The Ugly. It has been said many times that he was
a man of immense wit, very articulate, and like a walking encyclopaedia of
Jamaican music.

In 1969 King Stitt recorded exclusively for Clancy Eccles over rhythms
from Clancy's session band The Dynamites. His work was released in the
UK on Clandisc and Duke with his sound finding immense favour with
the skinhead including Fire Corner released on the Duke label DU-30 in
1969, and Herbsman on Clandisc CLA-207 in 1970, which also credits
Any Capp on the label. An album was issued on Trojan TTL-21 in 1969
by The Dynamites featuring tracks from King Stitt including Fire Corner
from which the album took the title. Other singles during the skinhead
years included Virgorton 2 and Dance Beat. Following a battle with cancer
the legendary DJ passed away at his home in Kingston on 31 January 2012
at the age of 72.

"Haul it from the top to the very last drop".

JIMMY LONDON

Jimmy London was born on the 30th November 1949 in the parish of St. Catherine. Jamaica. His early work saw him recording as a member of The Inspirations and spending some time with both Lee 'Scratch' Perry and Joe Gibbs.

His success came when he teamed up with the Impact All Stars at Randy's Studio recording several well received singles including a cover of Simon & Garfunkel's Bridge Over Troubled Water released on Randy's RAN-507 during 1970.

Randy's, one of the Trojan subsidiary labels, was set up to release productions from the late Vincent Chin's Jamaican Randy's and Impact Labels with A Little Love RAN-520 released the following year. Both singles were substantial hits in Jamaica with Bridge Over Troubled Water featuring on Trojan's budget album Tighten Up Volume 5. Both tracks also appeared on his debut album Bridge Over Troubled Water released on Trojan TRLS 39 in 1972.

THE MAYTONES

A Jamaica tradition has always been for a group to form their name reflecting their respective birthplace and The Maytones are no exception. The Maytones formed in the late 1960s and consisted of Vernon Buckley, Alvin Ranglin and Gladstone Grant. All three grew up in May Pen in the parish of Clarendon, Jamaica. May Pen has produced several recording artists over the years and perhaps one of its most famous sons is Toots Hibbert who formed the Maytals. Much of The Maytones early material was recorded for Alvin Ranglin who had left the group to become their manager.

The first recording session in 1968 saw the subsequent release of Billy Goat a record that was snapped up by Trojan for release in the UK on Blue Cat BS-149. The captivating boss reggae track Sentimental Reason was issued on Pama's Camel label CA-27 in 1969. The single Black And White Unite with a prominent bass line was released in 1970 on Camel CA-47 and featured on the first volume of Straighten Up with the title changed to Straighten Up. Trojan launched the GG label in 1970 primarily as an outlet for Alvin Ranglin productions and over its time The Maytones became the labels most featured artists. The group released several notable singles including their excellent version of Greyhound's Black And White on GG-4522 in 1971.

In 1972 the group recorded two versions of As Long As You Love Me GG-4531, a first-rate vibrant reggae number with the B side a slowed down ballad version. The pulsating A side made it onto Trojan's Tighten Up Volume 6 released towards the latter part of 1972.

JACKIE EDWARDS

Wilfred Gerald 'Jackie' Edwards was born in Jamaica in 1940 and spent his teenage years performing covers of American R&B hits. His rich voice was often compared to Nat King Cole and this enabled him to build a solid reputation. Jackie started penning songs when the import of records from America dried up as the focus in America had turned from rhythm & blues to rock & roll, however this led to a demand for more local productions.

The home grown Jamaican R&B was produced primarily for the sound systems of the day with writers blending R&B and calypso and most significantly shifting the accent of the drum from the first and third beats to create ska. Jackie Edwards work was seen as equally influential as the likes of Prince Buster. He worked for Studio One before linking with the up and coming independent producer, Chris Blackwell.

His early Jamaican releases included You're Eyes Are Dreaming, Tell Me Darling and What's Your Name, the song later used as the inspiration for Boy Friday's Version Girl in 1970. Jackie Edwards relocated to the UK in the early sixties where he renewed his acquaintance with Chris Blackwell who by now had the beginnings of his business empire, selling singles to specialist shops, often for large amounts of money.

Chris Blackwell identified that Jackie had a talent as a writer and could help Blackwell's groups under his management. One in particular at that time were The Spencer Davis Group. The group had previously released three singles but they all failed to reach the top 30. Very much in need of new material Chris Blackwell asked Jackie to write a song for them, initially as a B side and he penned Keep On Running.

The song earned the group a massive number one hit and remains perhaps their most enduring song. Their follow up number one was also penned by Edwards, Somebody Help Me, a worldwide hit for the group and Chris Blackwell.

Throughout the transition from ska to rocksteady and eventually reggae Jackie Edwards produced some excellent recordings including Julie On My Mind released on Island WIP-6026 in 1968, Johnny Gunman on Bread BR-1107 and In Paradise on Trojan TR-7833, both released during 1971.

White Christmas was a track originally recorded in 1965 and re-released as a single on Trojan TR-7883 in 1972. Also released the same year was an album I DO LOVE YOU on TRLS 47.

Side 1
1. I DO LOVE YOU 2. DON'T STOP
3. BEWILDERED 4. WHO TOLD YOU SO
5. YOU'RE EYES ARE DREAMING
6. JULIE ON MY MIND

Side 2
1. ON THE RUN (WITH A GUN)
2. A LITTLE STORY 3. DO WHAT YOU WANNA DO
4. JOHNNY GUNMAN 5. WHY MAKE BELIEVE
6. MISS BLACK AND BEAUTIFUL
7. COME ON GIRL

Sadly Wilfred 'Jackie' Edwards died in Jamaica on the 9th August 1992, however five years previous to that he had visited the UK to take part in a veterans reggae performance concert in London, an event that he received no money for and paid all his own travelling expenses.

THE ETHIOPIANS

The Ethiopians were formed by Leonard Dillon a native of Port Antonio, Jamaica, who was born on the 9th December 1942. Dillon's early influence in the world of music came from the church before moving to Kingston in 1963.

A chance discussion with Peter Tosh who then introduced Dillon to The Wailers gained him an appointment with Clement 'Coxone' Dodd. The other members of the group were Stephen Taylor and Aston Morris. The group began recording for Dodd as early as 1966.

After Morris the group songwriter left The Ethiopians began recording at Dynamic Studios. They later released the time honoured classic hit Train To Skaville issued on the Rio label during 1967, a record that made it to number 40 in the UK chart in September that year.

Further ska classics followed including Engine 54 and The Whip. 1968 saw the release of their early reggae hit the ghetto lament Everything Crash, the track later covered by Prince Buster was released in the UK in 1970 on JJ Records, prefix JJ-3303. The song was criticising the political situation in Jamaica at a time when power and water were being rationed, a move that lead to unrest and in one incident 31 people were shot by the police.

Dillon continued to change producer and between 1969 and 1971 The Ethiopians released material under several producers with singles released on Nu-Beat, Trojan, Bamboo, Duke Reid, GG, Treasure Isle, Big Shot, Explosion and Song Bird. One of the most notable recordings Lot Wife was released on Song Bird SB-1062 in 1971.

The group released two albums on Trojan, in 1969 Reggae Power TTL 10 and Woman Capture Man TBL 112 in 1970.

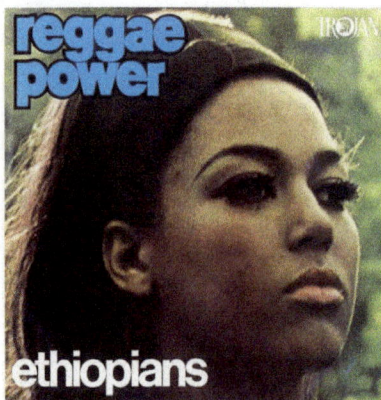

ROY SHIRLEY

Roy Shirley was born on the 18th July 1944 in Kingston's Trench Town where he grew up. His early recordings were never released so he joined Leslie Kong with his first record co-arranged with his close friend Jimmy Cliff. After a spell with Ken Boothe he joined the original Uniques. In 1966 he recorded Hold Them said to be the first record to slow down the infectious ska beat, therefore creating rocksteady. The story goes that the song just wouldn't work with ska so Gibbs suggested he slowed down the rhythm, a move that inadvertently created a massive hit in Jamaica.

With no further success following that release Roy teamed up with Bunny Lee. During 1968 he set up his own Public label releasing amongst others Flying Reggae and Prophecy Fulfilling. A Jamaican hit came in 1971 with A Sugar. Roy Shirley wrote the lyrics to the song and asked a deejay Altyman Reid to sing it, but there was a problem with some of the vocals so the producer asked Roy to sing it again. The record was released in the UK in 1972 on both Trojan's Green Door GD-4026 and Pama's Punch PH-108. The original Jamaican release gives credit to both Roy Shirley and Altyman Reid.

KEN BOOTHE

Ken Boothe was born in Denham Town, Kingston in 1948. His recording career began as one half of the duo formed with his friend Stranger Cole, releasing recordings under the title Stranger & Ken. Ken's solo career was launched while working with Clement 'Coxone' Dodd, releasing several records including the popular single The Train Is Coming, backed by The Wailers.

In 1970 Ken switched to Leslie Kong's Beverley's Records and met with immediate success with the launch of Freedom Street. Released in the UK on Trojan TR-7756, and Why Bay Why with the latter featured on a compilation album titled Reggae Party, produced by Leslie Kong and released courtesy of Trojan Records in the UK on the Music For Pleasure (MFP) budget album MFP 5176, in 1970.

The tragic and untimely death of Leslie Kong in 1971 had far reaching effects on many artists such as Desmond Dekker and Ken Boothe who continued recording for various producers. Ken had to wait a further two years beyond the golden age of reggae for chart success, but when it came it was huge.

His lightened version of reggae awarded the fading Trojan a number 1 hit in the UK with TR-7920, Everything I Own. A sweetened adaptation of the original release was hastily re- launched with the same prefix as the record became popular, aiding its airplay and progress up the chart. Produced by Lloyd Charmers the record was unusual as the title Everything I Own is never mentioned on the release as Ken referred to anything I own. The record remained at number 1 for three weeks in 1974 and although it only charted for twelve weeks six of those were in the top five.

PHYLLIS DILLON

Phyllis Dillon was born in Linstead St. Catherine, Jamaica on the 1st January 1948 and was very much influenced by American singers Connie Francis and Dion Warwick. As has happened with many famous reggae artists Phyllis began here musical career singing at talent shows and it was at one of those competitions that Duke Reid session guitarist Lynn Taitt discovered Phyllis.

At the tender age of 19 she recorded her first single for Duke Reid on Treasure Isle, Don't Stay Away featuring Tommy McCook and The Supersonics. Her original recording of Its Rocking Time was later used by Alton Ellis as Rocksteady. Another of her popular recordings during the rocksteady era was Perfidia.

From 1967 until 1971 she lead a double life, living in New York but returning to Kingston twice a year to continue recording for Duke Reid. Treasure Isle released an album in 1970 titled One Life To Live.

1971 saw the release of one of her biggest UK successes with the title track One Life To Live, One Love To Give released on Treasure Isle TI-7058, with the track making it onto Trojan's very impressive Club Reggae Volume 2. By the time of the release of Midnight Confession on Treasure Isle TI-7070 in 1972 Phyllis had already decided to retire from the recording industry whilst still only 23. In 1998 Phyllis returned to the recording studio to work once again with Lynn Taitt.

The world of reggae lost one of its most enduring talents when Phyllis died of cancer at the age of 56 in 2004.

THE MELODIANS

The band were formed in the Greenwich Town area of Kingston in 1965 by Tony Brevett, Brent Dowe and Trevor McNaughton and had their first record cut at Coxone Dodd's famous Studio One. The latter part of the rocksteady era saw the release of several excellent Jamaican hit singles on Duke Reid's Treasure Isle, most notably, You Have Caught Me, I'll Get Along Without You, You Don't Need Me and A Little Nut Tree released on Doctor Bird DB-1125, in 1968.

Their biggest commercial success came when they joined forces with Leslie Kong, who was by now enjoying unprecedented international success for a Jamaican producer, with the release of Sweet Sensation in 1969. The record was issued in the UK by Trojan on TR-695 and spent one week in the UK chart In January 1970, later that year it featured on Trojan's first Reggae Chartbusters album. The record had an equally impressive B side with It's My Delight. Another notable release on Trojan with two excellent offerings was Rock It With Me on TR-7764 with the flip side featuring Oh Say Darling Say.

Rivers Of Babylon followed the same year, a massive Jamaican hit and a popular song in the UK released on Summit SUM-8508. Despite failing to chart it enjoyed international success featuring on the outstanding soundtrack of the Jamaican film The Harder They Come.

As with many musicians The Melodians didn't escape the effect of the untimely death of Leslie Kong in 1971, eventually moving to record with Lee 'Scratch' Perry and Byron Lee.

Their lead singer Brent Dowe released a solo recording in 1971, a cover of Dawn's Knock Three Times, that seemed to suit the pop-reggae idiom superbly. The record produced by Leslie Kong was released on Summit SUM-8521 with the track featuring on the superb Trojan Club Reggae Volume 2 the same year.

SLIM SMITH

Slim Smith has often been described as the greatest vocalist to emerge during the rocksteady years. Born in Kingston in 1948 the world of reggae lost another of its famous sons as early as 1973. Despite this several great reggae tracks remain as his legacy. He began his recording career with The Techniques singing as lead vocalist and recording under Duke Reid on his Treasure Isle label.

In 1967 he established an association with Bunny Lee and reformed The Uniques. The highly successful My Conversation was issued on Island WIP-3122. After releasing more hit singles and a successful album Slim left the group to pursue a solo career remaining with Bunny Lee. Everybody Needs Love was released on Lee's Unity label UN-504 in 1968. The single The Time Has Come was released on Pama PM-850 and also on Trojan's Explosion label prefix EX-2074 the same year. The album Just A Dream was released on Trojan TRLS 186 in 1972 and also on Pama prefix PMLP 3242.

Unable to gain entry to his parents house he broke a window badly cutting his arm. He bled to death before he could receive treatment. His death at the time stunned Jamaica and the world of reggae.

PAT KELLY

Pat Kelly was born in 1949 in Kingston Jamaica. His big break in the music industry came when Slim Smith left The Techniques in 1967. His falsetto voice harmonized well and Pat continued where Slim had left off. In 1968 he took on a solo career moving to Bunny Lee's studio.

Working with Bunny 'Striker' Lee he released in his homeland How Long Will It Take. The record became the biggest selling Jamaican single of 1968. When released in the UK on Pama's Gas label GAS-115 it was believed to have been the first reggae record to be overdubbed with strings. UN-511 the Twelfth Of Never has been well documented as having the label crediting Max Romeo but was in reality sung by Pat Kelly. Bunny Lee had released Pat Kelly's rocksteady version on Island WI-3124 in 1968 and the vocals were allegedly overdubbed on to a reggae rhythm for the 1969 release.

Pat Kelly was reportedly offered a lucrative contract to sign to Apple Records but had to decline due to his contract commitment to Pama. Bunny 'Striker' Lee has described Pat Kelly as being one of the greatest singers ever.

THE HIGH PRIEST OF REGGAE

LAUREL AITKEN

Lorenzo Aitken better known as Laurel was born in April 1927. Unlike most of his compatriots it wasn't until the late 30s that his family settled in Jamaica. He moved to England in 1960 but returned to Jamaica to release a plethora of ska and then rocksteady working alongside Duke Reid with backing supplied by The Skatalites. Laurel returned to England to work with Pama, recording tracks issued mainly on the Nu Beat label, including Fire In Me Wire, Pussy Price on NU Beat NB-046 and Skinhead Train NB-047 in 1969.

In 1970 he released the classic single Guilty on Pama's Camel label under the guise of Tiger. Several other singles followed including It's Too Late on Trojan TR-7826, which deservedly had an outing on their Club Reggae Volume 2 TBL 164 in 1971. Kingston Town was issued on Doctor Bird DB-1203B in 1969, not the Lord Creator version but a cover of Harry Belafonte's 1956 recording Jamaica Farewell. An album The High Priest Of Reggae was released on Pama PSP 1012 in 1970. It was Laurel who brought Ian Smith's all-white Inner Mind reggae band to Pama's attention. He continued to perform classic ska and reggae until his death in 2005 when at the age of 87 he suffered a heart attack and passed way.

14'6 **19'11** **99½** NEW PENCE

THE ALBUMS

Trojan Records had dominated the UK reggae market since their launch in 1968 to cater for the growing West Indian community and had released over 180 singles on various labels by the dawn of 1969. Traditionally Jamaican music, ska and rocksteady, found success in the singles market with albums seen as a luxury item. Trojan launched their TRL album series as early as 1968 with just a handful of releases issued by the dawn of 1970. Pama had also released their SECO series featuring the best of their subsidiary labels including Unity, Crab, Nu-Beat, Gas and Bullet.

Trojan helped to transform the album market by launching the budget price series TTL in early 1969. Its inaugural release Tighten Up was a compilation of the most popular recent releases, a format that would give wider access to the music. Priced at just 14/6d it was a must have for the skinheads. The budget priced albums had a modest expectation from Trojan but soon became a winning formula and the Tighten Up series had arrived.

Reggae Chartbusters followed with the album that brought the sounds of reggae to the mainstream and made the records that were hitting the charts or just bubbling under the top 50 available through the main high street outlets. Most importantly it enabled the emerging skinheads to own their favourite tunes for a modest outlay of 19/11d. The first was released in 1970 and showcased the original tracks that made the breakthrough from the clubs and disco's and brought the sound of reggae to a wider audience, a sound that the skinheads had fully embraced by the summer of 69, starting a love affair that was to last until 1972.

The Club Reggae series launched in 1971 was compiled as the title suggests from singles that were most popular in the clubs, giving a different offering to the chart hits that were outpouring from Trojan at the time, perhaps a more non commercial sound. The best of the compilation albums now follows with some fantastic collections of early reggae sounds to appreciate, beginning with the original Tighten Up series.

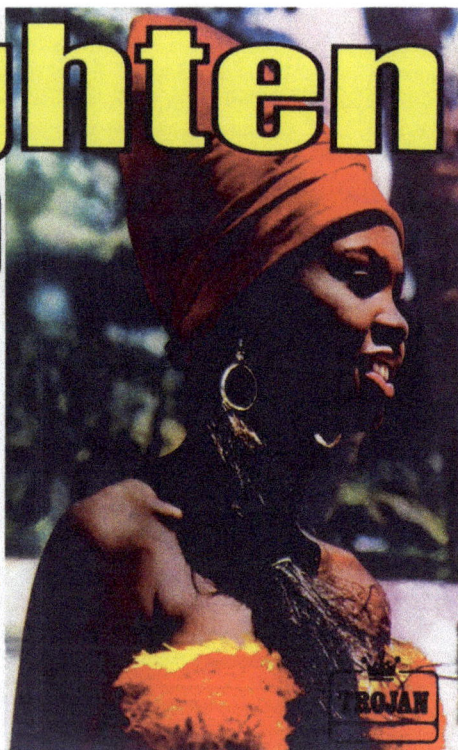

TIGHTEN UP
TROJAN RECORDS TTL 1 1969
(Re Issued as TBL 120)

TIGHTEN UP

14⁶

The opening track would inevitably have to be **Tighten Up** the record that gave the series its name. A tune with rocksteady and early reggae influences from the stable of Lee 'Scratch' Perry. The Untouchables recorded several tracks for Lee before perusing solo careers as Jimmy London and Billy Dyce. Joya Landis an American based singer had spent time in Kingston and recorded some songs for Duke Reid; one was her inspirational version of **Kansas City**.

Lee 'Scratch' Perry forged a long association with Trojan and is here enjoying an outing on track three with a tune that needs no introduction, a fine instrumental release from Val Bennett, **Spanish Harlem**.

Another of Lee 'Scratch' Perry's productions feature as track four, a Stevie Wonder number, **A Place In The Sun**. Covered by David Isaacs, the song was recorded at Coxsone Dodd's Studio One in Jamaica during 1968. **Win Your Love For Me**, a Sam Cooke number, was produced by Lynford Anderson and was credited to George A Penny. Side one concludes with **Donkey Returns** by Brother Dan All Stars, AKA Robert Thompson, who was resident in the UK taking influence from Trojan's successful Ride Your Donkey by The Tennors.

Side two gets the proceedings underway with **Ob-La-De, Ob-La-Da**, a version of The Beatles heavily influenced rocksteady hit penned by Paul McCartney making reference to Desmond Dekker. The reggae version somehow never quite cut it.

Another outing from Joya Landis, a follow up to Kansas City, was **Angel Of The Morning**, a song that proved even more popular being a fabulous lilting version of a recording from a US top ten pop hit of the same year. **Fat Man** by veteran Derrick Morgan was an updated version of a song he had recorded way back in 1960 as a teenager, a record that became one of Jamaica's biggest hits of that year.

Byron Lee And The Dragonaires began their career on the hotel circuit. They featured in the James Bond film Dr No, set in Jamaica, and by the time they had released their own version of Booker T & The MG's **Soul Limbo** the group had become steadfastly established. Incidentally the MG's track was used for decades by the BBC for their cricket theme tune, ironic given the corporations early reluctance to give airplay to West Indian music.

The Kingstonians featured on the next two Tighten Up volumes but their first offering in the series **Mix It Up** was a sound typical of the time, lively and exciting, a fusion of rocksteady and the emerging sounds of reggae.

The album came to a close with **Watch This Sound** from The Uniques, a famous trio composed of Slim Smith, Lloyd Charmers 'Tyrell' and Martin 'Jimmy' Riley.

The first album of Tighten Up proved to be a successful formula and within a few months a second volume was launched, the series being the spring board for the future compilation albums in the Chartbusters and Club Reggae series. The inaugural Tighten Up released during 1969 as TTL 1 appeared on the all orange label. The Album was then re-issued as TBL 120 in 1970 on the more familiar orange and white label. Volume 2 and 3 were initially issued with the TTL prefix, later to resurface on the popular TBL series.

SIDE ONE

1. TIGHTEN UP (Prod. Lee Perry)   Untouchables
2. KANSAS CITY (Prod. Duke Reid)   Joya Landis
3. SPANISH HARLEM (Prod. Lee Perry)   Val Bennett
4. A PLACE IN THE SUN (Prod. Lee Perry)   David Isaacs
5. WIN YOUR LOVE (Prod. Winford Anderson) George A. Penny
6. DONKEY RETURNS (Prod. Bunny) Brother Dan All Stars

SIDE TWO

1. OB-LA-DI, OB-LA-DA (Prod. Les Carter)   Joyce Bond
2. ANGEL OF THE MORNING (Prod. Les Reed) Joya Landis
3. FAT MAN (Prod. Clancy Anderson)   Derrick Morgan
4. SOUL LIMBO (Prod. Byron Lee)   Byron Lee
5. MIX IT UP (Prod. J.J. Johnson)   Kingstonians
6. WATCH THIS SOUND (Prod. Winston Lowe)   Uniques

HAVE YOU HEARD THESE OTHER GREAT ALBUMS?

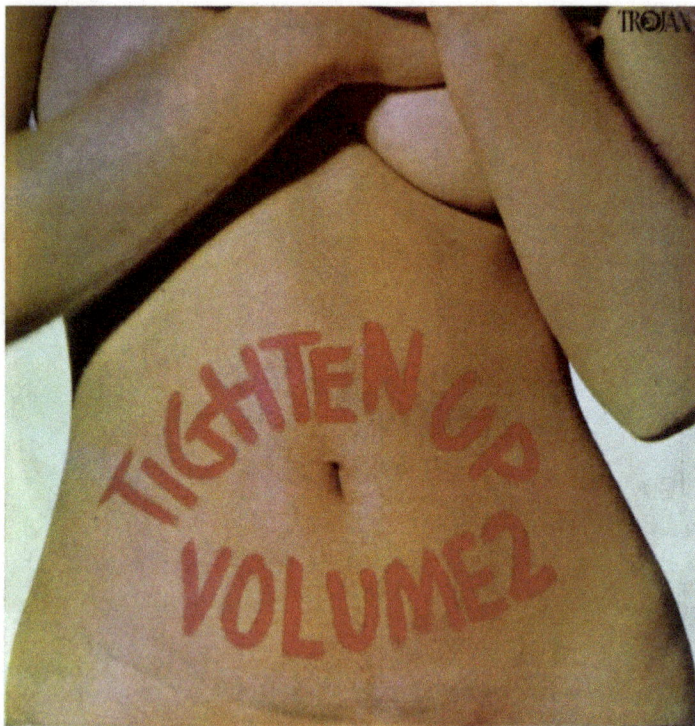

TIGHTEN UP VOLUME 2
TROJAN RECORDS TTL 7 1969
(Re Issued as TBL 131)

TIGHTEN UP Volume 2

14⁶ (in green circle)

Probably the best, but almost certainly the most relevant as the second in the series was launched at a time when reggae and the skinheads were truly entwined in a musical love affair. Few would know, and how could they, that this would be the height of that love affair. The album was a must have for the clean cut cropped headed youth of the day.

The Pioneers had a popular hit with **Long Shot kick The Bucket**, one of three chart successes to feature on Volume 2, making it onto the Chartbuster series along with Reggae In Your Jeggae and Return Of Django. Long Shot kick De Bucket, to give it the original Jamaican title, tells of the demise of Long Shot after 202 races at Kingston's famous Caymanas Park race course.

Rudy Mills **John Jones** was a hit in Jamaica and quickly released in the UK where it became a firm favourite with the skinheads, though never gaining chart success. However that isn't what Tighten Up was all about, it was about boss sounds that found favour with the skinheads and their West Indian friends. **Fire Corner** from King Stitt, a D.J. who perhaps paved the way for the toaster to make the transition to recording artist, although the album credits Clancy Eccles, and **Wreck A Buddy**, a risqué outing from The Soul Sisters continues the no nonsense reggae theme.

Dandy's **Reggae In Your Jeggae** comes next, a lyrically challenged but none the less highly infectious success, the track released on Thompson's own Downtown label, a subsidiary of Trojan. **Fattie Fattie** completes an impressive collection on side one, yet another outstanding offering from Clancy Eccles.

Return Of Django from Lee Perry's Upsetters, one of the other chart success to feature on this volume, gets side two under way and was Trojan's biggest hit to date reaching number 5 in the British charts.

The Kingstonians feature again this time with **Sufferer**, a record that had become a huge hit in Jamaica. They would return again on the forthcoming Volume 3. Joya Landis also featured on the first album in the series and returns with **Moon Light Lover**.

Come Into My Parlour by The Bleechers was a lively outing as was **Them A Laugh And A Ki Ki** from The Soulmates, a group made up of Glen 'Capo' Adams, Alvin Lewis, Max Romeo and George Agard from The Pioneers, who penned the song.

An infectious instrumental **Live Injection** from the Upsetters is track six and concludes the proceedings in a most appropriate fashion on what was the true sound of skinhead reggae.

The tracks on Volume 2 were danceable and energetic and at the budget price distribution of the incessant rhythms was available on the high street for the first time. Reggae was now being sold by one of the major record outlets of the time, Woolworths, for just 14/6. Tighten Up Volume 2 proved to be a huge success with the third in the series released in 1970.

The labels on TTL 7 and TBL 131 refer to just Tighten Up.

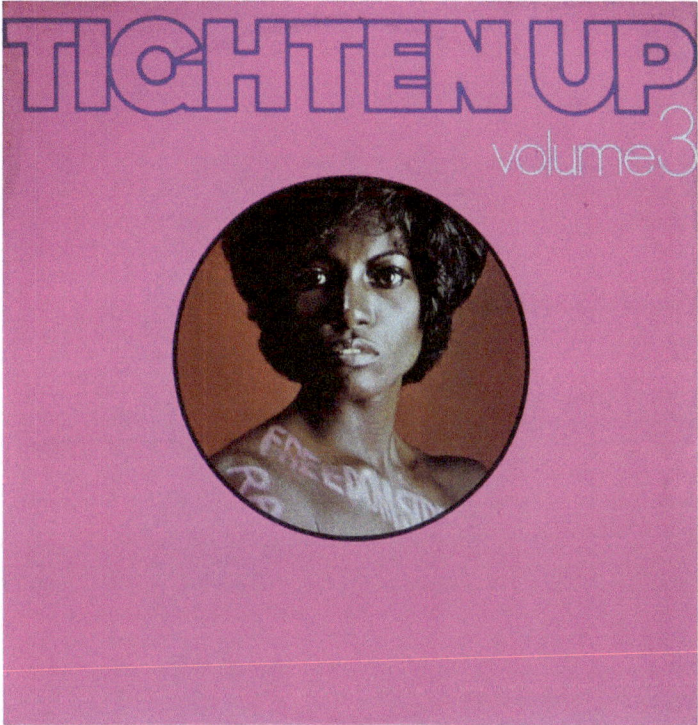

TIGHTEN UP VOLUME 3
TROJAN RECORDS TBL 145 1970

TIGHTEN UP Volume 3

TBL 145 was a reissue of TTL 32 with an altered sleeve.

Trojan had launched the series in 1969 originally on the budget TTL label. Tighten Up TTL 1 showcased the most popular reggae records available in the UK at the time. The decision was taken to continue with the series so here is volume 3.

The Maytals get the proceedings underway with their only UK chart hit **Monkey Man** which reached number 47 in May 1970 and needs no introduction. The second offering comes from the Upsetters featuring on vocals Dave Barker, one half of Dave & Ansel Collins. The Upsetters had enjoyed chart success in 1969 with the instrumental Return of Django but **Shocks Of A Mighty** is a completely different offering showcasing the vocal talents of Dave Barker that would later come to the fore on Double Barrel.

Ken Boothe's career began way back in the early sixties as part of the duo Stranger & Ken. He later began recording solo with his own inimitable style of soulful vocals displayed here on the Trojan release of **Freedom Street**. Ken went on to achieve cult status with his massive UK number one Everything I Own, a recording that topped the charts for three weeks in 1974.

Next up is Dandy with **Raining In My Heart**. The prolific producer, writer and singer had previously enjoyed success with Reggae In Your Jeggae and Rudy A Message To You. Like Ken Boothe he was destined to enjoy further chart success during the early 1970s after the original golden age of reggae had come to an end.

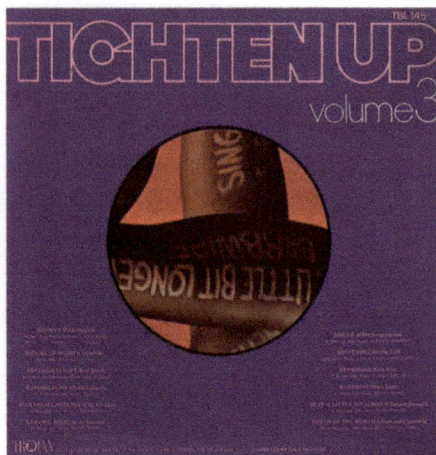

The Man From Carolina is next up from the GG All Stars, a favourite with the skinheads but failed to chart. Side one concludes with an instrumental **Leaving Rome** from Jo Jo Bennett who was an established Jamaican musician with the rhythm the same as used on the recording Rome, a Lloyd Jones song issued on Pama's Bullet BU-429 in 1970.

Side two sees the return of a group having featured on the first two Tighten Up volumes, The Kingstonians, this time with **Singer Man**, a track released on the Song Bird label in 1970. Jimmy Cliff needs no introduction as the singer songwriter later to be actor had already featured on Trojan's Reggae Chartbusters with Wonderful World Beautiful People. **Suffering In The Land** was his penultimate release on Trojan before his move to Island Records where he would enjoy chart success once more with Wild World before his foray into the film industry.

King Stitt was a disc jockey in Kingston and successful singer with his single Fire Corner in 1969 toasting over reggae rhythms. Further success followed for King Stitt, sometimes referred to as the 'Ugly One' with the track featured here **Herbsman**.

Songs with innuendoes in the lyrics have always proved popular with Prince Buster and Max Romeo to name but two leading the way. That risqué theme continues here with Nora Dean's **Barbwire**, a big hit both in the UK and back in Jamaica. The penultimate offering comes from Delano Stewart who began his career as a member of The Gaylads, although he frequently released solo efforts as here with **Stay A Little Bit Longer**, a song with an up tempo beat. The album concludes with a very popular recording amongst the skinheads, **Queen Of The World**, by Lloyd & Claudette, but despite that popularity the record failed to chart.

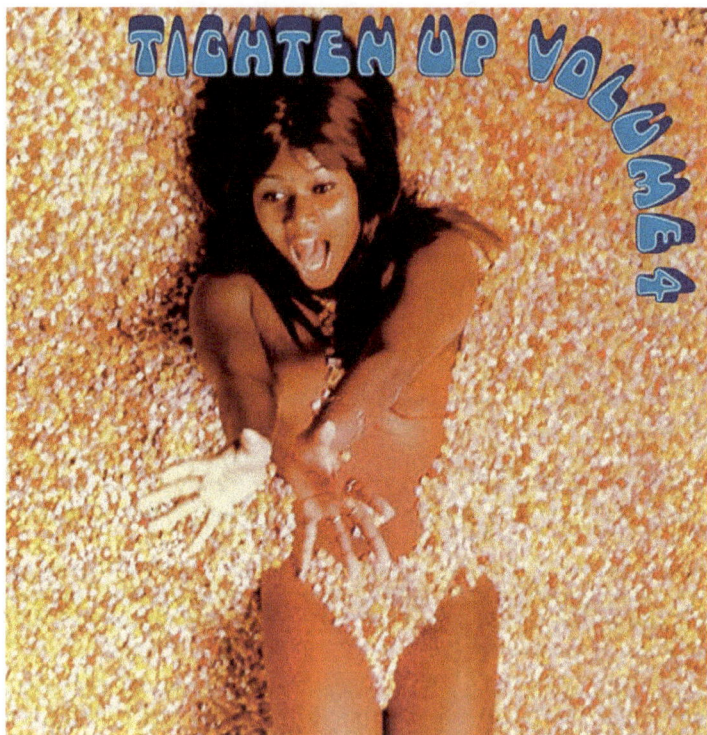

TIGHTEN UP VOLUME 4
TROJAN RECORDS TBL 163 1971

99½
NEW PENCE

TIGHTEN UP Volume 4

By 1971 reggae had been well and truly accepted into the mainstream although influences were beginning to creep in that would eventually, but not just yet, lead to the undoing of its early success. The album opens with the Rastafarian influenced **Blood And Fire** from Niney The Observer. Track two needs no introduction and went on to feature on the soundtrack of the forthcoming film The Harder They Come. **Johnny Too Bad** was released on the Dynamic label by The Slickers, a record drawing attention to the Jamaican Rude Boys who were responsible for violence and crime in their homeland. The legendary group The Ethiopians from the sixties came in with a distinctive sound on **The Selah** and feature again on side two with **Good Ambition**.

The unmistakable sounds of the Maytals keep the infectious rhythm running with their up tempo **One Eye Enos**, continuing where they had left off with Monkey Man, a track that featured on Volume 3. The next track highlights Merlene Webber performing well with a heavily accentuated rhythm on her **Hard Life**. The first side concludes with Judy Mowatt proclaiming that **I Shall Sing**, though sung under the pseudonym of Jean with the backing from The Gaytones. Judy became a member of Bob Marley's I Three's with fellow vocalist Rita Marley and Marcia Griffiths.

Side two opens with a classic number from Hopeton Lewis showcasing his talented vocal skills as he slows the pace on **Grooving Out On Life**. The Pioneers also featured on Tighten Up Volume 2 and continued their catchy rhythms with **Starvation**, a track highlighting the plight in Africa. **Bush Doctor** was an offering from the British based session players The Music Doctors. Track four is the second offering from The Ethiopians, a track that continued in their traditional style.

Lloydie & The Lowbites became infamous for the risqué album Censored and The Lowbites feature here with **I Got It** . Censored was issued through Trojan on the Lowbite label prefix LOW-001 but a second album volume 2 although planned was never issued. Pama had earlier released an album of ribald but infectious skinhead reggae material titled Birth Control on Pama SECO 32 in 1970, and Censored came off second best. The title track was utilised by The Specials for their number one hit Too Much Too Young a decade later. **Stand By Your Man** brought about a total change of style from Marlene Webber with her resounding version of a famous Tammy Wynett number and concluded yet another exceptional collection of reggae.

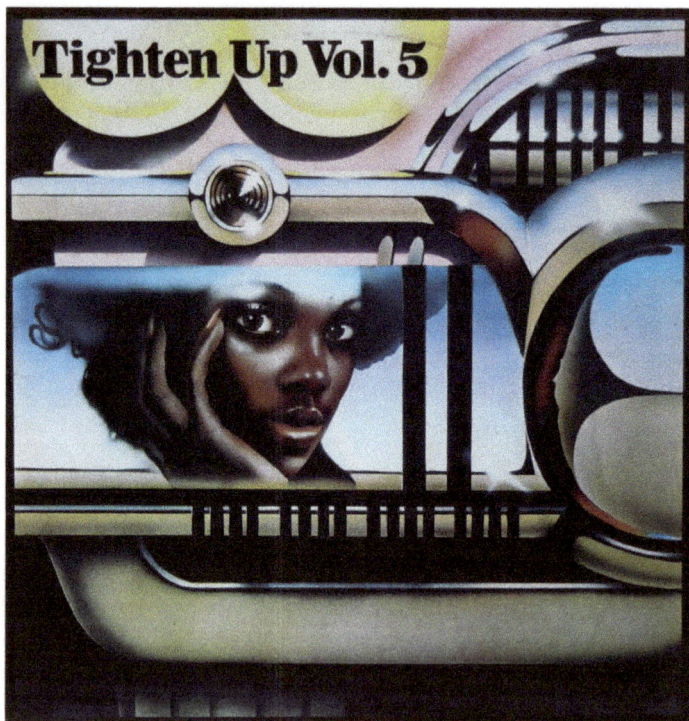

TIGHTEN UP VOLUME 5
TROJAN RECORD TBL 165 1971

TIGHTEN UP volume 5

Number five in the series came some three years after the inaugural release, the series having gone from strength to strength, although perhaps not known at the time this would be the last truly authentic offering in the series.

The opening track featured Delroy Wilson with his classic **Better Must Come**. Delroy had started out at Coxone Dodd's Studio One and was now somewhat of a veteran on the reggae circuit at the young age of 22. The track was released on the Jackpot label, JP-763 in 1971.

Track two, **In Paradise**, is a soulful ballad in Jackie Edwards imitable style and was issued on Trojan TR-7833. The song was a duo performed with Judy Mowatt, although credited on the label as Julie Anne. Next up is a change of pace from Clancy Eccles prodigies The Dynamites with their own rendition of **Hullo Mother**, a somewhat interesting instrumental. Clancy himself is up next with **Rod Of Correction**, a distinctive Clancy rhythm with his characteristic vocals enduring throughout.

Dennis Alcapone comes in with his talk-over version of his fellow studio artist Eric Donaldson's rendition of Cherry Oh Baby. Dennis' distinctive vocals are showcased here on **Ripe Cherry**, the same combination was used on his famous Guns Don't Argue utilising Eric's Love Of The Common People. A medley concludes side one from Errol Dunkley aptly titled **Three In One**. The single was a collection of old hits released on Big BG-327 with the B side titled One In Three.

Side two gets under way with a record that suited the pop reggae idiom, **Joy To The World** from Julien And The Chosen Few, actually Julie Anne who as we have already discovered on the album is in fact Judy Mowatt. The record was produced by Sonia Pottinger and released on High Note HS-054.

Next up is **Know For I**, a track from Bongo Herman and Bunny who as the sleeve notes mentioned sound very much like the Ethiopians on this infectious medium tempo number. No mistaking who is up next on track three, it is of course The Maytals with their **It's You**, slightly slower than their normal pace but still maintaining an intense feel.

The pace changes again with track four from Jimmy London with his rendition of the Simon & Garfunkel classic **Bridge Over Troubled Waters**. The track was released on Randy's RN-507 in 1970, and incidentally the inspiration for an album of the same name issued during1972.

The penultimate is another well know cover, this time **Shaft,** from the Chosen Few, the well known theme tune from the popular film of the day. The album concludes with a record already well documented in the book **Duppy Conqueror** from Bob Marley And The Wailers.

There were reputed to have been three different pressing of Tighten Up Volume 5 TBL 165. The pressing listed here but also one with Peter Tosh's Memphis in place of Duppy Conqueror and another with Know For I featuring twice.

TIGHTEN UP VOLUME 6
TROJAN RECORDS TBL 185 1972

TIGHTEN UP Volume 6

Although not the last in the series volume 6 was the last that held true to the previous offerings at a time when reggae was rapidly declining in favour with the skinheads, the youth who four years earlier helped elevate reggae to the world stage. However sweetening many of the releases with sophisticated string arrangements would prove costly for Trojan at a time when the traditional skinhead movement was also in decline.

The collection here although not quite on par with previous compilations in the Tighten Up series does contain a few more gems. The Maytones maintain an incessant rhythm on **As Long As You Love Me** released on the GG label in 1972. The Maytones were formed in the late sixties and comprised Vernon Buckley and Gladstone Grant, both originating from May Pen, Clarendon, Jamaica which had inspired the their name.

Harry J All Stars **Down Side Up** was another notable offering from the talented producer Harry Johnson and was released in 1972 on the Harry J label. Side one ends with a chartbuster, a rare outing for Tighten Up, from Dandy AKA Robert Thompson to name just one. **Suzanne Beware Of The Devil** was a big hit for Dandy Livingstone in the late summer of 1972, one of the last as the golden age of reggae was drawing to a close. The only others to make the top 30 would be Johnny Nash, with There Are More Questions Than Answers, and Judge Dread with Big Seven, ironically using the same rhythm track featuring on **President Mash Up The Resident**, a good offering on the album from Shortie.

Side two kicked off with a cover version of Jimmy Cliff's **Struggling Man** by the British based group the Cimarons who performed admirably with a good up tempo version, although very pop influenced. Next The Maytals with **Redemption Song**, yet another excellent addition from the legendary group.

The penultimate track came from the soulful Jackie Edwards with **Who Told You So**. The album closes with a reverberating sound from Clancy Eccles in his usual upbeat quality vein with the rousing **Unite Tonight**.

To complete the album Trojan included **Pitta Patta** by Ernie Smith, **Do Your Thing** by the Chosen Few, **Breezing** from Mike Chung and **Hot Bomb** by I Roy & The Jumpers.

The Tighten Up series continued with another two volumes with volume 7 and 8 acting as an outlet for Trojan's continued production into 1973. A further album was scheduled, Tighten Up volume 9, TBL 211, but was never issued.

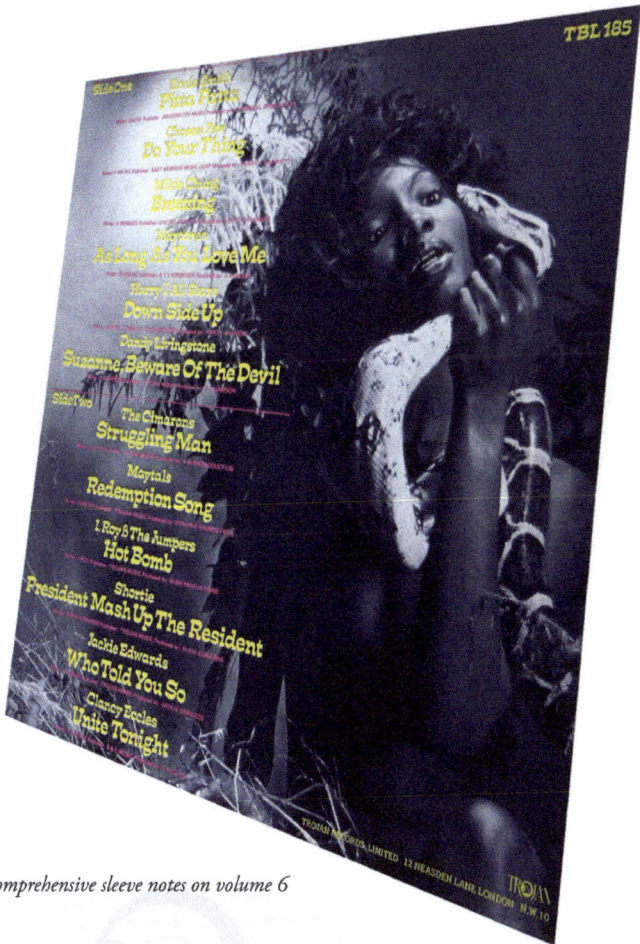

No comprehensive sleeve notes on volume 6

REGGAE CHARTBUSTERS
TROJAN RECORDS TBL 105   1970

19'11

REGGAE CHARTBUSTERS

The Chartbusters series is launched with **Wonderful World Beautiful People** by Jimmy Cliff. Released in 1969 the record made it to number 6 in the UK chart, one of three chart successes for Jimmy over the next year or so. Following up on track two is a record by producer Dandy, **Reggae In Your Jeggae**. Although it never made the British charts it was a popular choice with the skinheads. Next up was **Israelites** released on Pyramid in 1968, the record seen by most as the defining influence for reggae. On its release it had little airplay but became popular with the skinheads who heard it in the clubs and disco's. It started to receive air play in early 1969 presenting a total new sound to those not familiar with Jamaican music. Israelites entered the charts in March 1969 and by mid April was sitting proudly at the top of the pile, the first reggae number one in the UK.

The skinheads who embraced reggae from its evolvement from rocksteady in 1968 had a tribute paid to them with the next track **Skinhead Moonstomp**. The moonstomp theme no doubt influenced from the events of July 1969 and man's first landing on the moon. It was a foot stomping offering from Symarip, popular of course with the skinheads but never breaking into the top 50. The famous album followed with a host of bracer snapping tracks suited to the skinhead theme. The penultimate track on side one features The Pioneers **Poor Rameses**, a record released after their massive hit Long Shot Kick The Bucket that features on side two.

Side one concludes with an instrumental that became an anthem for the skinheads, **Liquidator** by Harry J All Stars, a Harry J production who also had his own record label back in Jamaica. The single was released in the UK through Trojan on the Harry J label in 1969. Liquidator peaked at number 9 in November 1969 and spent some twenty weeks on the chart. November 1969 was a month that saw three reggae records in the top 10 and a further two within the top 50.

Liquidator was adopted as an anthem played before matches by some football clubs but was dropped as it was said to have encouraged violence amongst rival skinheads. 1970 was truly a heady time of chart success for Trojan and reggae in general.

Side two opens with another instrumental, this time by the Upsetters. **Return Of Django** was released on Trojan's Upsetter label in 1969 and the title track for the LP TRL 19 released by Trojan in 1970, again on the Upsetter label. Composed by Lee 'Scratch' Perry in the true vein of pure reggae it spent a respectable three weeks at number 5 in November 1969.

Another popular choice for the skinheads was Tony Tribe's rendition of **Red, Red, Wine** . The single featured on track two with the original release on the Downtown label DT-419 in 1969 having some copies miss credited to Tony Tripe. Despite its popularity and an appearance on Top of The Pops dressed as a skinhead it only made it to number 46. Another record followed but tragically the singer was killed in a car crash in 1970.

Third up needs no introduction, the 1969 release by The Pioneers telling the tale of **Long Shot Kick The Bucket**. Recorded for Beverley's as Long Shot Kick De Bucket the record had a true Jamaican feel to it. The single received little air play on its release but by the autumn of 69 it was added to the BBC play list. Reaching number 21 in November it charted for a total of eleven weeks. Track four features another instrumental to find popularity with the skinheads, this time it was **Elizabethan Reggae**. The single was released on Trojan's Duke label and made it to number 14 in March 1970. The record was the only chart success for Boris Gardner of the era but he achieved a number one spot with a vocal offering almost two decades later.

Desmond Dekker makes a second appearance up next with **It Miek,** sometimes spelt It Mek, released in 1969 as a follow up to Desmond's massive hit Israelites, a record incidentally that was still on the charts when It Mek was climbing. The single spent two weeks at number 7 in July of that year. **Sweet Sensation** was a record that managed just one week on the chart at number 41 in January 1970 and completes the line up of a dozen chartbusters. A first rate offering from The Melodians being a fast moving melodic reggae number in a similar vein to many tracks that feature on the forthcoming and eagerly awaited Reggae Chartbusters volume 2. The Melodians later recorded their biggest success Rivers Of Babylon, a song that featured on the soundtrack of the forthcoming Jamaican film The Harder They Come.

REGGAE CHARTBUSTERS VOLUME 2
TROJAN RECORDS TBL 147 1970

REGGAE CHARTBUSTERS Volume 2

Following on from the highly successful Reggae Chartbusters a second volume was issued in 1970 on Trojan's budget TBL series priced at 19/11, or as we would say today 99 pence. The series proved popular as it allowed the emerging skinheads to get hold of all their favourite reggae records as many could not afford the scores of singles that were being released at this time, remembering volume one was only issued in April of the same year.

It was obvious by now that reggae was not to be the flash in the pan that several commentators of the time were predicting. Reggae had moved on a pace from the original releases on volume one as that album covered records released in 1969 through to 1970.

The Chartbusters albums should never be underestimated for their promotion of reggae as for the first time reggae was being sold in the mainstream outlets, and was now being heard outside of the school disco and the clubs for the first time.

As the hits continued to come reggae began to receive far more airplay at the BBC and began to lose the stigma of being crude and basic, with this volume highlighting the melodic harmonies and strings of the evolving music. Not perhaps as authentic as the original sounds of 1969 but nevertheless reggae was now appealing to the masses and enjoying a period of unprecedented success.

The first track needed no introduction, nor the artist, it had reached a respectful number 2 in the charts and rewarded Desmond Dekker with his first chart hit since parting from The Aces. Desmond had previously enjoyed fleeting chart success with The Aces in 1970 with Pickney Gal also featured on this album, and prior to that in 1967 with 007 and Israelites and It Miek in 1969. **You Can Get It If You Really Want** was a huge hit for Desmond, a song penned by Jimmy Cliff, and another song to feature on the soundtrack of The Harder They Come albeit Jimmy Cliff's original version. Following his previous chart success Desmond had now moved to England where he would remain.

Second up is Freddie Notes And The Rudies with **Montego Bay**, just charting at number 45, being a cover of Bobby Bloom's version that enjoyed considerable chart success at the same time. The song tells of life in Montego Bay with the opening line telling that Vernon will meet him when his Boeing lands.

Track three had launched Nicky Thomas to a worldwide audience with **Love of The Common People**, a very melodic song that peaked at number 9 enjoying fourteen weeks on the charts earlier in 1970. Following the records success Nicky moved to England. It was however to be Nicky's only chart success but as has been said before good records do not always achieve charts recognition and Nicky continued to produce and record several excellent tracks before his untimely death in 1990.

Fourth up was **What Greater Love** by Teddy Brown who only released a few singles, this being his most popular with a follow up Rose Garden, tracks that were very pop- reggae influenced and very melodic. Teddy's voice was used on many records to help sweeten the sound.

Next comes **Pickney Gal** a hit for Desmond Dekker And The Aces earlier in the year, the last of Desmond's recordings with the Aces reaching number 42 in January 1970, before going solo with the release of You Can Get It If You Really Want. The concluding track of side one is **Message From A Blackman** by Derrick Harriott who enjoyed a good number of releases during the ska and rocksteady years. Message From A Blackman was released on the Song Bird label in 1970, an offering that was somewhat different than the rest of the tracks on this album delivering as the title suggests a message with a somewhat surreal feel to the record. Although selling well it never entered the British chart.

Side two kicks off again with a record that requires no introduction and very little explanation, **Young Gifted And Black** by Bob And Marcia. Bob is of course Bob Andy and Marcia is Marcia Griffiths both individual performers in their own right. The record was released on Trojan's Harry J label with strings added to the original Jamaican version, reaching a respectable number 5 and spending a creditable twelve weeks on the chart.

Track two, **Monkey Man** by Toots And The Maytals, was a Leslie Kong produced record although it has been said that Toots was having an affectionate dig at him. Surprisingly the record only achieved a number 47 in the UK and was the only British chart success for Toots and The Maytals. Now that old saying about not getting into the chart certainly runs true for The Maytals. They became one of the most popular and prolific reggae groups with their own distinctive style.

A complete change of style came next with a track from Horace Faith. **Black Pearl** was a record perhaps over cooked, and a far cry for the pure reggae that endeared the skinheads, amongst others. However it sold well and gained the only hit for Horace reaching number 13. It was described at the time as swamped with pop hooks, nevertheless it became a huge hit spending some ten weeks on the chart.

Nicky Thomas features again with his follow up to Love Of The Common People, an extremely hard act to follow and he never enjoyed its success with **God Bless The Children**. The record lacked the same melodic commercial appeal and failed to make the chart.

The penultimate offering, the second on the compilation from The Rudies, was **Patches**, a cover of a huge hit for Clarence Carter. A cover version of a pop hit in reggae was often released and did sometimes work, on this occasion it worked extremely well, despite this the record failed to provide a second chart success for The Rudies who shortly after reformed as Greyhound.

The album comes to a close with Jimmy Cliff's rendering of **Vietnam**, a hard hitting account of the troubles of the time. Surprisingly this was only Jimmy's second chart hit but not gaining the heady heights of his first, only reaching number 46, and charting for just three weeks. That completed the line up of Chartbusters but reggae was still at its height and more chart success was following on.

The charismatic 45 sleeve for the orange and white label promoted the albums available from Trojan at the budget price of just 19/11.

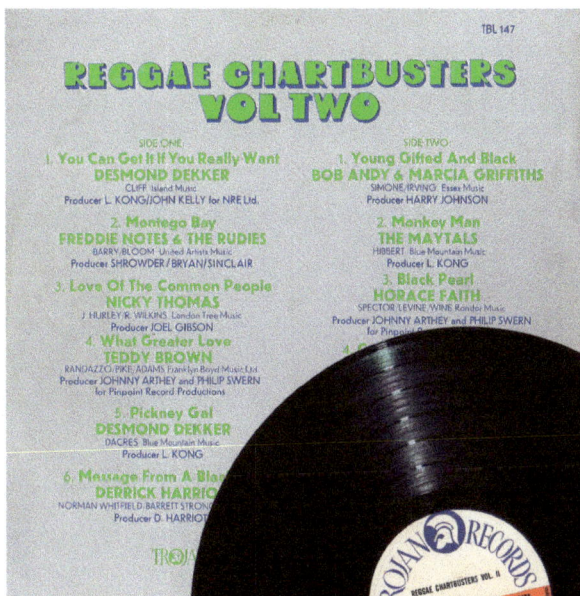

REGGAE CHARTBUSTERS VOLUME   3
TROJAN RECORDS TBL 169   1971

REGGAE CHARTBUSTERS Volume 3

The third and final in the series of Reggae Chartbusters continued the theme with the records that had entered the charts or flirted just outside. The difference in the style of reggae from that first volume is very evident here, the album kicking off with The Pioneers Jimmy Cliff penned song, **Let Your Yeah Be Yeah**.

A lot of water had flowed under the bridge since The Pioneers previous chart success with Long Shot Kick The Bucket back in 1969. This was a change in direction for The Pioneers who had several excellent releases since that hit including Black Bud and Samfie Man, but chart success had eluded them. Now offering a more pop driven string laden sound that brought them a top 5 hit in September 1971, spending twelve weeks on the chart.

Track two sees Nicky Thomas back following his Love Of The Common People with a somewhat different offering of an Aaron Neville tune but despite good sales it failed to make the charts. **Tell It Like It Is** was the A side of TR-7830 with the B side featuring BBC, the singer having a dig at the reluctance of the nations radio station to give reggae the airplay it deserved.

Track three was the second of the massive chart success for Dave & Ansel Collins with **Monkey Spanner**. A refreshing change for the purists of raw reggae, released on the Techniques label it was a true unpretentious sounding track with the opening line declaring that "This is a heavy, heavy monster sound". Monkey Spanner spent three weeks at number 7 in July 1971, however not quite reaching the lofty height of its predecessor earlier in the year.

Greyhound continue the commercial sounds on track four with **Follow The Leader**, but alas didn't follow on the previous success achieved with Black And White. The record was short of the brilliance of that previous offering but they enjoyed renewed chart success later with their rendition of Moon River, a track that would have almost certainly featured if there had been a follow up album Chartbusters Volume 4.

Track five sees another outing for Bob And Marcia following on from their previous hit Young Gifted And Black with **Pied Piper.** The record continued in the same melodic vein but with a change of content from their previous outing. As with several of their compatriots the follow up failed to emulate the previous offering but Pied Piper did achieve a respectable number 11 during July 1971, a month that saw three reggae records in the top 30. Side one is concluded with **One Big Happy Family** by Bruce Ruffin, a track fully aimed at the pop-reggae market, although it failed to achieve the same impact as his previous hit Rain with chart entry eluding him this time.

Side two begins with a number one, we have already covered Monkey Spanner but earlier in 71 **Double Barrel** introduced Dave And Ansel Collins, incidentally the duo who were assumed by many to be brothers were in fact Dave Barker and Ansel Collins. Double Barrel was a huge hit in Jamaica. Released in the UK on Trojan's Techniques label it was initially given little airplay but before long was storming the charts entering at 43 in March 1971, and by now receiving good coverage on radio. It reached the heady heights of number 1 in May where it remained for two weeks, spending seven weeks in the top 10 and a total of fifteen weeks on the chart.

Track two was performed by Daniel In The Lion's Den, AKA The Rudies. **Dancing In The Sun** continues the pop-reggae vein, a catchy tune featuring Carl Douglas who later found fame with Kung Fu Fighting. Moving onto track three we find Greyhound again with a single already mentioned.

It seems that the tracks for Chartbusters were not in chronological order but were set out to provide a good overall variety of reggae and it worked. **Black And White** was Greyhound first outing having reformed from The Rudies and was the first of three chart successes they would enjoy, the others mentioned previously were Moon River and later in 1972 they came again with I Am What I Am, a certainty for that elusive volume 4.

Dandy is next up with **Salt Of The Earth**. Dandy would have to wait until the summer of 1972 before enjoying chart success with Suzanne Beware Of The Devil as this bouncy number, a cover of a Jagger Richardson song, failed to chart. Track eleven is another from Bruce Ruffin, **Rain** . The track was released before his previous offering on the album but unlike One Big Happy Family it peaked at number 19 during May of 1971, spending eleven weeks on the chart. Bruce moved to London to continue his career after the success of Rain.

You can't keep a good man down and Desmond Dekker returns to conclude side two with **The Song We Used To Sing**, a catchy number, being the follow up on Trojan to Desmond's smash hit You Can Get It If You Really Want. The track was perhaps over produced moving away from the raw sound of Desmond's earlier patois influenced hits and the free flowing excellent You Can Get It If You Really Want. It failed to give Desmond another run at the chart.

With 1971 drawing to a close the previous chart success would never be emulated with only a handful of chart entries to follow before the end of 1972. Trojan never released a Chartbusters Volume 4. They did however continue to produce a few good records that featured on later volumes of Tighten Up and Club Reggae through the remainder of 1972.

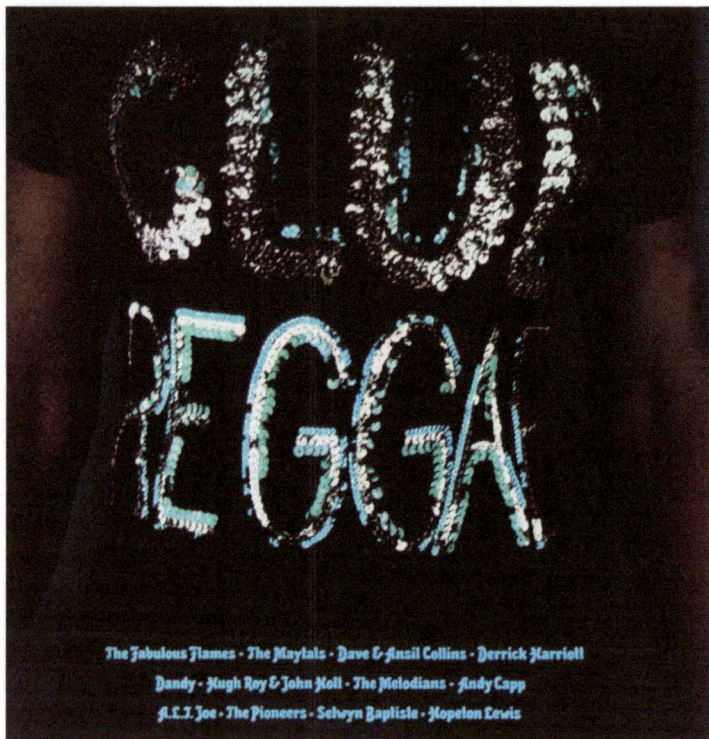

CLUB REGGAE
TROJAN RECORDS TBL 159   1971

CLUB REGGAE

The first in Trojan's successful Club Reggae series was launched on the TBL prefix and was soon followed by Volume 2 the same year. Jamaican music hadn't fallen well into the album market until Trojan came up with the idea of the budget priced albums using singles that had so called peaked in sales then compiling them onto budget priced LP's. The idea proved to be very successful allowing many of the working class youth, who in most cases could not get hold of the many singles being released in ever increasing numbers, to own their favourite tunes.

The Club Reggae series was compiled as the title suggest from singles that were most popular in the clubs giving a different offering to the chart hits outpouring from Trojan at the time, although some tracks crossed over most notably here with Dave And Ansel Collins number one chart hit Double Barrel.

The Club reggae series was said to have run a close second to the popular Tighten Up, certainly the first three in the series were packed with some excellent sounds. The Club Reggae idea was not a new venture as Island had previously issued Club Ska and Club Rocksteady compilation albums.

Side one gets underway with **Holly Holy** from the Fabulous Flames, a record written by Neil Diamond and produced by Clancy Eccles. Released on Clandisc CLA-224 in 1970 it featured Lord Creator's Kingston Town on the B side. Track two however requires no introduction, **54-46 Was My Number** from The Maytals was an updated reggae version of the groups rocksteady hit from 1968, 54-46 That's My Number. The track here was issued on Trojan TR-7808 with a version on the flip side by Beverley's All Stars. Both tracks were produced by the legendary Leslie Kong who sadly passed away the same year. Track three is the chart topping hit from early 1970 by Dave And Ansel Collins, **Double Barrel**, the second release on the new Techniques label TE-901.

The tempo then slows with Derrick Harriott's **Groovy Situation,** released on the Song Bird label prefix SB-1042. The perpetual Dandy is up next with **Take A Letter Maria** this time released under his own name, a track issued on Trojan TR-7800 in 1970. Side one concludes with an emerging talk over song, **Wear You To The Ball**. Sung by Hugh Roy & John Holt, the track produced by Duke Reid and released on Duke Reid DR-2513 in 1970. The song was a re working of The Paragons Jamaican rocksteady hit of the same name who included John Holt as a member of the group.

Side two gets under way with a record that featured on the soundtrack of the forthcoming blockbuster Jamaican film The Harder They Come. **Rivers Of Babylon** from The Melodians, a track also produced by Leslie Kong and released on Summit SUM-8508 in 1970. Rivers Of Babylon continued the theme of including records that had peaked in terms of sales but were still very much a part of the current sounds of the day.

Track two is a complete change of pace with an offering from Andy Capp, **The Law**, a Byron Lee production issued on Duke DU-69 again being a single from the previous year. **Hitching A Ride** by A.L.T. Joe AKA Trevor Aljoe was a cover version of a hit for Vanity Fair from 1969.

The Pioneers featured just the once on Club Reggae and are up next with **I Need Your Sweet Inspiration,** a far more commercial sound than they had previously found chart success with, the track being released on Trojan TR-7795 in 1970. The penultimate track features an up tempo instrumental from Selwyn Baptiste of Freddie Notes And The Rudies Montego Bay complete with accompanying steel drum on **Mo' Bay.** The first volume of Club Reggae signs off with another upbeat sound this time from Hopeton Lewis with an admirable delivery of **Boom-Shacka-Lacka**, an excellent Duke Reid production issued on Duke Reid DR-2505 and released in 1970.

Soon to follow hot on the trail of Club Reggae would be one of the most exciting compilation albums that Trojan released; Club Reggae Volume 2 was issued a few months later the same year.

261

CLUB REGGAE VOLUME 2
TROJAN RECORDS TBL 164   1971

CLUB REGGAE Volume 2

1971 witnessed the release of the second in the Club Reggae series and an album of great diversification and distinction, with every track a true masterpiece of Jamaican music. Following on from the successful launch of what was seen as the best reggae album released in 1971, Club Reggae. This new compilation came with a truly comprehensive set of sleeve notes from Rob Bell, so good that here they are in full.

One of the best reggae albums released in 1971 was Club Reggae (TBL 159) which featured those records most popular in the discotheques. Such a successful compilation had to be followed by a second volume, so voila.

Kicking off side one is twenty three year old Eric Donaldson singing his big hit of the year **Cherry Oh Baby** amid stiff competition, the song won the 1971 Jamaican Festival Song, gaining a festival Gold Medal, the Desno and Geddes award and a cash prize for Eric. Quite a feature for his first recording! The song has a hypnotic bass-dominated rhythm and features Eric's acrobatic voice feeling the way around the lyric.

Little Boy Blue is uncompromising reggae with a tight yet swinging guitar and organ. Verne and Son sound in fine fettle on this song; their first recording I believe. Produced by A. Ranglin of G.G. Records, who has been responsible for such past hits as African Melody and Man From Carolina.

There was a time when instrumental reggae was the order of the day, and, although now it is usually the vocal records which are more popular, the occasional instrumental is still a force to be reckoned with, for instance **To The Fields** by Herman. From the opening insinuating words from Herman to the closing bars, the number really moves. Herman is in fact Herman Chin-Loy, owner of Aquarius Records and also co-producer of Bruce Ruffin's recent hit Rain.

Organ and piano lead the intro for Clancy Eccles' **Sweet Jamaica** and indeed the organist holds the rhythm together all the way through the number, employing the 'creeping' technique which proved so popular on Clancy's production of Holly Holy. Clancy is of course, one of the veterans of the Jamaican entertainment scene, and is also an accomplished songwriter Sweet Jamaica being one of his own compositions.

263

Laurel Aitken is another pioneer of West Indian music, and was indeed one of the first Jamaican artists to settle in the U.K. **It's Too Late**, his own composition, is somewhat reminiscent of the style of the Drifter's records of the early sixties, although completely stamped with Laurel's own personality. Laurel also produced the number himself, an activity which is taking up more and more of his time these days.

Jamaica has produced some great female singers, from Patsy and Millie to Cynthia Richards, Marcia Griffiths and the greatly underrated Phillis Dillon. Phillis has been recording for quite some time, but up to the time she teamed with top producer Duke Reid, she had not met with the success she really deserved. **One Life To Live, One Love To Give** was the turning point, and reached the Top Ten in Jamaica. She possesses a most distinctive voice which seems to float from note to note with her seemingly effortless ease on this number, a perfect foil for her accompanying group.

Every now and then a pop number turns up which is ideally suited to the reggae idiom, and the mammoth pop hit of 1971 **knock Three Times** falls neatly into that category. Brent Dowe, lead singer with the Melodians, made his first solo recording with the Dawn number, and scored immediately. The record was produced by Leslie Kong of Beverley's records, who so sadly passed away in the summer of 1971.

Former label mates of Brent Dowe and the Melodians were the Gaylads who hit the Jamaican charts with **Can't Hide The Feeling**, and it is possibly the best record they have ever made, with a great vocal arrangement and a superb production. One to play to those people who still put down Jamaican music as being crude and monotone.

Byron Lee and the Dragonaires have been the top band in the Caribbean for nearly ten years now and are now on the verge of achieving international acclaim. They have toured America, the UK, Canada and many other countries, and everywhere they go, the most requested item is their version of George Harrisons' **My Sweet Lord**, featuring band vocalist Keith Lynn. Keith, although fairly diminutive in size, is very much a giant in terms of vocal stature as any follower of the twelve piece band will testify.

The last year has seen the emergence of the 'Version' either being the instrumental of a vocal, or a record brought 'up to date' by dubbing the voice of a D.J. over the old tape.

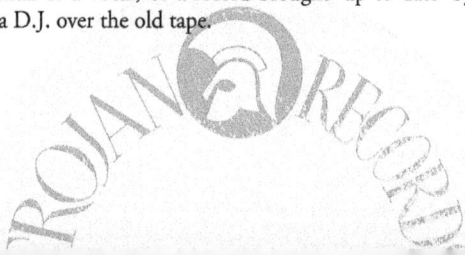

Examples of the latter are any U-Roy or Dennis Alcapone records, both noted for their fast talking rhymes using local slang and dialect, and thus quite often making the words completely unintelligible to an English audience. Producer Dandy gently satirizes the situation with his **Version Girl** sung by Boy Friday, a relatively unknown singer whose voice sounds suspiciously familiar!

One of the longest established vocal groups from Jamaica are The Wailers who were hitting he high spots back in the early sixties with such titles as Hooligan, What's New Pussycat and many more. The two lead singers are Peter Touch and Bob Marley, although it seems to be Bob Marley who now takes the leading role. They have hit the Jamaican charts several times this year, the biggest success being Duppy Conquer and Small Axe. **Small Axe** is a superb example of their fine harmonizing and Bob Marley's controversial lyrics.

The last few months have seen a rash of songs praising Jamaica – Clancy Eccles Sweet Jamaica, Honey Boy's Jamaica, Greyhound's Funky Jamaica and Neville's I **Love Jamaica**. Neville wrote, sung and produced I Love Jamaica for Ken Khouri's Federal Records, and what a success it has been! It is a strange record - predominantly a reggae although the vocal is very much calypso influenced. Nevertheless - a fine record, as indeed is the whole album. I hope you enjoy it as much as we enjoyed putting it together.

Rob Bell.

These sleeve notes on Club Reggae Volume 2 are the most comprehensive issued on the Trojan TBL label at a time when an LP cost just 19/11. Looking back now it is pleasing to see that Rob Bell had an eye for talent when recognising the remarkable Bob Marley before he became famous on the world stage admirably supported by the great Peter Tosh or as the record labels back then referred to Peter Touch

Was this the most complete and best album of Jamaican music ever released by Trojan? I will leave that up to you.

The budget priced Club Reggae TBL series continued only out sold by the most famous of Trojan's collections Tighten Up with Club Reggae Volume 3 released in 1972. A further album was issued later 1972 Club Reggae Volume 4 but by this time the pop infused reggae produced in the UK was very different from those early sounds emanating from Jamaica.

99½
NEW PENCE

Cherry Oh Baby
Eric Donaldson

Little Boy Blue
Verne and Son

To The Fields
Herman

Sweet Jamaica
Clancy Eccles

It's Too Late
Laurel Aitken

One Life To L
One Love To
Phillis Dillon

Knock Three Times
Brent Dowe

The Feeling

CLUB REGGAE VOLUME 3
TROJAN RECORDS TBL 178 1972

CLUB REGGAE Volume 3

I recall that the release of Club Reggae Volume 3 was eagerly awaited and even the BBC made reference to its release. It did not disappoint with the album art work looking superb. Opening the proceedings was Dennis Alcapone with his scorching **Alcapone Guns Don't Bark**. Dennis Alcapone was one of the original DJ's, a gifted performer with amazing talent. Influenced by U Roy, his excellent DJ skills are to the fore here as he toasts over Eric Donaldson's Love of the Common People.

Next up after featuring on Trojan's Reggae Chartbuster following huge success in the British charts with hits such as Wonderful World Beautiful People is Jimmy Cliff making his debut on the Club Reggae compilation with a rather different outing, **Those Good, Good Old Days**. Track three features The Uniques with a rather vivacious version of Paul Simon's **Mother And Child Reunion** a record that was riding high for Paul Simon in the UK charts peaking at number 5 in March 1972. Paul Simon, one half of the famous duo Simon & Garfunkel had travelled to Jamaica to record the track at Dynamic Studios to capture an authentic Jamaican sound.

Another debutant to the Club Reggae series is Desmond Dekker with **Live And Learn,** a medley of his previous hits including Sabotage. King Iwah and the Upsetters **Give Me Power** and the Deltons instrumental **Chopsticks** concluded side one of the album.

Side two continued in the same vein as side one with tracks from God Sons with **Merry Up**, Rocking Horse with **Hard Time** and Soul Syndicate with **Riot** all continuing the sound of the clubs, a sound that would have received very little if any air play from the BBC.

The Fabulous Five are listed up next with a brilliant pulsating tune on **Come Back And Stay,** although the track featured is actually the B side Come Back And Stay-Version, sounding very much like Scotty. The group had only formed in 1970 with Come Back And Stay being their first single, a record incidentally that made it to number one in Jamaica. The Fabulous Five provided the backing for Johnny Nash on his album I Can See Clearly Now, an album that inevitably helped to establish Bob Marley as a major international songwriter following the success of Stir It Up and Guava Jelly.

The penultimate track, **Just A Dream**, came from Slim Smith who was one of the most soulful and accomplished singers of rocksteady and reggae. He performed solo as well as being a member of The Techniques. He also had a stint with The Gaylads before joining The Uniques. Many different stories surround the death of Slim in 1973 but what is certain is that his untimely death left the world of reggae music a whole lot poorer. The album concluded with the highly regarded offering of **Johnny Gunman** from Jackie Edwards. Other hits followed for Jackie including In Paradise. Jackie was a prolific singer from the sixties and songwriter and his talents were demonstrated with the songs penned for The Spencer Davis Group in 1965, providing them with two popular number ones in the UK, Keep On Running and Somebody Help Me.

15'6

STRAIGHTEN UP FROM PAMA

Pama and Trojan began putting out compilation budget priced reggae albums in 1969, Trojan with their Tighten Up series and Pama with their greatest hits from Pama's subsidiary labels, both featuring a collection of hits from the previous year. Tighten Up was a massive success for Trojan with volume 2 reaching number two in the UK album chart, alas only to disappear from the chart after a couple of weeks as budget priced albums were then excluded from the chart. I wonder why?

The art work for Trojan featured scantily clad young ladies but Pama who had traditionally used shots of singers and club scenes on their album covers went a step further with sleeves often more explicit than Trojan. The first Straighten Up from Pama was issued in 1971, a good two years after the inaugural Tighten Up from Trojan with the third released towards the end of 1972.

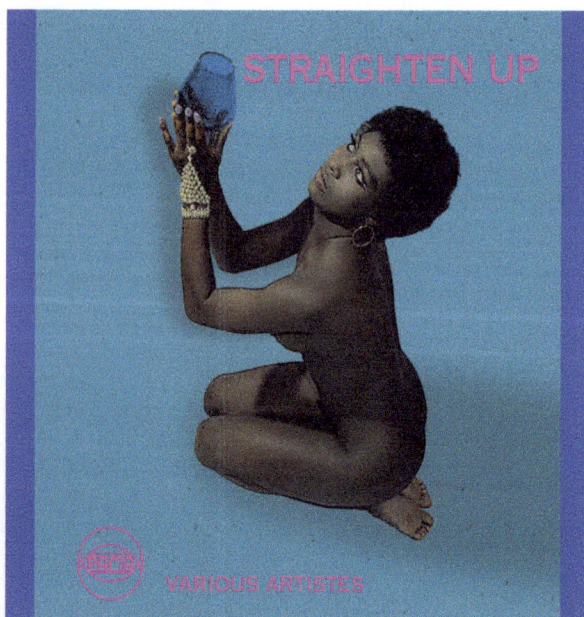

STRAIGHTEN UP VOLUME 1
PAMA   PMP 2002   1971

STRAIGHTEN UP VOLUME 1
PAMA PMP 2002 Released 1971

Side 1
1. LET IT BE - The Mohawks
2. LAST GOODBYE - Norman T Washington
3. WITHOUT MY LOVE - Little Roy
4. GOT TO GET YOU OFF MY MIND - Shel Alterman
5. CHARIOT COMING - The Viceroys
6. STRAIGHTEN UP - The Maytones

Side 2
1. GIVE HER ALL THE LOVE I'VE GOT - John Holt
2. BRING BACK YOUR LOVE - Owen Grey
3. YELLOW BIRD - Winston Groovy
4. SOMEDAY WE'LL BE TOGETHER - The Marvels
5. TOO EXPERIENCED - Winston Francis
6. PICK YOUR POCKET - The Versatiles

Let It Be is a cover version of the Beatles number 2 hit from March 1970, incidentally the same week saw Young Gifted And Black and Elizabethan Reggae in the top 30. The cover version issued on Supreme SUP-204 in 1970 kicks off the Straighten Up series and is performed admirably by The Mohawks in true skinhead reggae style. **Chariot Coming** by The Viceroys was released on Bullet in 1970 and has another outing on the excellent Sixteen Dynamic Reggae Hits Pama album. Side one concludes with the sound that gave the series its title, **Straighten Up** from The Maytones. The single with a prominent bass line was released in 1970 on Camel CA-47 but under the title Black And White Unite. **Bring Back Your Love** from Owen Gray also gets an outing. **Yellow Bird** was originally released on the re-branded New Beat label NB-055 in 1970, a some-what traditional offering from Winston Groovy when compared to other releases. **Someday We'll Be Together** is a vocal outing from The Marvels with backing from The Mohawks. The single was issued on Gas GAS-139 in 1970. The group Alex and Cornell Hinds and Eddie Smith specialised in Doo-wop harmonies. Perhaps one of their most endearing hits came later during 1972 with their version of Then He Kissed Me, issued on Trojan TR-7872 and plugged as a Christmas hit along with Big Seven from Judge Dread and Big City from Dandy Livingstone by Trojan. Winston Francis comes in with a rocking sound on **Too Experienced** issued on Punch PH-5 in 1969. The Versatiles continued their tradition concluding the album with a classic skinhead reggae sounds on **Pick My Pocket** released on Nu Beat NB-060, one of the last few to appear on the original Nu Beat label before a complete transition to New Beat.

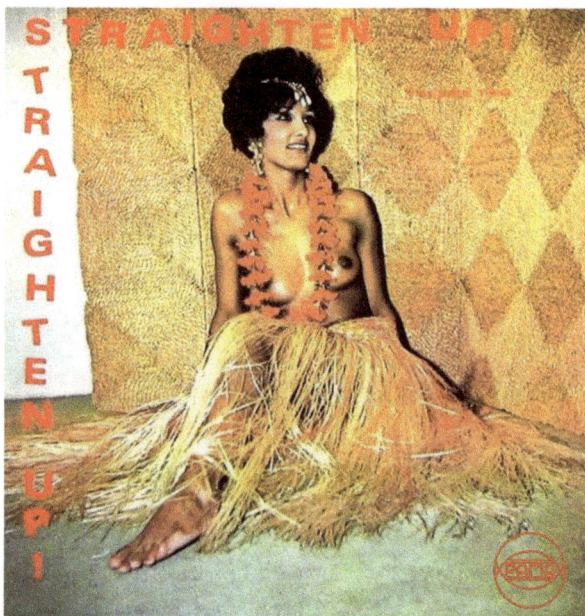

STRAIGHTEN UP VOLUME 2
PAMA PMP 2007 1971

Side 1
1. GUILTY Tiger
2. JUST MY IMAGINATION - Dave Barker
3. FAREWELL MY DARLING - Eugene Paul
4. DON'T YOU WEEP - Max Romeo
5. JOHN CROW SKANK - Derrick Morgan
6. FREE THE PEOPLE - Winston Groovy
7. MY GIRL - Slim Smith

Side 2
1. MONKEY SPANNER - Larry And Lloyd
2. LOVE AND EMOTION - The Righteous Flames
3. PUT YOUR SWEET LIPS - Raphael Stewart
4. I WANNA BE LOVED - Winston Groovy
5. CHEERIO BABY - The Classics
6. SAMETHING FOR BREAKFAST - Winston & Pat
7. EVERY NIGHT - Rudy & Sketto Ritch

The notes on Straighten Up Volume 2 declared the phenomenal success of Straighten Up bringing numerous requests for a second volume. *' We have selected just about the very best reggae numbers available today, bearing in mind your favourite artistes, adding two extra numbers for a bonus and giving you a dish of Old Jamaica's grass skirted damsels on the cover'.*

15'6

Volume 2 gets off in great style with **Guilty** by Tiger AKA Laurel Aitken, the single released on Camel needs no introduction, featuring on several of Pama's compilation albums. Dave Barker, the vocal part of the famous duo is up next, this time with Lloyd Charmers with a Jamaican single **Just My Imagination**. Eugene Paul gives a good rendition over a catchy rhythm with **Farewell My Darling** released on the Pama Supreme label PS-317 in 1971. Another Pama Supreme label release on PS-321 is **John Crow Skank** performed admirably although a change of direction by Derrick Morgan, with the track utilising the rhythm from Cherry Oh Baby. **My Girl** from Slim Smith completes side one, a catchy number from the man heralded as the greatest vocalist of the early reggae era.

A cover of **Monkey Spanner** was always going to be difficult for Larry & Lloyd to pull off with their release on New Beat NB-080. The single was poles apart from Dave & Ansel Collins. They did however keep the original single format with an instrumental Version 2 on the B side. **Love And Emotion** from The Righteous Flames and **I Wanna Be Loved** from Winston Groovy are up next, the latter a recognisable Winston Groovy sound. The skinhead reggae sound is back with **Cherrio Baby** from The Classics issued on Punch PH-70 in 1971, who were in fact The Wailing Souls from Jamaica who also recorded under the name of The Little Roys. This one differs from the tight Eric Donaldson version where his fine acrobatic voice skilfully negotiated the lyrics, nevertheless a cracking sound. **Samething For Breakfast** from Winston & Pat who are better known as Winston Groovy and Pat Rhoden was issued on Bullet BU-475 in 1971, with the B side Sweeter Than Honey from Winston Groovy equally as good.

The album concludes with an excellent revived number from Ruddy & Sketto Ritch with **Every Night** issued on Supreme SU-218 in 1971 and produced by Laurel Aitken. Every Night was the inaugural release on the Doctor Bird label in 1966 on DB-101 with the full artist credit as Joe White & Chuck and Baba Brooks Band.

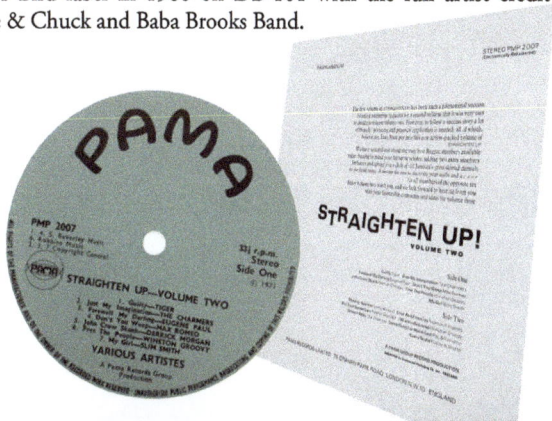

STRAIGHTEN UP VOLUME 3
PAMA PMP 2014   1972

Side 1
1. RUM RHYTHM - Shirley & Charmers
2. SOUTH OF THE BORDER - Denzil Dennis
3. NANNY SKANK - Hugh Roy
4. BEND DOWN LOW - The Groovers
5. OWEN GRAY GREATEST HITS - Owen Gray
6. ROCK STEADY - The Marvels
7. A SUGAR - Roy Shirley

Side 2
1. PRAY FOR ME - Max Romeo
2. LINGER A WHILE - John Holt
3. AILY AND AILALOO - Niney &Max
4. SEARCHING SO LONG - Derrick Morgan
5. WAY DOWN SOUTH - Hugh Roy
6. NOTHING CAN SEPARATE US - Owen Gray
7. PLENTY OF ONE - Derrick Morgan

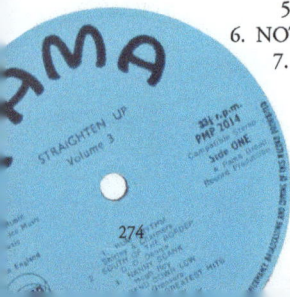

Kicking off Volume 3 is **Rum Rhythm** from Shirley & Charmers, better known as Roy Shirley and Lloyd Charmers, released on Bullet BU-502 in 1972. The Jamaican release was titled Mucking Fuch by The Muckers. **South Of The Border** is a well travelled song from a film dating way back to 1939 describing a road trip to Mexico. Probably easier to list who hasn't released the song than who has. This excellent version, issued on Pama Supreme PS-350, is performed admirably by Denzil Dennis who was the other half with Jennifer on the re-issued Escort release of Young Gifted And Black. Hugh Roy or U. Roy is up next with **Nanny Skank** although the single issued on Punch PH-104 reads Nannyscrank, presumably a take on Larry Marshalls Nanny Goat. Next up is a cover version by The Groovers of **Bend Down Low** issued on Escort ERT-863. The original Bob Marley & The Wailers single issued in Jamaica in 1966 is still perhaps the best. **Owen Gray Greatest Hits** gives an outing for Owen Gray with a compilation single of his greatest hits, not always a favourable option up against the singles in their original form. **Rock Steady** from The Marvels is next then side one concludes with the well documented **A Sugar** from Roy Shirley and Altyman Reid, issued on both Trojan's Green Door label, GD-4026B and the Pama Punch label PH-108 in 1972.

Side two opens with Max Romeo, this time in a completely different mood with **Pray For Me,** highlighting a change in style with politically motivated influences showing that his musical talent went far beyond risqué lyrics. John Holt comes up with a scorcher on Camel CM-78 with **Linger A While** in true boss reggae fashion. A change of pace with **Aily And Ailaloo** from Niney And Max issued on Bullet BU-503. Max is of course Max Romeo and Niney is Winston 'Niney' Holness. **Searching So Long** is a track composed, produced and sung by Derrick Morgan issued on Crab CRAB-67 in 1970, having the distinction of the ultimate record issued on the Crab label. Hugh Roy is back with **Way Down South**, a resounding talk over version of Billy Dyce's brilliant Take Warning issued on Trojan's GG label. Hugh Roy's true reggae classic was issued on the main Pama label PM-835 in 1972. To keep it in the family The B side features Be My Guest by Billy Dyce. Duplications of recordings were not uncommon as often Jamaican producers would license the same record to both companies and a release on Trojan's GG label highlights this having the A side of GG-4532 as Be My Guest and the B side Way Down South. **Nothing Can Separate Us** comes from Owen Gray, refreshing to listen to an original single issued on Camel CA-73 in 1971. Derrick Morgan concludes the last Straighten Up of 1972 with **Plenty Of One** issued on Punch PH-107, produced and preformed by Derrick. Alas another of those compilations, this time of Derrick's earlier recordings kicking off with Tougher Than Tough, a track previously issued on Pyramid PYR-610 in 1967.

STRAIGHTEN UP!

PAMA ALBUMS

Pama released several compilation albums during 1969 - 1970
on their budget ECO and SECO (Stereo) labels

BULLET A WORLD OF REGGAE
PAMA SECO 19   1970

Side 1

1. THROW ME CORN - Winston Shan And The Sheiks
2. HEART DON'T LEAP - Dennis Walks
3. COPY CATS - The Clan
4. EACH TIME - The Ebony Sisters
5. COME BY HERE - Winston And Rupert
6. WHAT'S YOUR EXCUSE - The Hippy Boys

Side 2

1. THEME FROM 'A SUMMER PLACE' - Ranny Williams
2. I AM JUST A MINSTERL - The Kingstonians
3. LOVE OF MY LIFE - Dennis Walks
4. HOG IN A ME MINTI - The Hippy Boys
5. THAT'S MY LIFE (BECAUSE YOU LIED) - Fitzroy Sterling
6. LET ME TELL YOU BOY - Ebony Sisters

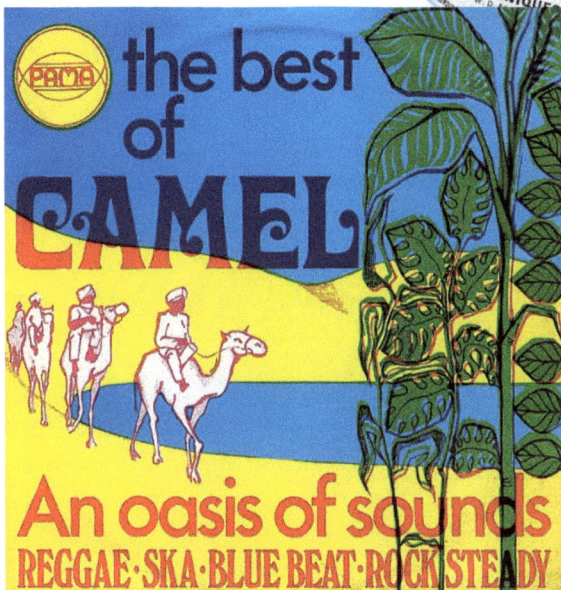

THE BEST OF CAMEL
PAMA   SECO 18   1970

Side 1
1. STRANGE WHISPERING - The West Indians
2. WHO YOU GONNA RUN TO - The Techniques
3. GIRL WHAT YOU DOING TO ME - Owen Grey
4. THE WARRIOR - Johnny And The Sensations
5. CONFIDENTIAL - Lloyd Charmers
6. BONGO NYAH - The Little Roys

Side 2
1. EVERY BEAT OF MY HEART - Owen Grey
2. IN THIS WORLD - The Federals
3. GO FIND YOURSELF A FOOL - The Techniques
4. DANNY BOY - King Cannon
5. SINCE YOU BEEN GONE - Eric Fratter
6. YOUR SWEET LOVE - The Soul Cats

CRAB BIGGEST HITS
PAMA ECO 2   1969

Side 1
1. PRIVATE NUMBER - Ernest Wilson
2. RUN GIRL RUN - G.G. Grossett
3. FIRE A MUSS MUSS TALL - The Ethiopians
4. CHILDREN GET READY - The Versatiles
5. SEVEN LETTERS - Derrick Morgan
6. REGGAE HIT THE TOWN - The Ethiopians

Side 2
1. WORK IT - The Viceroys
2. RIVER TO THE BANK - Derrick Morgan
3. SPREAD YOUR BED - The Versatiles
4. WHAT A BIG SURPRISE - The Ethiopians
5. REGGAE CITY - Val Bennett
6. LONELY HEARTACHES - The Tartans (The Clarendonians)

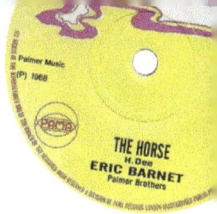

While the music was great the album covers for the Gas, Nu-Beat and Unity compilations were more than a little underwhelming in comparison to the usual flamboyant artwork from Pama.

GAS GREATEST HITS
PMA ECO 4 1969

Side 1

1. 1,000 TONS OF MEGATON - Roland Alphonso
2. HOW LONG WILL IT TAKE - Pat Kelly
3. REGGAE IN THE WIND - Lester Stirling
4. WALKING PROUD - Martin Riley
5. AIN'T TOO PROUD TO BEG - The Uniques
6. THE HORSE - Eric Barnet

Side 2

1. SOUL CALL - The Soul Rhythms
2. WANTED - Baba Dise
3. NEVER GIVE UP - Pat Kelly
4. TE TA TOE - Eric Barnett
5. RING OF GOLD - The Melodians
6. CHO CHO TRAIN - Soul Cats

NU-BEAT'S GREATEST HITS
PAMA ECO 6 1969

Side 1

1. LA LA MEANS I LOVE YOU - Alton Ellis
2. RESCUE ME - The Reggae Girls
3. ANOTHER HEARTACHE - Gregory Isaacs
4. RHYTHM HIPS - Ronald Russell
5. HALIE SELASSIE - Laurel Aitken
6. MY TESTIMONY - The Maytals

Side 2

1. TRAIN TO SOUTH VIETNAM - The Rudies
2. HEY BOY, HEY GIRL - Derrick And Patsy
3. BLOWING IN THE WIND - Max Romeo
4. RHYTHM AND SOUL - The Carltone All Stars
5. SUFFERING STILL - Laurel Aitken
6. GIVE YOU MY LOVE - Derrick And Paulette

UNITY'S GREATEST HITS
PAMA   ECO 7   1969

Side 1
1. BANGARANG - Lester Stirling & Stranger Cole
2. LAST FLIGHT TO REGGAE CITY - Tommy McCook
3. LET IT BE ME - Slim Smith & Paulette
4. EVERYBODY NEEDS LOVE - Slim Smith
5. REGGAE ON BROADWAY - Lester Stirling
6. TWELFTH OF NEVER - Max Romeo (actually Pat Kelly)

Side 2
1. SPOOGY - Lester Stirling
2. FOR ONCE IN MY LIFE - Slim Smith
3. IF WE SHOULD EVER MEET - Stranger Cole
4. THE AVENGERS - Tommy McCook
5. ON BROADWAY - Slim Smith
6. BRIGHT AS A ROSE - Lester Stirling

REGGAE HITS 69 VOLUME 1
PAMA   ECO 3   1969

Reggae Hits 69 came with its own sleeve notes from John Jones in Jamaica although not in chronological order:

Children Get Ready surely one of the best in modern reggae beat very good backing along with good singing and fine lyrics. The Versatiles - a group of young Jamaicans first began singing together at school but soon graduated to the professional field. This is their first release and after listening we feel sure there is plenty more good stuff where that came from. Best of luck boys.

Last Flight To Reggae City a combination of great talent here which has gone into the making of this entertaining record. The spoken comedy of Stranger Cole coupled with the fine flute work of Mr. Lester Sterling has put Flight To Reggae City into the ska charts without any fuss whatsoever - and just listen to that beat - keep dancing.

Bangarang like the song says mama no want Bangarang and who would with such authentic rhythm to dance to. Stranger Cole and company again, and this time Bangarang went straight to number one in the Jamaican charts and stayed there for several weeks, while in England and the USA it created havoc over Christmas and was the most popular ska record for many weeks.

The Horse, now here is a surprise hit. Some time ago a gentleman called Cliff Noble made an instrumental and called it The Horse round about the same time a gentleman called Mr. Eric Barnett in another part of the world made another instrumental and he too called his The Horse as a follow up to a local hit, The Donkey. Both discs were issued in England and both were hits, one a R&B the other a ska hit, great eh!

Rhythm Hips on release was voted discotheque record of the week by a well known disc columnist The Swinger. Ronald Russell the artiste tells a story all men love to hear, about the young mini-skirted girls who when they walk are living poetry in motion. Good story, good record.

Reggae In The Wind. Why not? if you feel you should, then go on Reggae In The Wind. A great beaty number dished up by those hit-makers Lester Sterling & The Soulmates, great fun.

River To The Bank. Derrick Morgan and friends have served us with an old Jamaican ring play song. River To The Bank brings back memories of great fun, thoroughly enjoyable so join in and sing.

Push Push, the ruder variety of ska music but very subtle and the children will not be able to detect any rudeness at all in this song. Well composed and very well performed indeed by those stalwarts of ska, The Termites.

Hey Boy, Hey Girl. This song is very well known in the United Kingdom, played quite often over the radio and a discotheque hit. The mums and dads as well as the teenagers go for this one in a very big way, nice to find it on an album with so many other good numbers. Artistes Patsy and Derrick, both no strangers to the scene and it's the same Derrick Morgan that dishes up **I Love You** another good reggae number that is sure to go down especially among the romantics.

Have Some Fun. New artistes Devon and The Tartans are surely off to a grand start with their very own composition Lets have Some Fun. Nice harmony with some good voices, ska music is surely glad to enrol them.

Reggae Hit The Town. Once again The Ethiopians, higher tenor voices, individual styling and right in rhythm with the great reggae beat when Reggae Hit The Town - and it will with this album.

Happy listening and have lots of fun with this record and mind you - learn the new dance - THE REGGAE

John Jones - from Jamaica

REGGAE HITS 69 VOLUME 2
PAMA ECO 11 1969

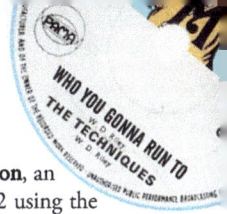

Side one gets under way with the powerful **1000 Tons Of Megaton**, an outing from the great saxophonist Roland Alphonso on GS-112 using the rhythm from Slim Smith's Everybody Need Love. **Who You Gonna Run To** by Winston Riley was the inaugural release on Camel CA-10, a vibrant early reggae sound that credits The Techniques but the artist is believed to be The Shades. Next up is **Down In The Park** by The Inspirations who were in fact Jimmy London and Billy Dyce. Their voices are recognisable on this track with great harmonies, their first release on Camel CA-11. The Versatiles are back with **Spread Your Bed**, another boss reggae sound issued on CRAB-5. **Take Your Hand From My Neck** issued on CRAB-13 is an offering from The Viceroys, a track sure to get the skinhead on the dance floor, although the label credits The Paragans (Paragons) who feature on the B side. **Throw Me Corn** released on Bullet BU-399 gives the full credit to Winston Shand & The Shieks, another vibrant skinhead reggae sound guaranteed to get those old boots stomping.

Side two kicks off with **Soul Call** from The Soul Rhythms, an instrumental with a clever blending of horns to a good rhythm released on GAS -113. **Work It** from The Viceroys is a boss reggae sound, pulsating with a driving beat and one that is guaranteed to get the dance floor quaking from those skinhead boots, issued on CRAB-12. **Run Girl Run** is a record in a similar vein to the previous by G.G. 'George' Grossett, produced by Harry Mudie and issued on CRAB-10. Ernest Wilson the former lead singer with The Clarendonians is up next with a cover version of **Private Number**, catchy tune but not all songs suit the reggae idiom. **Since You've Been Gone** is a record from Eric Fatter released on Camel CA-20, an excellent beat and outstanding vocals help make this another dance crasher. The album concludes with **Spoogy** from Mr Bangarang, Lester Sterling, another to get the dance floor crashing, this time a live recording from the National Stadium in Jamaica and released in the UK on Unity UN-509, with the label credit as Lester Sterlin.

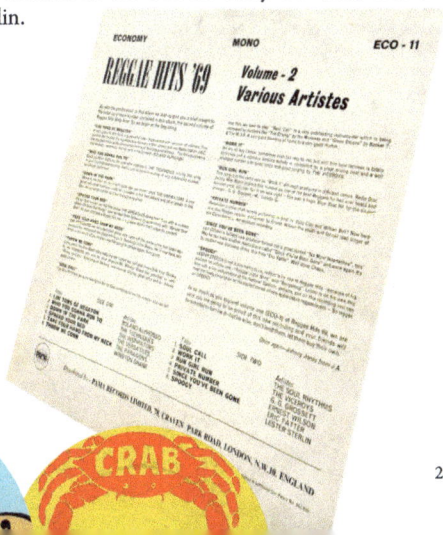

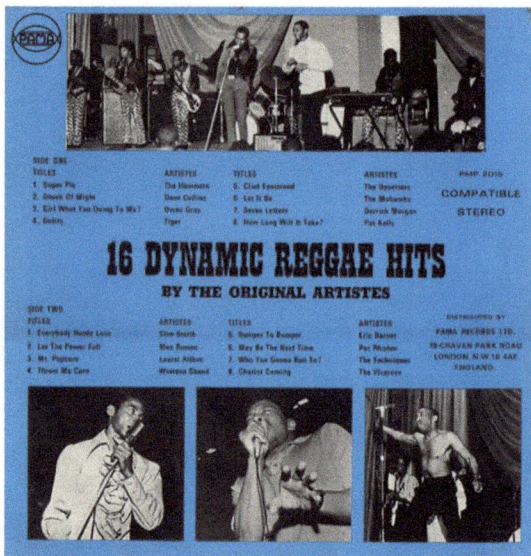

SIXTEEN DYNAMIC REGGAE HITS
PAMA PMP 201   1972

Side 1
1. SUGAR PIE - The Hammers
2. SHOCK OF MIGHT - Dave Collins
3. GIRL WHAT YOU DOING TO ME - Owen Gray
4. GUILTY - Tiger
5. CLINT EASTWOOD - The Upsetter
6. LET IT BE - The Mohawks
7. SEVEN LETTERS - Derrick Morgan
8. HOW LONG WILL IT TAKE - Pat Kelly

Side 2
1. EVERYBODY NEEDS LOVE - Slim Smith
2. LET THE POWER FALL - Max Romeo
3. MR. POPCORN - Laurel Aitken
4. THROW ME CORN - Winston Shand
5. BUMPER TO BUMPER - Eric Barnet
6. MAY BE THE NEXT TIME - Pat Rhoden
7. WHO YOU GONNA RUN TO - The Techniques
8. CHARIOT COMING - The Viceroys

Sixteen Dynamic Reggae Hits was issued by Pama in 1972, Trojan released
an album of the same name during 1973 with sixteen different sounds
from the Dynamic Studios in Jamaica.

Notable outings on the album come from **Shock Of Might** by Dave Barker. The record needs no introduction, released on Punch PH-25. The A side was actually Set Me Free with the B side the well known Hit Me Back, also released on Trojan's Upsetter label which only credits Upsetters.

Girl What You Doing To Me by Owen Gray was another dynamic sound living up to the album title, the single released on Camel CA-25 in 1969.

Guilty by Tiger needs little introduction, another classic release from the Camel stable, produced by Laurel Aitken and according to many sources Laurel was indeed Tiger.

Seven Letters by Derrick Morgan and **How Long Will It Take** from Pat Kelly are also stand out tracks. The Pat Kelly single sold very well but never charted as the sales were predominantly from non chart retailers.

Throw Me Corn released on Bullet BU-399 in 1969 gives the full credit to Winston Shand & The Shieks, another vibrant skinhead reggae sound.

May Be The Next Time is a very melodic outing from Pat Rhoden, backed amiably by The Mohawks on Pama PM-811.

Where You Gonna Run To has already had a mention on Reggae Hits 69 Volume 2. Produced by Winston Riley and the inaugural release on Camel CA-10. The vibrant early reggae sound is credited to The Techniques but the artist is believed to be The Shades.

The album concludes with **Chariot Coming** by The Viceroys issued on Bullet BU-441 in 1970. As with some singles, including the instrumental version of Bob & Marcia's hit Young Gifted & Black on Trojan's Harry J label, the B side Stacko by Syndey Allstars, is well worth a spin. The record produced by Sydney Crooks was a favourable skinhead reggae instrumental track in its own right.

All in all Sixteen Dynamic Reggae Hits really does lives up to its title!

THIS IS REGGAE
PAMA PSP 1003 1970

This album is up there with the best, and almost certainly one of the most relevant compilations from Pama as most of the tracks on This Is Reggae are laid down in true boss skinhead manner with the album launched at a time when reggae and the skinheads were truly entwined in a musical love affair.

Derrick Morgan had a huge hit with **Moon Hop** released on CRAB-30 in 1969 reaching number 49 in the UK chart during January 1970. It was written to commemorate the 1969 Apollo moon landing but as has been well documented Skinhead Moonstomp seemed to hold back further chart success for Derrick and Pama. The skinhead reggae beat and the screeching lyrics made for a foot stomping classic and was the catalyst for the Moon Hop album issued on PSP 1006 in 1970. Owen Grey, sometimes spelt Gray, is no stranger to the music scene, he was recording as far back as 1960 in Jamaica and comes up with a dance crashing sound finding his way around the lyrics in falsetto style on **Girl What You Doing To Me,** another favourite with the skinheads released on Camel CA-25 in 1969.

Pay Kelly's well documented **How Long Will It Take** comes next. Another top tune, the record issued on Gas GAS-115 in 1969 is seen by many as his greatest soulful tune. Reggae with strings added was not as common for Pama as it became for Trojan but the record sold well only failing to chart as the sales were predominantly from non chart return stores. Another record that narrowly failed to chart, again due to non chart retailers and perhaps a lack of distribution options was **Clint Eastwood** issued on Punch PH-21 in 1969 by The Upsetters. The track was a take on Yakety Yak over a vibrant Lee Perry rhythm, again another favourite boss reggae sound.

Sometimes the term 'needs no introduction' is clichéd but not the case with Max Romeo's risqué **Wet Dream**. If ever there was a skinhead favourite this is it, an up-tempo number with a very strong melody, almost unique at the time, and had already made a name for Max in his native Jamaica. **Sentimental Man** from Ernest Wilson concludes side one, the track issued on Crab CRAB-45 in 1969.

Side two kicks off with **Pretty Cottage**, a vocal led single issued on Escort ES-810 in 1969. The label credits Stranger 'Soul' Cole but is actually accompanied by Gladdy Anderson. Next up comes **Sentimental Reason** reigniting the boss skinhead sounds running right throughout the album. Admirably preformed by The Maytones the captivating boss reggae track was issued on Pama's Camel label CA-27 in 1969.

Derrick-Top The Pop as the title suggests is another classic track credited to Derrick Morgan and issued on Unity UN-540 in 1969. But maybe there is a twist to the story as the track sounds very much like Pop A Top Part 2 from Andy Capp released on Duke DU-71B, with a touch of Fat Man. Lynford Anderson AKA Andy Capp was a studio engineer and producer. He produced this track and the original version titled Popatop issued on Treasure Isle TI-7052, a release that fashioned quite a shift for the reggae beat. Perhaps his most endearing song was The Law (Part 1) released on Trojan's Duke DU-69 during 1970. A boss sounding album without an offering from Laurel Aitken would be out of character so here he is with a self produced number **Jessie James**, issued on Nu Beat NB-045 in 1969. A chugging infectious beat with intermittent gun fire declaring Jessie James rides again. The penultimate offering was **Cat Nip** issued on Camel CA-29 in 1969 from The Hippie Boys, another infectious beat this time with organ running through, defiantly one to get those old boots on the dance floor. The album concludes with **Honey** from Slim Smith issued on Unity UN-542, always great vocals from Slim but the rhythm track seems a little at odds to the rest of this excellent album.

BANG BANG LULU   PAMA PMLP 4 1969
(The album was issued with three different coloured sleeves, black orange and red)

Jamaican music has a long history of risqué lyrics dating back to the days of calypso and continuing with the shift through to reggae.

Lloyd Tyrell AKA Lloyd Charmers or Lloyd Terrel gets the album under way with **Bang Bang Lulu,** rock steady at its best with cheeky vocals released on Pama PM-710 in the spring of 1968. Track two is listed as Wet Dream but is in fact **Mr Rhya**, another offering from Lloyd Tyrell with a driving rhythm released on Nu Beat NB-023 in 1969. Devon And The Tartons are up next with **Making Love** issued as a B side on Nu Beat NB-021 the previous year, although lacking a storming instrumental rhythm. **Push Push** by the Termites gets the album back on track so to speak with a vocal inspired recording. A look to the future will see Judge Dread rule the roost with the rude version of nursery rhymes, but here Eric 'Monty' Morris gives us a Clancy Eccles production **Simple Simon,** another Nu Beat B side issued on NB-011 in 1968 gets a good run out. Lloyd Terrel opened side one and closes with **How Come**, or does he? as the track issued on Pama PM-740 sounds very much like How You Come performed by Lee Perry And The Gaylets.

Lulu Returns to open side two with another risqué offering from Lloyd Tyrell released on Pama PM-752 in 1969. As the title suggests Lulu has returned with good vocals over a hypnotic beat.

The melodic rhythm track from **I Love You** issued on Nu Beat NB-16 in 1968 by Derrick Morgan can be described as storming and one to get the DM's moving. Why? well it's the rhythm track Max Romeo utilised for his massive hit. **Soul Food** is an early Pama recording on PM-723 from Lyn Taitt And The Jets with a distinctive vocal led track that takes a while for the dance floor to beckon. **Push It Up** from The Termites is another Pama recording issued on PM-729 in 1968, the number produced by Clancy Eccles has a good rock steady early reggae beat. **Money Girl** from Larry Marshall is another of the B sides to feature, issued on Nu Beat NB-022, the A side sported Max Rome's Blowing In The Wind. The album concludes with **Rhythm Hips** from Ronald Russell, the track is another rock steady early reggae dance crasher produced by Eric Barnet and issued on Nu Beat NB-019 during 1968. If the tune sounds familiar that's because The Horse from Eric Barnett is an instrumental version and the initial release on Gas GS-100 in 1968.

REGGAE HIT THE TOWN AGAIN

Much has changed since the skinhead reggae days of 68-72. Tighten Up Volume 2 or the new shiny 7" single Monkey Spanner from Dave & Ansel Collins was tangible, you could hold it in your hand or tuck the LP under your arm, you could feel the texture of the printed cardboard and vinyl, and the fact it was your very own recording made it special. Of course there was always a possibility of what would happen if you dropped it, lost it, or it fell into the wrong hands?

The world of reggae has been blessed with the Trojan back catalogue readily available on many compilation CD albums and the digital download platform for many years. What has been missing is the vast amount of recordings issued under the Pama label, but reggae is hitting the town again with the anomaly being addressed as the boss sounds from Pama are now being made available digitally re-mastered in high quality audio for the first time. We can now down-load Pat Kelly's Twelfth Of Never on Unity, Rome from Lloyd Jones on Bullet, the fore-runner of Leaving Rome by Jo Jo Bennett, and Black & White Unite AKA Straighten Up from the Maytones. The Straighten Up series, the rival to Trojan's popular Tighten Up, are now available as complete albums to down-load.

THE HARDER THEY COME
ISLAND RECORDS ILPS 9202 1972
The Harder They Come soundtrack,
original recording re-mastered available on Island Records.

THE HARDER THEY COME

West Kingston Jamaica, a shanty town, on a small island in the Caribbean where the best grass in the world it was said sold for 2 dollars an ounce in the street, a place where reggae was born and where hundreds of kids flock from all over Jamaica drawn by the promise of fame and fortune.

It was here that the raw world of reggae and Jamaica was brought to the big screen for the first time. Jimmy Cliff declaring You Can Get It If You Really Want. He portrayed one of those kids, Ivanhoe 'Ivan' Martin, based on a real-life Jamaican character called Rhyging who achieved fame and notoriety in the 1940s. Looking for a break in music is his only way to escape from the ghetto and shanty towns.

The sound track introduced reggae to the world, a world that the skinhead had embraced since late 1968, but it also brought the harsh reality of the shanty towns of Jamaica to the fore with undeniably one, if not the best ever, collection of authentic reggae sounds put together on one album.

The opening track by Jimmy Cliff declares that **You Can Get It If You Really Want** a tracked penned by Jimmy Cliff himself. **Draw You Brakes** by Scotty portrays the grief that ensues in the heart of the Jamaican ghetto. The Melodians **Rivers Of Babylon** and Cliff's **Many Rivers To Cross** continues the theme of oppression.

A change of tempo from Toots And The Maytals who feature in the film, comes with **Sweet And Dandy** a song about a young couple about to get married, having last minute nerves. The first side of the album concludes with the title track **The Harder They Come**.

Side two tells the story of the rude boy walking down the road with a pistol in his waist, **Johnny Too Bad** warn The Slickers. Crime runs through the shanty towns echoing the incessant rhythms of the sound of reggae. Desmond Dekker tells of the 'rudie' route, looting, shooting and wailing in shanty town with his hit **007**.

Another track to feature from Toots And The Maytals is the vivacious **Pressure Drop** followed by Cliff's emotively slower paced **Sitting In Limbo**. The album concludes with an instrumental version of **You Can Get It If You Really Want** followed by **The Harder They Come,** a very appropriate track portraying the end of the film and the closing credits.

The Harder They Come was the first feature film produced in Jamaica. The movie is in Jamaican Patois which can be understood to some extent by English speakers. There are subtitles in English for much of the original movie.

Picture the scene if you can outside the Carib Theatre in Kingston Jamaica, when the first screening of The Harder They Come was due to take place. By 1pm a large crowd started gathering, despite the film scheduled for later that evening and by 6pm the crowd was estimated to have swollen to tens of thousands with traffic at a standstill.

By the time it was all over the doors had been ripped from their hinges with three people to a seat, and many seats torn up. The vastness of the crowds who had gathered there to witness for the first time Jamaican's on the big screen prevented many, including Jimmy Cliff, attending with event he prime minister said to have shared a single seat with his wife.

Perry Henzell had achieved success with the film, a production that had taken three years to complete with what has been described as a limited budget that kept running out, untrained actors and at times ad hoc dialogue. Despite the success in his homeland many critics advised against promoting the film overseas. Some four year ago the youth in Britain had warmed to the sounds of Jamaica but how would the people react to the film, the test would be the first screening in Brixton.

The UK premier could not have been more different than that opening night in Jamaica, with many critical of the films portrayal of poverty and drug running, not their vision of sundrenched beaches and a land of milk and honey.

Attendances steadily improved and eventually The Harder They Come became a London phenomenon, in due course spreading through Europe and the World. Today over 40 years on the film has achieved cult status, thanks to Henzell's dedication to his creation.

As a boy Perry was educated in England at boarding school then a stint working for the BBC followed before returning to Jamaica in the 50s. Perry Henzell died in 2006 at Treasure Beach aged 70, an accomplished man who rightfully became a true legend in Jamaica.

The sleeve notes told how day and night the studios scattered about in shanty town turned out tunes, adding life to the incredible outpouring for a small island in the Caribbean. The sleeve notes continued to reveal that it was however a cry to stay alive telling that although everybody wants it maybe nobody wanted it as badly as the Jamaican's and certainly nobody has ever expressed that need better in song.

CONCLUSION

Rosko gave us his top ten and I was going to finish with a little indulgence of my own but it is impossible to list as such a wide-ranging amount of quality recordings were issued during the period 68-72. The person who has described reggae as monotonous should maybe take time out and listen to the sounds of Desmond Dekker's You Can Get It If You Really Want, Max Romeo's Wet Dream, Monkey Spanner by Dave & Ansel Collins, Liquidator from Harry J All Stars or Long Shot Kick The Bucket from The Pioneers and of course Desmond's Israelites. My list would just go on and on and on and would certainly include Love Of The Common People, Pickney Gal, 54-46 Was My Number and Wonderful World, Beautiful People. There perhaps I may just have done it, or have I? What about Samfie Man from The Pioneers and Moon Hop from Derrick Morgan or Johnny Too Bad from The Slicker, I said it would go on and on.

The music that originally brought a sense of belonging for the skinheads had by early 1972 changed beyond all recognition from those early hard hitting sounds, with Trojan being the main instigator of the sweetened recordings. Pama were still to some extent remaining faithful to the original sound but the quality of the output was a far cry from those early days and they never enjoyed the distribution of Trojan.

To make matters worse the quality clothing that became as much a part of the skinhead identity as reggae was now being turned out in inferior quality from the manufacturers. It was a direction that saw the discerning skinhead lose faith. Some who by now were a second generation, following on from their brothers, became disillusioned with the sound. Some hanging onto the lasting hope for a resurgence of the original skinhead era which never came. The love affair was over by the autumn of 1972. The clock was also ticking for both Trojan and Pama and unfortunately for skinhead reggae.

Times winged chariot has moved on but those quality skinhead reggae sounds of 68 to 72 have stood the test of time and although half a century has passed those original recordings still sound as fresh today as they did way back then. I hope the book has helped you reminisce back to a unique time when Symarip said *"'Get your braces together and your boots on your feet"*.

Got your boots.... Dr Marten boots.

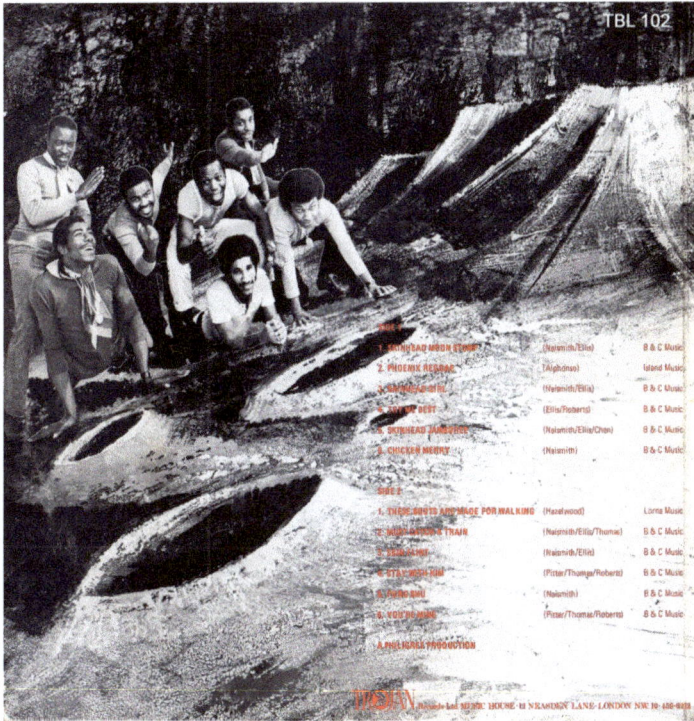

SKINHEAD MOONSTOMP
SYMARIP TBL 102 1970

Ben Sherman only costs 59/6

INDEX

A

Ace, Charlie 33
Aces, The 22, 67, 69, 71, 128, 129, 139, 250, 251
Adams, Glen 79, 164, 233
Agard, George 4, 80, 233
Aggrovators, The 214
Aitken, Laurel 20, 22, 23, 39, 50, 54, 60, 61, 226, 264, 273, 285, 287
Alcapone, Dennis 33, 49, 180, 197, 198, 203, 241, 265, 268
Alcapone, Dennis & Lizzy 52
Aljoe, Trevor (ALT Joe) 260
Alphonso, Roland 164, 283
Anderson, Gladdy 287
Anderson, Lynford 229, 287
Andy, Bob 21, 54, 98, 99, 143, 251
Andy, Horace 163
Andy & Joey 287
Ann, Julie 37
Arkin, David 113, 144
Arthey, Johnny 21, 47, 98, 140, 157
Auty, Don 61

B

Babb, Errol 60
Baptiste, Selwyn 261
Barker, Dave 21, 39, 45, 49, 58, 108, 141, 163, 236, 256, 273, 285
Barnett, Eric 281, 289
Barrett, Aston 'Family Man' 134
Barrett, Carlton 134
Beatles, The 67, 229, 271
Beckford, Ewart 31, 198, 202
Bell, Rob 263, 264, 265
Beltones, The 10, 31, 175
Benn, Tony 61
Bennett, Faye 77
Bennett, Jo Jo 237
Bennett, Val 45, 164, 229
Beverley All Stars 159, 259
Binge, Ronald 135
Binns, Sonny 113
Blackburn, Tony 130
Blackwell, Chris 4, 10, 18, 49, 95, 158, 162, 166, 175, 205, 206, 218
Bleechers, The 233
Bloom, Bobby 113, 250
Bob And Marcia 19, 21, 35, 47, 51, 54, 98, 99, 140, 143 175, 205, 251, 256, 285
Bond Joyce 20
Bongo Herman & Bunny 43, 241
Booker T & The MG's 229
Boothe, Ken 35, 51, 159, 163, 221, 222, 236
Bowie, David 62
Boy Friday 29, 37, 180, 265
Boys Jay 136
Brevett, Tony 224
Brooks, Baba 273
Brother Dan All Stars, The 45, 229
Brown, Chris 4, 63

B

Brown, Glen 108
Brown, Teddy 251
Buckley, Vernon 217, 244
Busters All Stars 164
Buster, Prince 16, 22, 60, 126, 154, 157, 164, 192, 198, 218, 220, 237

C

Cacia Mike 4
Campbell, Cornel 163
Capp, Andy 31, 45, 215, 260, 287
Carter, Clarence 252
Charles, Sonny 140
Charmers, Lloyd 43, 56, 222, 230, 273, 275, 288
Charmers, The 16, 33, 35
Checkmates, The 140
Chin, Vincent 41, 216
Chosen Few, The 37, 241, 242, 244
Chrystallites, The 214
Chung, Junior 135
Chung, Mike 244
Cimarons, The 127, 244
Clarendonians, The 56, 283
Classics, The 56, 58, 273
Claudette & The Corporation 35
Clay, Cassius 64
Cliff, Jimmy 5, 19, 22, 47, 49, 62, 67, 69, 81, 92, 93, 94, 95, 133, 138, 139, 146, 158, 159, 192, 205, 221, 237, 244, 247, 250, 253, 255, 268, 291, 292
Cole, Nat King 218
Cole, Stranger 20, 58, 222, 236, 281, 287
Collins, Ansel 45, 108, 109, 141, 256
Collins, Dave & Ansel 5, 18, 19, 45, 82, 108, 109, 141, 145, 205, 236, 255, 256, 259, 273, 293
Cooke, Sam 163, 229
Cooper, Henry 64
Crooks, Derrick 79, 132
Crooks, Sydney 4, 79, 86, 132, 285
Curved Air 82

D

Dandy 5, 13, 18, 29, 37, 45, 54, 153, 166, 179, 180, 233, 236, 244, 247, 257, 259, 265
Dandy & Audrey 29, 179, 180
Daniel In The Lions Den 256
Dawn 43, 232, 270
Dean, Nora 237
Dekker, Desmond 5, 13, 18, 19, 22, 47, 49, 51, 62, 67, 68, 71, 88, 93, 113, 126, 128, 129, 133, 139, 158, 192, 205, 222, 229, 248, 250, 251, 257, 26, 291, 293
Deltones, The 268
Dennis, Denzil 56, 275
Denzil & Jennifer 21, 54
Derrick & Patsy 282
Diamond, Neil 259
Dillon, Leonard 220
Dillon, Phyllis 45, 223, 264
Dodd, Clement Coxone 51, 67, 98, 99, 126, 128, 162, 163, 164, 168, 175, 186, 198, 202, 215, 220, 222, 224, 229, 241

INDEX

Donaldson, Eric 5, 33, 49, 162, 189, 190, 198, 241, 263, 268, 273
Douglas, Carl 262
Dowe, Brent 43, 224, 264
Dragonaires, The 56, 135, 210, 229, 264
Dread, Judge (Alex Hughes) 5, 27, 33, 126, 127, 154, 181, 211, 244, 271, 288
Drifters, The 264
Dunbar, Lowell (Sly) 141
Dunn, Earl 113
Dunkley, Errol 25, 241
Dyce, Billy 203, 229, 275, 283
Dylan, Bob 62
Dynamites, The 186, 215, 241

E

Eccles, Clancy 5, 10, 18, 20, 29, 31, 56, 186, 187, 215, 233, 241, 244, 259, 263, 265, 288, 289
Edwards, Jackie 27, 50, 163, 180, 218, 219, 241, 244, 269
Edwards, Rupie 25, 99, 156
Ellis, Alton 22, 54, 60, 163, 223
Emotions, The 73
Eternals, The & Campbell, Cornel 39
Ethiopians, The 43, 51, 52, 164, 220, 239, 241, 282
Everley Brothers, The 137

F

Fabulous Five, The 35, 269
Fabulous Flames, The 29, 186, 259
Faith, Horace 113, 140, 252
Fatter, Eric 283
Feliciano, Jose 142
Flames, The 287
Flip, Bunny 41
Francis, Connie 223
Francis, Willie 52
Francis, Winston 164, 271
Freeman, Alan 130

G

Gardner, Boris 31, 99, 135, 214, 248
Gaylads, The 25, 37, 159, 237, 264, 269
Gaylets, The 288
Gaytones, The 239
GG All Stars 33, 54, 237
Gibbs, Joe 25, 41, 79, 103, 132, 163, 168, 216, 221
Gladiators, The 10
God Sons 260
Goodall, Graeme 4, 16, 25, 45, 49, 158
Gopthal, Lee 10, 18, 126, 179
Gordon, Henry 'Raleigh' 120
Gordon, Rosco 163
Grant, Gladstone 217, 244
Gray, Owen 22, 52, 60, 163, 164, 271, 275, 285, 286
Groovers, The 275
Grossett, GG George 283
Greyhound 5, 19, 47, 82, 98, 113, 114, 115, 116, 119, 144, 147, 150, 151, 205, 211, 252, 255, 256, 257 265
Griffiths, Marcia 54, 98, 99, 143, 239, 251, 264
Groovy, Winston 22, 52, 60, 271, 273

H

Hales, Samantha 4
Hall, Audrey 179
Harlesden Monks, The 23, 61
Harriott, Derrick 43, 103, 251, 259
Harrison, George 264
Harry J All Stars 35, 62, 93, 134, 175, 244, 247, 293
Henry & Liza 77
Henzel Juliet 4
Henzell, Perry 4, 67, 95, 292, 293
Heptones, The 31, 35, 51
Herman (Chin-Loy) 31, 263
Hewitt, Winston 79
Hibbert, Frederick 'Toots' 4, 5, 120, 121, 217, 251
Hinds, Alex & Cornell 271
Hinds, Justin & The Dominoes 45
Hippy Boys, The 37, 134, 287
Holness, Winston 'Niney' 275
Holt, John 37, 52, 73, 99, 163, 202, 259, 275
Honey Boy 265
Howard, Easton Barrington 129
Hudson, Keith 198
Hugh Roy 41, 275
Hurley, John 137

I

Impact All Stars 41, 52, 216
Inner Circle 60
Inner Mind 4, 22, 23, 60, 61, 62, 226
Inspirations, The 216
Invincibles, The 108
I Roy 39, 244
Isaacs, David 45, 168, 229
I Threes 99, 239

J

James, Wilson 129
Jennifer 275
John, Elton 82, 127
Johnson, Harry (Harry J) 18, 35, 98, 134, 175, 244, 247
Johnson, JJ 189
Jones, John 282
Jones, Lloyd 237
Jumpers, I Roy & The 244

K

Kelly Pat 75, 78, 163, 225, 285, 287
Kennedy, Nicola 4
Khouri, Ken 128, 265
Killowatts, The 189
King Iwah 268
King, Rita 166
Kingstonians, The 27, 43, 230, 233, 237
Kong, Leslie 5, 18, 19, 20, 43, 47, 67, 68, 69, 72, 80, 85, 86, 87, 92, 120, 122, 123,125, 129, 132, 139, 146, 158, 159, 160, 161, 163, 192, 221, 222, 224, 251, 259, 260, 264

INDEX

Koningh, Michael De 5

L

Landis, Joya 229, 233
Larry & Alvin 175
Larry & lloyd 273
Lee, Bunny 'Striker' 4, 10, 12, 19, 20, 33, 39, 41, 54, 58, 73, 75, 77, 156, 162, 163, 164, 165, 166, 167, 193, 198, 202, 221, 225
Lee, Young Striker 5, 167
Lee, Byron 18, 33, 56, 120, 135, 189, 210, 214, 224, 229, 260, 264
Lewis, Alva 134, 233
Lewis, Hopeton 20, 25, 31, 239, 261
Lincoln, Junior 4, 21, 50
Lindsay, Simon 4
Little Roys, The 273
Livingstone, Dandy 29, 37, 98, 153, 179, 180, 181, 244
Lizzy 52, 204, 271
Lloyd & Carey 25, 35   Lloyd & Claudette 237
London, Jimmy 41, 216, 229, 242, 283
Lord Creator 259
Lowbites, The Lloydie 56, 239
Lynn, Keith 264

M

Mancini, Henry 114, 118
Manley, Michael 77
Mansano, Joe 39
Marley, Bob 35, 45, 49, 51, 58, 95, 99, 126, 149, 158, 164, 169, 175, 192, 205, 206, 210, 242, 265, 269, 275
Marley, Rita 205, 239
Marshall, Larry 10, 164, 275, 289
Martens, Dr 13, 14
Marvels, The 179, 271, 275
Mathias, Mat 61, 62
Mayfield, Curtis 163
Maytals, Toots And 4, 12, 25, 43, 51, 120, 125, 158, 159, 205, 217, 236, 239, 241, 244, 251, 259, 291
Maytones, The 27, 33, 217, 244, 271, 287
McCartney, Paul 67, 229
McCarthy, Nathaniel 'Jerry' 120
McCook, Tommy 223
McNaughton, Trevor 224
Mediators, The 287
Melodians, The 43, 45, 224, 248, 260, 264, 279
Mercer, Johnny 118
Millie 264
Mills, Rudy 27, 233
Mittoo, Jackie 287
Mohawks, The 61, 271, 285
Moreno, Roddy 5
Morgan, Derrick 5, 16, 20, 22, 52, 54, 58, 73, 158, 163, 164, 165, 192, 193, 194, 195, 229, 273, 275, 281, 282, 285, 286, 287, 289, 293
Morgan, Patsy 196
Morris, Aston 220
Morris, Eric 'Monty' 288
Muckers, The 275

Mudie, Harry 39, 283
Munro, Jessica 4
Music Doctors 37, 239

N

Nash, Johnny 35, 51, 62, 119, 149, 152, 155, 181, 205, 206, 210, 211, 244, 269
Neasden Connection, The 37
Neville 33, 265
Neville, Aaron 255
Niney 27, 239
Niney & Max 52, 275
Noble, Cliff 281
Notes, Freddie & The Rudies 35, 113, 115, 250, 261

O

Oakley, Glenroy 113
Omare, Max 62
Oppressed, The 5

P

Palmer, Carl 10, 20, 162, 166
Palmer, Harry 10, 14, 20, 56, 73, 162, 166
Palmer, Jeff 10, 20, 60, 61, 162, 166
Pan's People 64
Paragons, The 99, 202, 259, 283
Parker, ken 39
Parks, Lloyd 163
Paul, Eugene 273
Paulette & Gee 33
Perry, Fred 13
Perry, Lee 'Scratch' 5, 10, 18, 19, 20, 33, 49, 58, 108, 168, 169, 187, 189, 198, 202, 205, 209, 216, 224, 229, 233, 248, 287, 288, 297
Piglets, The 157
Pioneers, The 4, 5, 6, 10, 19, 25, 43, 47, 69, 79, 80, 81, 82, 85, 86, 87, 88, 93, 98, 127, 146, 151, 159, 205, 233, 239, 247, 248, 255, 261, 293
Pottinger, Sonia 37, 202, 241
Priest, Maxi 138
Pyramids, The 16, 25, 31, 142

R

Randy's All Stars 41
Ranglin, Alvin 33, 189, 202, 203, 217, 263
Ray, Danny 27, 127
Reid, Alytman 35, 221, 275
Reid, Duke 18, 31, 45, 47, 67, 126, 128, 162, 163, 164, 166, 192, 198, 202, 223, 224, 225, 226, 229, 261, 264
Rhoden, Pat 52, 273, 285
Rhyging 294
Richards, Cynthia 56, 264
Righteous Flames 273
Riley, Desmond 13, 29
Riley, Jimmy 230
Riley, Winston 19, 45, 108, 109, 141, 283, 285
Robinson, Earl 113, 144
Robinson, Indiana 88
Robinson, Jackie 4, 79, 85, 86, 89, 132

INDEX

Robinson, Ralph 86
Rocking Horse 41, 269
Rodigan, David 5
Rodrigues, Rico 179
Rolling Stones, The 75, 175
Romeo, Max 5, 10, 12, 14, 18, 20, 25,31, 54, 56, 58, 62, 73, 74, 75, 77, 126, 130, 162, 163, 164, 233, 237, 275, 287, 289, 293
Rosko, Emperor 4, 5, 9, 20, 74, 88, 157, 293
RTL 29
Rudie & Sketto Rich 273
Rudies, The 61, 113, 113, 118, 179, 193, 252, 256, 257
Ruffin, Bruce 51, 109, 142, 151, 159, 214, 256, 257, 263
Russell, Ronald 281

S

Scott, Tony 54, 134, 175
Scotty 35, 269, 273
Scotty & Derrick 43
Seaga, Edward 128
Shades, The 283, 285
Shand, Winston & The Shieks 283, 285
Sherwood, Adrian 5
Shirley, Roy 35, 52, 221, 275
Shirley & Charmers 275
Shorty 35, 156, 244
Simon And Garfunkel 216, 242, 268
Simon, Paul 51, 119, 127, 148, 211, 268
Simon, Tito 127, 179
Simone, Nina 98, 136
Sinclair, Joe 35, 43 Skatalites, The 226
Sisters 33
Skatalites 287
Slade 127
Slickers, The 27, 33, 58, 186, 239, 291, 293
Small, Carlton 65
Small Faces 11, 60
Smith, Dennis 198
Smith, Eddie 271
Smith, Ernie 244
Smith, Ian R 4, 5, 22, 23, 60, 62, 226
Smith, Micky 4, 15
Smith, Slim 33, 73, 163, 225, 230, 269, 273, 287
Smithy All Stars 62
Soulmates 25, 233, 281
Soul Rhythms, The 283
Soul Sisters 25, 233
Soul Syndicate 269
Specials, The 56, 239
Spence Davis Group 60, 218, 269
Staple Singers, The 134, 175
Sterling, Lester 12, 58, 164, 281, 283
Stevens, Cat 49, 92, 93, 94, 138
Stewart, Delano 37, 237
Stitt, King 29, 186, 202, 215, 233, 237
Sugar & Dandy 179
Supersonics, The 223
Supremes, The 82
Sweet Confusion 54
Sydney Allstars 285
Symarip 16, 17, 247, 294

T

Taitt, Lynn (& Jets) 223, 288
Tartans, The & Devon 282, 288
Tattersall, Dave 22, 62
Taylor, Stephen 220
Techniques, The 214, 225, 269, 283
Tennors, The 229
Termites, The 281, 288, 289
The Boss, Joe 16
Thomas, Nicky 5, 47, 103, 104, 127, 137, 153, 179, 180, 205, 251, 252, 255
Thompson, Robert 29, 37, 229, 233, 244
Tiger 39, 52, 226, 273, 285
Tilley, Claire 4
Topham, Finley 22
Tosh, Peter 41, 52, 159, 205, 206, 210, 220, 242, 265
T. Rex 104, 127
Tribe, Tony 29, 179, 215, 248
Two Tones, The 108
Tyrell, Lloyd 56, 230, 288

U

Uncle Fee 64
Uniques, The 52, 127, 148, 156, 221, 225, 230, 268, 269
Untouchables, The 45, 168, 229
Upsetters 6, 18, 21, 49, 52, 62, 69, 87, 93, 131, 169, 174, 205, 214, 233, 234, 236, 248, 268, 285, 287
U-Roy or Hugh Roy 31, 45, 56, 180, 198, 202, 215, 265, 268, 275

V

Vanity Fair 260
Verne & Son 33, 126, 154, 263
Versatiles, The 52, 271, 281, 283
Viceroys, The 271, 283, 285
Virtues, The 175

W

Wailer, Bunny 205, 206, 210
Wailers, The 35, 45, 49, 134, 149, 169, 175, 186, 205, 206, 209, 210, 222, 242, 265, 275
Wailing Souls 273
Walsh, Jimmy 22, 62
Warwick, Dion 223
Webber, Marlene 41, 239
West Indians, The 189
White, Joe & Chuck 273
White, Trevor Ardley 113
Who, The 11
Wilkins, Ronnie 137
Williams, Andy 118
Williams, Virgil Jack 63
Willoughby, Neville 210
Wilson, Delroy 39, 52, 162, 241
Wilson, Ernest 283, 287
Winston & Pat 273
Wonder, Stevie 229
Wright, Winston 33, 175
Wynett, Tammy 239